Jan Grim

Reconsidering the Uniform

Religion und Biographie

Religion and Biography

herausgegeben von/edited by

Prof. Dr. Detlev Dormeyer (Dortmund)
Prof. Dr. Ruard Ganzevoort (Amsterdam)
Prof. Dr. Linus Hauser (Gießen)
Prof. Dr. Friedhelm Munzel (Dortmund)

Band/Volume 25

LIT

Jan Grimell

Reconsidering the Uniform

Existential and religious identity reconstruction
among Swedes after military service

LIT

This book is printed on acid-free paper.

Bibliographic information published by the Deutsche Nationalbibliothek
The Deutsche Nationalbibliothek lists this publication in the Deutsche
Nationalbibliografie; detailed bibliographic data are available on the Internet at
http://dnb.d-nb.de.

ISBN 978-3-643-90992-3 (pb)
ISBN 978-3-643-95992-8 (PDF)
Zugl.: Amsterdam, Vrije Univ., Diss., 2017

A catalogue record for this book is available from the British Library

© LIT VERLAG GmbH & Co. KG Wien,
Zweigniederlassung Zürich 2018
Klosbachstr. 107
CH-8032 Zürich
Tel. +41 (0) 44-251 75 05
E-Mail: zuerich@lit-verlag.ch   http://www.lit-verlag.ch
Distribution:
In the UK: Global Book Marketing, e-mail: mo@centralbooks.com
In North America: International Specialized Book Services, e-mail: orders@isbs.com
In Germany: LIT Verlag Fresnostr. 2, D-48159 Münster
Tel. +49 (0) 2 51-620 32 22, Fax +49 (0) 2 51-922 60 99, e-mail: vertrieb@lit-verlag.de
e-books are available at www.litwebshop.de

Contents

5

ACKNOWLEDGEMENTS

As I left full-time military service, the academic world and studies gradually became my new life and identity, and thus invited a lost spiritual depth of life. Prof. Dr. R. Ruard Ganzevoort, you allowed me to navigate deeper layers of this spiritual depth as you supported the acceptance of this PhD project at Vrije Universiteit, Amsterdam, and generously offered yourself to supervise it. Thank you very much. Your supervision and gentle invitations to new ideas and perspectives have tailored this project, even my own academic identity, to what it is today. Dr. Thomas Girmalm, thank you for your support throughout the early years at Umeå University and for your assistance as the second supervisor of this project.

Thanks to Dr. Mikael Lundmark (Umeå University), who in an early dawn introduced this research project proposal to Prof. Dr. R. Ruard Ganzevoort.

I also wish to thank the financial help from Helge Ax:son Johnsons Stiftelse, Teologifonden i Umeå and Härnösands och Luleå stifts råd för utbildning och forskning, which was received throughout this project.

Dear participants, thank you for your time, which was filled with openness and generously shared real life experiences, which you have invested throughout the project. Many thanks.

My gratitude goes to Seth Zeigler, who has edited the English in the dissertation, as well as assisted my pursuit of adequate translations of narrative accounts in Swedish to English. Thank you very much for the discussions and the time that you have generously given this process.

Prof. Dr. Dave Blackburn (University of Québec), thank you for reading and strengthening the first chapter on the Canadian Armed Forces.

I also would like to thank the Swedish Soldiers Homes Association for the interest that you have shown this research project.

I would furthermore like to thank my parents Ingegerd and Anders Grimell, who have supported me throughout the intensive years of the project by going the extra mile to support my children with your endless love, from time to time, which assisted me greatly in finding the time to write and refine many of the articles and chapters within the dissertation. And likewise to my wife, Lindha Grimell, many thanks for your patience and support throughout this project.

CHAPTER 1

Introduction: Identity Reconstruction in Transition from Military to Civilian Life

1.1 Military cultures shape military identities

A transitional journey must, by the very definition of transition, begin somewhere in space and time. Therefore, in an introduction of identity reconstruction amid transition from military to civilian life, it is necessary to begin in the military cultures that have shaped the military identities. The goal is to more profoundly explore the starting point for the identity reconstruction that ensues during the process of transition from military into civilian life. Without this background we may undermine the full understanding of how military cultures may influence and operate on the construction of a military story of who I am as a service member and the possible impact that process may have on the self. Military cultures shape the narrative identities of service members which may resonate deeply in the individuals' selves (Adler, Zamorski & Britt, 2011; Bélanger & Moore, 2013; Brunger, Serrato & Ogden, 2013; Grimell, 2015; Haynie & Shepherd, 2011; Rosenberg, 1993; Thornborrow & Brown, 2009). This implies that the military transition to civilian life begins in an existing narrative definition of a person, to which the journey to new civilian presuppositions calls for a narrative re-definition or reconstruction of the story of who I am which may be experienced as a challenge, perhaps even as a threat, by the self. A greater awareness of military identities, in sufficient detail to reveal even their nuances, may help during transition through potential military and civilian cultural obstacles, advances and challenges as the individual grapples with his or her own identity reconstruction (Bragin, 2010; Coll, Weiss & Yarvis, 2012; Hall, 2012a, 2012b). A shift from military service to a civilian life equates to a transitional journey from one culture to another, from one identity to another wherein the different cultural content likely shapes rather different narrative identities of the self. The aspiration behind elaborating on military cultures and identities is to present a prelude to the actual focus of this dissertation: existential and religious dimensions in identity reconstruction among Swedish military personnel in the process of becoming civilians. The term *civilian* is selected in order to underscore that the process of leaving service is emphasized. The term *veteran* in a Swedish context could be understood in several ways (e.g., someone who has been employed by the Swedish Armed Forces and served nationally or internationally with or without weapon, or someone who has participated in a military international mission)[1], but the selection of *civilian* should eliminate

---

[1] For more information see Försvarsmakten (2017) in regards to definitions.

any ambiguity in this case as to what the transition is about: military personnel who undergo transitions to civilian life.

The way military culture is understood in this dissertation is not as a way of life that is necessarily universally shared by all those who live in it, rather culture is as a collection of "values, meanings, and practices unevenly distributed" (Gregg, 2005, p. 6) and adopted by its members in the very shaping of military identities. The emphasis in this section is not to present a final position on military cultures but rather to consider some of the common themes in the research on military cultures, contextual differences, military identities and potential by-products thereof. A military identity is understood is as a story of who I am shaped by a military culture, a personal narrative which serves as a claim of identity made by the self as a service member due to a specific set of military values, meanings and practices. Moreover, it is suggested that this story, be it military or civilian, has a corresponding I-position in the self (Hermans, 1996a, 1996b, 1999, 2001a). Therefore it is suggested that the self, by preexisting and new I-positions, is indeed involved in a narrative identity reconstruction (Hermans, 2003). Thereby the terms *self-identity work* and *identity reconstruction* assume and include the same self-identity process, but with different words. Self-identity work and identity reconstruction are used somewhat interchangeably throughout this dissertation. However, the term *narrative identity reconstruction* refers more to the narrative process of empirically changing the story of who I am into something different (Hermans & Hermans-Jansen, 1995). A conceptualization of the self as a dialogical narrator (Hermans, Kempen & van Loon, 1992) will be elaborated in chapter two. Now, after introducing some clarifications of core concepts, some features of military cultures will be sketched and discussed.

The military world and way of life is more or less separated from the civilian world and way of life. But the degree of isolation is not constant across societies and time, and even within the same context this isolation is nonetheless subject to different perspectives. Huntington (1957) emphasized the distinctions and dichotomy between military and civilian worlds, whereas Janowitz (1960) documented more of the interactive relationships spanning between these two realms. This study is only drawn from Swedish service members in transition, yet even a brief comparison to the relatively similar (yet much larger) Canadian Armed Forces can begin to illustrate the intricacies and nuances of these distinctions and isolations and how they are filtered and accentuated or softened by different perspectives.[2] In the case of a Cana-

---

[2] The idea to expound upon the theory with an empiric comparison between the Canada Armed Forces and the Swedish equivalent was not only influenced by the availability of literature but also the fact that the researcher

dian context the distinction between civilian and military is relatively pronounced (Park, 2008), as the Armed Forces function more as military mini-societies - including for example their own health care systems, living arrangements, and judicial systems - all encapsulated within the larger civilian societies. However, in a Scandinavian context there is much more sharing and overlap between and among military and civilian cultures. The Swedish Armed Forces cannot easily be understood as a mini-society within the larger society when compared to the Canadian system. Swedish service members are to a large degree dependent upon the civilian society for their health care and living arrangements. Swedish service members tend to live part of their actively serving lives outside of the military bases and instead within the civilian population, and there is no general system of mandatory postings across the Swedish country or elsewhere. However, the opposite may often be the case in a Canadian military context which typically includes mandatory postings and provides both housing and these services on base or nearby. Yet, in regards to housing, the potential accommodations for soldiers on base is typically insufficient, and thus often only low ranking military personnel inhabit these Canadian Armed Forces quarters, so even in this context the distinctions between civilian and military can be blurred, variable, and debatable.

This prelude serves to introduce examples of contextual differences between military cultures, including a blend of culturally specific elements which influence the construction of military identities. This is why it is critically important to instead understand any military culture as a composite of somewhat diverse cultures; they really do differ. Additionally, the contexts within in a military culture may change across time, and within such a military culture subcultures may exist corresponding to a variety of specific branches and units (Devries, Hughes, Watson & Moore, 2012; Edström, Lunde & Haaland Matlary, 2009; French, 2005; Haaland, 2009, 2011; Janowitz, 1960; Moskos, Williams & Segal, 2000; Thompson & Lockhart, 2015). Yet there are also similarities across military cultures, some of which are elaborated in the following parts of this section. This dissertation acknowledges that military cultures include contextual differences while also sharing common features, for example discipline, obedience, community, camaraderie and a chain of command or hierarchy that may sustain a kind of kinship among service members nationwide and worldwide.

---

visited Valcartier Family Centre, located close to Valcartier garrision, in 2016 (11-15 October), to exchange lessons learned and research on transition from military to civilian life. During that week Canadian researchers and personnel at the centre helped to broaden the structural knowledge entailing both differences and similarities between these military forces. Additionally, the researcher attended *Forum 2017*, a large conference hosted by The Canadian Institute for Military and Veteran Health Research (CIMVHR) which has a specific emphasis on transition from military to civilian life.

As men and women enter military service they are exposed to a new array of behaviors, rules and codes of conduct, language games, attire, equipment (including fire arms), combat vehicles, facilities and living quarters within gated military communities (Ben-Ari, 1998; Blackburn, 2016a; Boose, 1993; Brotz & Wilson, 1946; Burkhart & Hogan, 2015; Coll et al., 2012; Devries et al., 2012; Edström et al., 2009; Huntington, 1957; Wertsch, 1991). Military garrisons and communities are restricted areas for the general civilian population. Individuals of course enter the military for varied individually meaningful reasons, be it education or development or championing freedom and democracy, and with different intended and expected roles which may, in theory, exclude them from actual combat, but the ultimate underlying fact is that any military force is one cohesive machine which is designed and intended to destroy. Military communities train and condition service members in a variety of ways to face death, and potentially kill, during military service. Service members will learn many things, but the position of this dissertation is to describe the foremost purpose of the Armed Forces as lucidly as possible. Military cultures prepare their members in effective and systematic ways to break the (civilian) cultural taboos and otherwise legally punishable act of killing other humans, in organized ways, and this implies that military cultures stand in stark contrast to civilian entities within the western world (Bragin, 2010; French, 2005; Goldstein, 2001; Kümmel, 2011; Strachan, 2006; Verrips, 2006; Wilson, 2008).

The military community and life of service is tailored in a collectivistic way which appears to stand in a sharp contrast to an individualistic western way of life (Bragin, 2010; Franks, 2004; Huntington, 1957; Woodward & Jenkings, 2011). The authoritarian and hierarchical fundamentals inherent within military contexts are designed to shape a predisposition to conform and obey orders which indicates that freedom and democracy hold an ambivalent position within the Armed Forces (Hall, 2012a, 2012b; Wertsch, 1991). Within military organizations there is no such thing as democracy, freedom of choice, or even privacy, as these would make it impossible to reach a level of discipline and sacrifice necessary to conduct combat and war wherever and whenever it is supposed to be executed (Edström et al., 2009; Franks, 2004; French, 2005). The shaping of service members is a turbulent and on-going process. Everything from the standard military uniform, hair-cutting, and the removal of personal intimacy items (e.g., piercing, ear rings) is part of a de-individuation process which is designed to suppress the individual and to conform him or her to the military ideal, new military relationships and coordinated action, and context-specific behaviors required to do the job (Blackburn, 2016a; Goldstein, 2001; Verrips, 2006; Wertsch, 1991). The basic military training consists of

10

several rites of passage with an intense focus on camaraderie, discipline, physical training, marching, medics, shooting exercises and demanding group-oriented exercises in the field environment. Throughout the basic military training the relational ties are likely to grow between service members emotionally, behaviorally, and cognitively. In this process, service members will learn to suppress individuals' needs for the collective requirements. Soon service members develop camaraderie which is reinforced at every turn (Brotz & Wilson, 1946; Brunger et al., 2015; Burkhart & Hogan, 2015; Woodward, 2008). Deep bonds and relationships develop between military personnel through their service, and these bonds are rarely found outside of military cultures. Actions and attitudes of loyalty, duty and even self-sacrifice are manifested among military personnel (Franks, 2004; Haaland, 2009; Hall, 2012b; Sørensen, 2011). It has been suggested that the military ethic is basically corporative in spirit and fundamentally anti-individualistic (Huntington, 1957; Woodward & Jenkings, 2011). Unification myths play a vital role and depict the transformation from separate units into a whole. The narration of these unification myths serves as a moral imperative for military personnel. Service members will learn to trust each other to the point that one literally could lay one's life in the hands of a battle buddy. When tactical groups are formed after basic military training and live missions are conducted for longer periods of time, maybe even during real combat, the relational bond between service members grows deeply consolidated. Some have suggested, using theological terminology, that the group, and the battle buddies, perhaps even the larger military organizations, may become sacred and worth dying for (French, 2005; Grimell, 2016b; Lunde, 2009). The military relationships, community and service will likely become the primary focus of meaning in a service member's life.

Even so, presented elsewhere, service members are not passive recipients who simply absorb institutional messages throughout their socialization processes (Grimell, 2017b). Service members are active agents who may appropriate and interpret military cultures to fit or resonate with their own selves and preexisting I-positions in various unique ways, and therefore individuals position themselves differently within military institutions. As active agents military personnel uniquely interpret the institutional contexts and construct a variety or multiplicity of perspectives according to their personal aspirations. This implies that beyond the mainstream sociological perspective on military socialization presented above, each individual's psychological processes of internalizing the institutional ideas may be much more complex and heterogeneous than is often initially assumed. The psychological impact of military socialization may therefore be more nuanced, and this suggests that the military voices of service members may be divergent and thus influence their selves to varying degrees. Therefore, the term and category *military I-positions* may rather serve as a broad umbrella which envelopes both personal appropriations of the cultural and institutional ideas and more collective voices of the institutions which articulate critical institutional messages such as, for example, obedience, discipline, loyalty and duty-willingness.

But beyond this pro-militaristic cultural description there are also darker aspects or elements within military cultures and practices. Beside the most obvious aspect of destruction and the killing of other humans, military cultures also likely include a number of by-products. As military communities in general tend to be populated or dominated by men, females may be ascribed as the other by the majority of service men who implicitly or explicitly, conscious or unconscious, reproduce the cultural content based on male superiority (Andreassen & Ingalls, 2009; Goldstein, 2001; Higgins, 1993; Ruddick, 1993; Wertsch, 1991). Female service members may be exposed to an array of difficulties; moreover they may have a hard time to be acknowledged by their male peers for their expertise and capabilities solely because of their gender (Badaró, 2015; Bell & Reardon, 2012; Boose, 1993; Burkhart & Hogan, 2015; Estrada & Berggren, 2009). Additionally, as heterosexuality may be the culturally expected sexual predisposition among tightly bonding service men, homosexuality may be perceived as a threat to masculinity, as well as a threat to close emotional and bodily relationships among service men (Alvesson & Due Billing, 1997; Goldstein, 2001; Porter & Gutierrez, 2012). Lately the existence of warrior cultures has drawn attention, for example among the Armed Forces in Scandinavia related to the long-lasting campaign in Afghanistan (Abrahamsson, 2011; Agrell, 2013; Edström et al., 2009; Haaland, 2009, 2011). A warrior culture may, among many things, include the development of military ideals that reach extreme levels. A warrior culture could accentuate, but is not limited to, the glorification of combat and killing, radical dehumanization the enemy by the unit members during deployments, and emphasis on masculinity and strength whilst weakness, psychiatric and/or psychological issues are instilled and perceived with shame and guilt (Bryan & Morrow, 2011; Dickstein, Vogt, Handa & Litz, 2010; Malmin, 2013; Haaland, 2009). Other by-products that should be included as potential outcomes of military cultures as practices are disablement due to military training or wartime combat, mental health issues such as Posttraumatic Stress Disorder (PTSD). The Diagnostic and Statistical Manual of Mental Disorders (DSM–5), published by the American Psychiatric Association, provides standard criteria and common terminology for the classification of mental disorders (American Psychiatric Association, 2013). The fifth revision (DSM-5) was released in 2013 and includes changes to the diagnostic criteria for PTSD which has moved PTSD from the class of anxiety disorders into a new class of trauma and stressor-related disorders. Conditions included in this classification require exposure to a traumatic or stressful event as a diagnostic criterion.[3] Depression and reoccurrence of panic or anxiety attacks are experienced as part of PTSD symptoms. Operational Stress Injury (OSI) is a term that has been widely adopted within the Canadian Armed Forces and Veterans Affairs Canada as a more inclusive term to refer to a broad range of persistent psychological difficulties related to service (Laforce, Whitney & Klassen, 2013; Thompson & Lockhart, 2015). However, OSI do not serve as a diagnostic tool but rather as a way of reaching out in less stigmatizing ways to a wider spectrum of service members and veterans in order to provide them, and their families, with support to enhance their quality of life in the aftermath of military practices (Kohler & Wigfield, 2013). Other war related psychiatric conditions, such as Traumatic Brain Injuries (TBI), result from physical brain trauma amid explosions, blast waves or accidents that can result in long-term disability because of the development of cerebral hemodynamic, metabolic dysfunctions and associated cognitive impairments (Mark & Pike, 2013; Parkinson, French & Massetti, 2012; Strong & Donders, 2012). Moral injury or moral concerns may also appear as an implication of the practice of military cultures (Brock & Lettini, 2012; Knowles, 2013; Litz, Stein, Delaney, Lebowitz, Nash, Silva & Maguen, 2009; Rambo, 2010). Litz and colleagues (2009) have defined moral injury as "Perpetrating, failing to prevent, bearing witness to, or learning about acts that transgress deeply held moral beliefs and expectations" (p. 700). Moral injury may be another way of understanding the implications of the difference between military and civilian cultures (Stallinga, 2013). As the (civilian) cultural taboos of killing other humans may be broken during active service or deployment, a service member may need to repair the clash of two opposite cultural parts of his or her self. The military part, or I-position, of the self condones killing under certain circumstances, whereas the other part, or I-position, of the self views killing as a taboo, legally forbidden, condemned act. However, as already implied above, research suggests that we do not need to advance so far as killing another human to develop moral injuries (Roth, St Cyr & McIntyre-Smith, 2013). Potential moral injuries may include a wide spectrum of relatively passive traumas such as being as a service member in a conflict, regret, emotional pain, perhaps even rage resulting from being

---

[3] As for diagnostic criteria, the four clusters of DSM-5 symptoms include: intrusion, avoidance, negative alterations in cognitions and mood, and alterations in arousal and reactivity. Three new symptoms have been added, two under negative alterations in cognitions and mood (1. persistent and distorted blame of self or others and 2. persistent negative emotional state) and one under the alterations in arousal and reactivity cluster (3. reckless or destructive behavior).

given the task locating and retrieving the body parts of a battle buddy scattered by improvised explosive device, or even the guilt of being the benefactor of a battle buddy's own self-sacrifice for his or her comrade (Drescher, Nieuwsma & Swales, 2013; Yalom, 1980). The implications of moral injury may have a profound effect on emotional, psychological, spiritual and social well-being.

In summary, from the middle of the twentieth century onward, many attempts have been made to describe features of the military cultures. Many researchers within the sociological and psychological field agree that a common thread among military cultures is a collective and anti-individualistic perspective, which places battle buddies and the group first and foremost; camaraderie is reinforced at every turn. Community, camaraderie, training, and operationalized values (i.e., loyalty, discipline, obedience, endurance) are all examples of military cultural phenomena which contextually design and shape military identities (French, 2005). Recently, researchers have suggested that important components of military identities are competence and expertise in professional skills, camaraderie and a fictive historical kinship with previous service members (Woodward & Jenkings, 2011). There are also a potential set of cultural by-products that may follow in the footsteps of military practice. As one has entered the doors to the military world, its way of life will likely have a major impact on one's self-identity from a vast range of perspectives (Bragin, 2010; Coll et al., 2012).

1.2 Transition from military to civilian life: The need of new identities

A shared conclusion among many researchers from a number of western countries is that the transition and reintegration into civilian life has the potential to become a challenge for military personnel and may impact service members on personal, social, familial, financial, and administrative planes (Adler, Bliese & Castro, 2011; Blackburn, 2016a; Bragin, 2010; Brunger et al., 2013; Burkhart & Hogan, 2015; Coll et al., 2012; Jolly, 1996; Moore, 2012; Pellegrino & Hoggan, 2015; Rumann & Hamrick, 2010; Wheeler, 2012; Yarvis & Beder, 2012; Zinger & Cohen, 2010). As introduced earlier, it is logical to begin with some cultural contextual differences in transitional processes due to their potential significance, and thus a thought provoking comparison with which to begin can be made around how structural differences between the Canadian and Swedish examples may influence transition to civilian life and self-identity work. If a service member has been serving in a Canadian context, for example, wherein much of the everyday life is included under the umbrella of the larger military organization, such as health care, living arrangements, and schools for the children located

14

close to the base, then a transition out of the military community will likely manifest as a much more radical change. The civilian systems of health care, governmental agencies and organizations will quite probably be experienced as much more confusing and foreign, and thus their benefits may not be fully realized; a potentially acute need to learn how to navigate and operate within these novel spheres may develop (Thompson & Lockhart, 2015). Quite probably a fresh need for the military veteran to find a new civilian job, will also manifest more or less simultaneously. In Canada, the occupational aspect of the transition is probably one of the most developed and resources are available, for example, if veterans decide to go to college or university. The process of transferring military cultural knowledge and identities into civilian contexts may be quite an energy-consuming challenge for a military veteran after ten, fifteen or twenty years of active service within a closed military mini-society (English & Dale-McGrath, 2013). However, the change and challenge is not necessary limited to the service member him- or herself (Thompson & Lockhart, 2015). If children are involved they may be relocated to a new school as the family moves to a new area or city. A spouse may need to find a new job. Regular reposting may include the consequence of being continually up-rooted from base to base and city to city, which may hamper the cultivation of stable social networks (Blackburn, 2016b). A transition may also warrant the need to once again build a new social network. The challenge of a transition is not necessarily isolated or limited to the service member him- or herself but may include a partner and/or a family too, as they may have become a part of the military cultural system and now also need to reintegrate into a new civilian cultural context. A service member is, on the other hand, not left unassisted in this process (Thompson & Lockhart, 2015). For example, in Canada transitional programs such as the Second Career Assistance Network seminar (SCAN), which is the main program for all military members who are taking their release, are designed to ameliorate these types of challenges. Additionally other programs may assist service members and families in the aftermath of military practice (Kohler & Wigfield, 2013; Skomorovsky, Thompson & Emeno, 2013). Recently Veterans Affairs Canada has received funding to launch a five year research program on transition called Road to Civilian Life (R2CL), intended to provide a more robust knowledge base about the mental health of transitioning CAF members (for more background read Thompson & Lockhart, 2015).

A Swedish military context, however does not share all of these contextual military presuppositions; Swedish service members are likely rather familiarized with navigation through civilian systems such as health care and living arrangements. Children of service members will go to public schools which are most likely marginally, if at all, influenced by or proximal to the base, and a partner will most likely be employed somewhere within the civilian society. The absence of mandatory postings, for service members in general, around the Swedish country or elsewhere allow for a more stable social network. This suggests that the service member, and any partner and child/children, will be relatively integrated into the civilian population prior to transition and may moreover have a stable military as well as civilian network. The Swedish Armed Forces have a career transitional program that can aid military personnel in transition; however, a person needs to apply for such a program and may or may not be accepted (for more background read Försvarsmakten, 2014).

But even as there is more interaction and shared ground between the Swedish military and civilian cultures, this can potentially make for a relatively lonely transition for the service member him or herself; if the partner is basically fully integrated into civilian society, and the children almost surely are, then there may actually be less sharing and support within this family during transition. The bulk of the transition may rest solely on the service member, while the ease of transition for the rest of the family in comparison to his or her individual burden may leave him or her feeling quite lonely. From such a perspective it could be suggested that for a Swedish service member with a family the transition out of military service into civilian life may be a rather lonely journey when compared with a Canadian military family as a whole in a similar transitional process. In the Canadian context the entire family may be experiencing transition and relocation, albeit somewhat differently and individually, simultaneously (Thompson & Lockhart, 2015). This could plausibly lead to compounding misery for a tightly knit and empathetic family, or this sharing and empathy may help all share the burden and support each other more effectively, especially if the family members are close-knit and involved enough to understand yet sufficiently unaffected personally so as to be able to shoulder more of the burden for the service member. This may suggest that the process in a Swedish context may be more individualistically taxing, whereas in cultural contexts with more pronounced military mini-societies the family members may be more prompted to share in the cultural upheaval and thus the transition may be perceived more so as a shared process, even if only by a few close relatives. On the other hand, those serving in military cultures characterized by a greater disparity between the military and civilian who do not have any family with which to share the transition may find the process even more lonely. In any case, and amid all contexts, a couple or a family may need to renegotiate how to interact with each other and live a new life together as postings, deployments and military ways of life are in the process of changing (Beder, 2012; Hall, 2012b; Jolly, 1996).

Another noteworthy dimension of a transitional process is the reason thereof. If a service member decides by him or herself to exit service voluntarily, then the process begins with a different presupposition compared with, for example, a medically released service member. A transition coupled with a form of anxiety disorder caused by a traumatic experience, such as Post-Traumatic Stress Disorder, may severely impact a life in the aftermath of military practice. Veterans diagnosed with PTSD symptoms frequently experience reoccurrence of panic or anxiety attacks, which might limit their successful transition to a peacetime civilian lifestyle (Wall, 2008). Still, even if a service member is voluntarily released it is not unlikely that a medical issue such as PTSD may develop later in life. A diagnosed Traumatic Brain Injury may also pose a challenge for a veteran continuing with life in the aftermath of service. In addition to diagnosed medical conditions, or the wider concept of Operational Stress Injuries or potential forthcoming medical symptoms which may accompany life after transition; there may also be more or less burdensome moral issues to solve that may be tightly connected to the self-identity necessitated during a transition progress. Suicide does exist among veterans in the aftermath of military practice as an escape from the suffering and trauma (Castro & Kintzle, 2014; Jackson & Branson, 2012; Kopacz & Connery, 2015; Malmin, 2013). Rightfully, the preponderance of military research focuses on service members and veterans with psychiatric diagnoses, such as PTSD, TBI, or related symptoms such as OSI, moral injury or moral concerns.[4]

In summary, much of what has been written about transition thus far, could be understood as a broad variety of aspects that need to be included and addressed by the self, if individually pertinent, within the self-identity work in the process of becoming a civilian. Moreover, with a specific reference to the self-identity work from a narrative point of view, as military service comes to an end so too does the story of who I am as a service member. This could plausibly

---

[4] In this section I also wish to acknowledge the important works of both Lifton (1992) *Home from the War* and Tick (2005) *War and the Soul* which specifically address transition from military to civilian life among US veterans who have served, for example, in Vietnam. Both Lifton and Tick give special attention to PTSD and war trauma, and Tick suggests that healing could be better nurtured through an understanding of PTSD as an identity disorder in and of itself. However, in consideration of myriad contextual differences between the United States of America and Sweden, the different use of troops in war and conflict areas, in combination with the low rates of PTSD in Sweden, and furthermore the absence of diagnosed PTSD among the participants within this empirical project, a decision was made not to elaborate further in this study on transitional paradigms of PTSD and war trauma, even as this is recognized as a promising avenue of investigation in other contexts and cases. Meanwhile the focus here was to draw from research more in resonance with the specific contexts and the narratives of the interviewees, to build a situational and context-specific theory rooted in the empirical investigation.

create a wide discrepancy, both within the self and in interactions with significant others, for those who attempt to sustain an explicit personal narrative of I as a service member. Adding even another potential layer to the struggles with transition, the internal narrative of self-identity may not be wholly congruent with the explicit narrative. Some degree of both explicit and implicit narrative identity reconstruction must be tailored to a transition. The story of who I am needs to redefined and reformulated both externally and internally, inter- and intrapersonally. Such self-identity work needs to be addressed, perhaps from different angles, by all of the individuals that are directly included in such a transitional process.

1.3 Review on self-identity work in transition from military to civilian life

Service members face many potential challenges throughout military transition and reintegration into civilian life, and, depending on contexts, their families will more or less share in these. A growing body of research portraying transitional experiences can be found within a British, American and Canadian context. As has already been stated, the preponderance of research has addressed mental health topics such as PTSD, OSI, TBI, and moral injury in active service, transition and in the aftermath of service.

Fewer researchers have focused on the seemingly mundane types of military transitions such as career retirement, and over the years the topic of transition has been approached from various angles; however, these researchers as a whole do share a common thread throughout their conclusions: that self-identity issues were of concern for many service members during the transition into civilian life (Adler et al., 2011; Bragin, 2010; Brunger et al., 2013; Buell, 2010; Burkhart & Hogan, 2015; Drops, 1979; Jolly, 1996; Savion, 2009; Yanos, 2004). In fact, several researchers suggest that a transition and reintegration into civilian life has the potential to become a challenge for military personnel due to their strongly built up and ingrained military self-identity (Beder, 2012; Bragin, 2010; Bryan & Morrow, 2011; Edström et al., 2009; Haynie & Shepherd, 2011; Higate, 2008; Moore, 2012; Verey & Smith, 2012; Woodward & Jenkings, 2011).

Narrowing in more specifically on what can be said about self-identity work in transition as tailored to the Swedish sample in this dissertation and using a level of focus wherein other aspects in transitional research beyond identity reconstruction are more or less excluded, six qualitative interview studies will be subsequently presented with relevance for the inquiry of this dissertation. Brunger, Serrato & Ogden (2013) suggested in their qualitative study on transition to civilian life among 11 ex-service members who had served in the United Kingdom's Armed Forces that "the concept of identity in relation to the military is by no means a new one", but much of the focus thereof has been upon the investigation of military identities and the construction of gender "rather than how one's identity might shift in response to contextual alterations" (p. 88). Little attention has been directed to exploring and describing the service member's transition into civilian life that addresses self-identity work exclusively. Brunger and colleagues utilized an interview design which displayed that self-identity issues and the reconstruction of identity were of concern for many service members throughout their transition into civilian life and "the present study therefore suggest that the transition from military to civilian life is representative of a shift in identity, whereby ex-service personnel must accept identity loss and the inevitable need for change therein" (Brunger et al., 2013, p. 95). In the same study Brunger and her colleagues (2013) described the experiences among the participants categorized within three broad themes: "characteristics of a military life; loss as experienced upon return to civilian life; and the attempt to bridge the gap between these two lives. Transcending these themes was the notion of identity, illustrating that the transition from military to civilian life can be viewed as a shift in sense of self from soldier to civilian" (p. 86).

Drops (1979) conducted in his dissertation a study which addressed changes in self-concept and identity during transition and the effect on future behaviour as an adult. Drops compared the data from questionnaires completed by forty service men from the United States with interview data garnered from ten former service men who had left active service some time between one month and twelve years prior to the interview. In the phenomenological interview study, the ten men who had completed a career in the military were interviewed, five of them in company of their wives. Two men went through major changes in identity, one changed his self-concept, and the other seven were still in the process of transitioning or had apparently changed very little from a self-identity perspective. A process of phenomenological reduction was used to analyse the data from the interviews and to identify specific themes that surfaced during the transition. Themes were then reorganized and validated to give a general picture of the experience of becoming a civilian after a career in the military. The results of the study suggest that service members see themselves primarily as workers providing for the security of their families, just as they have for years. Leaving the service tends to be a positive experience, though adjusting to civilian life and obtaining civilian employment are emotional experiences that most men (the US Armed Forces were at the time not very inclusive of females) find difficult. The focus was more on leaving the service than on becoming a civilian. General self-concept remained basically the same and was even enriched to some degree for all groups in the study: officers and enlisted, employed and unemployed. Employed individuals tended to have more expanded self-concepts than those who were unemployed. The mid-life transition for military personnel seemed different from the transitions identified in the literature of the time. The focus was on the job and the career, rather than on life-values. Security took precedence over growth and development needs at this point in their lives.

In her dissertational study Yanos (2004) explored the perceptions of three recently retired US Air Force officers and their wives concerning adjustment to civilian life and general well-being through in-depth personal interviews. The interviews took place in two waves: the initial interview and a follow up interview that was conducted approximately five years after the initial interview and which was designed to investigate happiness. The study confirmed the assumptions that military officers will require considerable amounts of time for the transition to retirement, personal identity will be disrupted due to the loss of the work role, and general well-being will be negatively affected by the transition to retirement. Military retirees represent a group of individuals whose retirement age may begin as early as forty-two years. These individuals must transition to a new work setting within a culture that is unfamiliar to them. A multidimensional model of adjustment to retirement was developed in the study which considers retirement to be a precipitating event and addresses changes in the domains she delineated: Economic Impact, Social Support, Identity Reconstruction, and Physical and Mental Health. Identity Reconstruction and Mental Health represented the area of greatest challenge. A new positive self schema has to be developed by synthesizing the new civilian self with the military self. This new self schema was seen as developing from a combination of civilian employment, roles in the civilian community and perceived civilian social status in comparison to and challenge by former status and rank as a military officer. Inconsistencies between these officers' perceptions of identity reconstruction and their spouses' perceptions of this reconstruction were evident. All three individuals experienced great difficulty in reconstructing an identity for themselves within civilian sector, plausibly in large part because they had held such advanced ranks within the Air Force so that it was very difficult to find anything correspondingly fulfilling within the civilian sector.

Savion (2009) also undertook a phenomenological study within an American context where she explored the life transitioning experience, and return to civilian society, among recently retired military officers. The study narrowed in on how retired senior officers, who have been living in civilian society for two to five years, navigated a change in cultural differences and attended to the identity, awareness, and self-renewal which can lead to new beginnings and potential for learning. Ten participants were purposefully selected to explore the life transitioning process that accompanies retired senior officers as a result of returning to civilian society after more than two decades of active-duty military service. Each participant was interviewed twice over a period of time using an in-depth phenomenological interview method. Individual profiles were developed for each participant, and the interview data was elaborated through a phenomenological analysis method. As a result of the phenomenological reduction, clustering, and thematising, eight themes and thirteen subthemes emerged on life transition process stages. Savion offered the following conclusions:

- Life transitioning experience is expressed in terms of how an individual conceptualizes self in relation to the culture change.
- Adjusting to a different environment is an evolutionary process for individuals exchanging a structured culture for an unstructured culture.
- Navigating the life transition process of letting go of the old situation and starting anew involves a shift in thinking, being, and doing.
- The life transitioning experience unfolds in three stages (i.e. an ending, a neutral zone, and a new beginning) as an individual adjusts to a culture change.
- Identity and attitude evolve as an individual becomes more aware of self, others, and the environment.
- Learning is transformative; through self-reflection and self-discovery, one learns to embrace change, which leads to self-renewal.
- A favourable life transition outcome is dependent upon a self–realizing frame of mind.

Buell (2010) launched a study to present the experiences of retired US naval officers during their transitions from military to civilian lives employing a phenomenological approach. The study focused on the perceptions, experiences, and attitudes of six retired Lieutenant Commanders from diverse geographical and socio-economic backgrounds, five males and one female. Winnowed using a variety of personal interview tools, the data sets compiled by Buell suggested three distinct phases: identity, transition, and change. Across these phases, a major theme for all participants was a sense of loss: loss of identity, structure, financial security, and career satisfaction. Based on the overwhelming evidence gathered, preparation for the inevitable transition into retirement is paramount for success in the civilian world.

Burkhart & Hogan (2015) conducted a study which focused on twenty female service members that had transitioned into civilian life. The study was conducted years after the actual transition had taken place as the female service members had served in the Gulf War and post-Gulf War era. The qualitative design was built on face to face and telephone interviews. The analysis of the interview results, ex post facto as for the transitional experiences, shows that several participants claimed to have had experience identity issues. Burkhart & Hogan suggest that (p. 122):

> Participants' identity became challenged when they re-entered civilian life. Life patterns and values of military and civilian life were different, particularly in relation to camaraderie, rules of behavior, and work ethic. This created confusion that led to living two lives as veteran and civilian. The only way participants could maintain their identity within the civilian sector was to re-establish connections with the military, friends from the military, and veteran groups.

These presented studies add to the body of life transition literature which emphasizes self-identity work, mainly within a British and American context, and thereby provide both active and former service members, their families and significant others, and even the Armed Forces at large and related organizations such as family support centres, with insights which can be of great benefit to consider not only during, but also long before a transition from a military to a civilian society manifests. But as powerful as these insights are, none of these previous researchers have engaged in research from or within a dialogical framework or through a spiritual, religious, or existential lens.

In general preceding studies were typically either carried out on a small number of participants in one, or at most two, interview occasions, and/or the focus on self-identity work was often combined with other perspectives in acknowledgement of the extremely multifaceted nature of transition, much as this dissertation takes a practical theological focus. Moreover, the research presented in this overview shows both common patterns and contextual differences which suggests that the results and conclusions may not be entirely transferable in all aspects into other contexts. In general, it would be fair to conclude that very little attention has been dedicated to solely and longitudinally exploring and describing from a narrative perspective the process of identity reconstruction among service members in transition to civilian life. If we further hone that inquiry to include the task of investigating existential, spiritual or religious elements in such longitudinal processes, then even fewer research reports could be found.

In summary, relatively little research has been carried out on narrative identity reconstruction among voluntarily or medically released service members, and therefore it appears prudent to better round out and augment the larger body of research with the addition of such focused research. One of the most significant aspects was to sustain through a longer period of time this exploration of identity processes since there was a paucity of such temporally long investigations, which implied a blind spot in the self-identity work among former service members. Moreover, there was a growing need to conduct contextual research on identity work in transition amid cultural differences. The Swedish campaign in Afghanistan, in combination with service members that serve actively only a shorter period of years and then transition to a civilian life, stressed the need of contextual research on identity reconstruction. There was a very real risk in using lenses designed for a somewhat different focus as we try to read and understand what will happen and what actually is happening during the process of transition. A contextually attuned lens could reveal the finer details in the process. Finally, existential, spiritual or religious dimensions in the longitudinal identity reconstruction among service members in transition were rarely found in preceding research. Taken all together, these observations imply that there were deficiencies in the knowledge base concerning self-identity work which needed to be investigated systematically and contextually by researchers.

1.4 The purpose of the PhD project, research question, contributions, and limitations

The overarching purpose of the present research project was to describe the role of existential and/or religious dimensions in identity reconstruction among Swedish military personnel during the process of becoming civilians. The formulated purpose, in combination with the literature review, called for a contextual, qualitative, empirical, and longitudinal focus with a narrative approach to lived life experiences among service members in transition. The research project has adopted a longitudinal interview design to cover the transitional process among the participants. The focus and approach of the project were located within the body of practical theology which means that the interpretation of the analysis was formulated in conversation with theological traditions and related areas of existential, spiritual and religious research.

The central research question derived from the purpose of the project was: What is the role of existential and/or religious dimensions in identity reconstruction among Swedish military personnel during the process of becoming civilians?

The following subquestions outlined the analysis of the project:

- What are the experiences of Swedish military personnel in the process of becoming civilians?
- How is the identity constructed and reconstructed in the transition from a service member's to a civilian's narrative?
- What are the existential and/or religious elements in this process?

A number of contributions from the research project have been identified and are described below:

- It helps to fill a specific void in the research on military transition to civilian life as it presents portraits of long term self-identity work with a specific emphasis on existential and religious dimensions.
- It presents a unique contextual longitudinal study of self-identity work among service members in transition.
- It provides the field of military research, which is primarily populated by voices from psychology, sociology, health care and medicine, with a practical theological voice.
- It offers existential and spiritual perspectives derived from service members in a pluralized and secularized context to those working with health care and spiritual care.
- It assisted the participants' self-identity work during transition.

One limitation of the project, due to the original interview design, should be addressed. In the research project proposal the idea was to follow twenty participants and to conduct the first interview cycle (Time 1) as each was about to leave service, thereafter the second interview cycle (Time 2) one year post exit, and the final interview cycle (Time 3) two years post exit. In theory this was a preferable design. However, the time that was required to recruit a sufficient number of participants who fit such restraining criteria in such a numerically limited military context created a dire risk of severely prolonging the already long data gathering process, and therefore the criterion for participation in the project relative to exit point was widened (this will fully discussed in chapter 4 on Method).

1.5 An overview of the dissertation

This dissertation is comprised of ten chapters. The idea and the function of the chapters is that they should aid and support, piece by piece, the understanding of existential and religious dimensions in identity reconstruction among Swedish military personnel in the process of becoming civilians. The fact that the project includes processual long term storied data has inspired this dissertation to move this narrative data to the centre of the dissertation. Therefore, it should be said that this dissertation is about empirical lived life experiences; that they are its heart. It may be useful to introduce the metaphor of pieces of a puzzle in regards to the disposition of and relationship between the chapters as these are supposed to connect into each other as pieces of a puzzle wherein the dissertation as a whole is the final puzzle in this book upon which others and myself can then continue to build. All the pieces are important for the dissertation's final picture of this evolving puzzle.

Chapter 1, *Introduction: Identity Reconstruction in Transition from Military to Civilian Life*, which is concluding here with this overview of the structure of the larger dissertation, introduced the ways in which various terms and notions are adopted and understood, a background of military cultures and their contextual differences, and how cultures may shape military identities in different ways, including by-products of practices in military cultures. Research on transitional experiences with a specific emphasis on self-identity work was also introduced. The chapter concluded with a presentation of the research project, research questions, contributions, and limitations.

Chapter 2, *Defining the Theological Features of this Project*, presents the interdisciplinary approach of the project, the context wherein it has been conducted, the utilization of methodologies such as lived religion, ordinary theology, implicit religion, and additional definitions. Moreover, it presents the existential shapes of the project. These features combine to lay the foundation for the theological theory building throughout this dissertation.

Chapter 3, *Narrative Identity and a Dialogical Self,* introduces narrative theory and the specific dialogical approach included in the dissertation. This section is committed to firstly present a general position on narrative theory in resonance with narrative psychology. Thereafter follows a presentation of Dialogical Self Theory which serves as a theoretical position of the self as a dialogical narrator. The dialogical self as a narrator equates a self with multiple I-positions, and each and every one of these I-positions has his/her own stories to tell. Moreover, I-positions are the authors of the Me's which become empirical agents in narrative stories of the self. Thus, according to the Dialogical Self Theory, each self has not just one cardinal story to tell, but instead many stories populated by different Me's with correspondingly varied I-positions. In narrative accounts there may be tension and conflict, or dialogue and cooperation between unique I-positions of self that have the capacity to engage in dialogue; these varied I-positions can even form alliances and coalitions. This chapter concludes with a presentation of the narrative methodology (within a dialogical framework) which has been employed throughout the narrative analysis.

Chapter 4, *Method*, provides a description of the qualitative, narrative and longitudinal approach of the project, followed by an explanation of the joint production or construction of knowledge as a way of understanding what occurs during an interview. Moreover, this chapter contains a particularly detailed presentation of the researcher's positions, followed by a description of sampling, participants and interview design including an. The final parts of the chapter include the means of analysis and a general description of the analysis. The chapter concludes with a discussion on criteria to assess a narrative research project such as this.

Chapter 5, *Experiences of Swedish Military Personnel in Transition*, presents both general and particular experiences of transition within the sample based upon the first subquestion. This analysis has been conducted as a narrative inductive inquiry wherein the content and process among the participants has been investigated and elaborated between and within the groups. The results of the analysis are presented. Additionally, a number of narrative portraits will be given to better chronicle the voices of the informants in regard to content specific themes and processes. The final part of the chapter will introduce the discovery of three narrative evolutionary paths of transition: a full transition, a hybrid outcome, and finally a full return to military service. The paths function as a bridge from chapter 5 onto chapter 6.

Chapter 6, *How is Identity Constructed and Reconstructed in the Transition*, presents the analysis of the second subquestion of the research study. This analysis has also been conducted as a narrative inductive inquiry within a dialogical framework wherein the content and processes have been elaborated and presented through the displayed narrative evolutionary paths recently presented in chapter 5. During this analysis a number of analytical discoveries and insights of the self-identity work on the traversed paths will be shared, followed by an array of narrative portraits that are presented to highlight content specific themes and processes among the dialogical selves in transition. The chapter concludes with theory building.

Chapter 7, *Existential and Religious Elements in the Process*, presents the response to the third and final subquestion. Once again the analysis has been conducted as a narrative inductive inquiry wherein the existential and religious elements have been organized and elaborated partly by the three evolutionary paths of self-identity work, in addition to the specific elements that emerged across the paths. Through this process a number of analytical patterns and themes have been displayed within and between the paths of the sample. Additionally, narrative portraits are described to allow the participants voices to populate the chapter.

Chapter 8, *Investigating the Influence of the Interviews*, presents (parts of) the evaluation letters which the participants were invited to respond to and return once the interview study was concluded. Their responses suggest that the interviews influenced the participants' self-identity work in positive ways. Chapters 5, 6, 7, and 8 provide the empirical results of the project which will engage in conversation with practical theology in the final theory building of chapter 9.

Chapter 9, *A Theological Theory on Transition from Military to Civilian Life*, introduces a theological theory on transition from military to civilian life built upon the empirical analysis in the previous chapters. This theological theory is existentially and spiritually oriented and integrated with a dialogical framework. This theory provides the research field on transition from military to civilian life with an alternate voice which presents a tentative and contextual, existential and spiritual theological proposal of such a journey, a journey of transition that can benefit from correlational and critical dimensions located in time and space.

Chapter 10, *Conclusions*, presents the lessons learned in regards to the central research question and the study as a whole. Implications and possible routes for future research are discussed.

CHAPTER 2

Defining the Theological Features of this Project

2.1 An interdisciplinary approach

This research project as a whole is interdisciplinary and thereby combines a narrative approach within a dialogical framework for analysis with material drawn from sources such as lived religion (Ganzevoort, 2009; Ganzevoort & Roeland, 2014; McGuire, 2008), implicit religion (Bailey, 1990; Hamilton, 2001), and spirituality (Ellens, 2008, 2011; Heelas, 2008; Pargament, 2008, 2011; Pargament, Lomax, McGee & Fang, 2014). Several case study articles have been published using extracted narratives from this project; all of these articles have employed an interdisciplinary approach even as several lean more to narrative and dialogical methodology (Grimell, 2015, 2017a, 2017b, 2017e) whereas others utilize a more spiritual and/or practical theological methodology (Grimell, 2016b, 2017c, 2017d, 2017f). The development and application of a narrative approach within a dialogical framework has been beneficial for this dissertation as this framework has been applied in the analysis of the empirical chapters, which in turn have served as the foundation for the theological theory building throughout the dissertation. The theoretical ideas of a dialogical self and the derivative assumption of a self which consists of I-positions have been integrated into the theological prerequisites of the theory building. The theological theory which will culminate the last chapter is built upon the suggestion that what is needed to advance self-identity work in military transition to civilian life is a theoretical framework and methodology which can take into account conflict, tension, contradiction and polyvocality in a storied self without reducing this plurality to a single personal narrative of ego-identity development across time. Instead, what is opted for is a more nuanced understanding of the self as a dialogical narrator with multiple I-positions which are displayed by a storied self (Grimell, 2017b; Hermans et al., 1992; Hermans, 1996a).

This narrative approach within a dialogical framework serves as a cornerstone for the idea of a self as presented in the theological theory building throughout the dissertation. Because a dialogical self consists of I-positions, which are themselves constantly positioning and counter-positioning in relation to each other within the space of the self, contradiction, tension, and resistance, but also cooperation, collaboration, and deeper inner peace, are all possible. The dynamics of such I-positions which populate the self are dependent upon their constructions within different cultural settings (e.g., family contexts, school contexts, church contexts,

28

sports contexts, university contexts, military contexts, job contexts) which bring complexity into the self. Across time, some I-positions may become positioned in the spatial and/or temporal shadowland of the self; meanwhile others may grow much more vociferous and narratively active on a spatial and/or temporal level within the self (Hermans & Hermans-Konopka, 2010). I-positions of a self can also develop an infected destructiveness and darkness, just as they can flourish though productiveness and brightness, depending upon both how each I-position is shaped and cultivated within and by the self, but also in response to the progression of life and the surroundings in which the self evolves.

A belief in God equates an I-position as a believer, one I-position among many other I-positions which also has the potential for cooperation, tension and/or conflict with the other positions in the self. Such an I-position is also constructed in some type of cultural context of a religious tradition, congregation, family and/or friends, etc. When considering a believer in God, it is suggested here that God primarily works through such an I-position, and that this believer I-position may evolve to be a very influential position in the self, or dependent on the evolution of the self exist in the shadowland of the self while other culturally produced I-positions may be more or less motivated to make dialogue and cooperate with this position. Likewise *I as a believer in God* may itself be more or less interested in collaboration with other positions depending upon how these positions have been culturally constructed, in combination with other factors which influence the positions of the self and their dialogical capacity. This topography of the self suggests multiplicity in an individual wherein God operates through an I-position which can steer much of the perception and experience of life, but wherein this is not the only influential position within a culturally constructed self.

2.2 Context specific considerations for theological theory building

Five participants had some type of belief in God, angels or religious/spiritual experiences in nature or church concerts, whereas the majority of the participants had their beliefs and world views anchored in other more obviously secular domains and aspects of life, which implies using the words of Ganzevoort (2009, p. 6) that "Theologically, we need to be careful not to imply Gods presence in the traces we perceive and still appreciate the traces for what they are. Transcendence after all means that God may have left traces, but that we never know whether traces we find are traces of God." The Swedish society is known to be a rather secular context wherein the status and role of Christianity has declined over a long period of time (af Burén, 2015; Ahmadi, 2006; Thurfjell, 2015; Wikström, 1993). Recent research has suggested that,

"During the past three centuries, Sweden has moved towards a more individualistic and secular society, where religion has become less organized and more private" (Ahmadi & Ahmadi, 2015, p. 1188). This does not necessarily implicate that a theological theory must become invalid or outdated in a contemporary Swedish society, but rather that a theologian must take into consideration the context, including the audience to which a theological theory is supposed to speak to, and make dialogue with these in order to be interesting and fresh. To use the words of Tillich (1957, p. 13) "Man cannot receive an answer to a question he has not asked." The theological answers to the dimensions and elements of the transitional processes presented in the previous chapters must first somehow resonate to the participants' explicit and implicit questions of life and experiences, and then theology may offer a potential to become an alternate dialogical voice for both a military audience and a research field which to a large extent lacks such a voice. This is important for practical theologians who work in the spirit of lived religion because "In pluralized, secularized, and deinstitutionalized contexts, these fields should not be limited to explicitly religious or specifically Christian domains, but include the broader field of spiritual and existential practices" (Ganzevoort & Roeland, 2014, p. 1).

2.3 Lived religion, ordinary theology, and implicit religion

The theological approach towards the development of theological theory building across this project, and in this dissertation, was inspired primarily by two approaches in practical theology, one of which is known as *lived religion* (Ganzevoort, 2009; Ganzevoort & Roeland, 2014) and the other as *ordinary theology* (Astley, 2002). These two approaches share a focus on praxis or action among ordinary people in lived life as the object of study and reflection for practical theology. The concept of praxis emphasizes what people do rather than focusing on official, organized and institutional religions, their sacred sources and doctrines, and such. Astley (2002, p. 56) calls this specific focus of study "ordinary people's articulation of their religious understanding" or *God-talk*, whilst Ganzevoort & Roeland (2014, p. 3) describe it as "the ways in which religion is lived", an even broader perspective which does not necessitate explicit God-talk but instead includes, for example, gardening as an activity which for some harbors existential and spiritual significance. This practical theological emphasis on the study of praxis as lived religion also resonates with the sociological approach of McGuire (2008, p. 12); she defined *lived religion* as the study of "how religion and spirituality are practiced, experienced, and expressed by ordinary people (rather than official spokespersons) in the context of their everyday lives". McGuire (2008) states that in order to understand any individual's lived religion it is first necessary to make visible all of the aspects of his or her religious lives which have been rendered invisible by the social construction of religion in western societies. According to McGuire (2008) lived religion is based more on practices than on religious ideas and beliefs and thus rather requires practical consistency in order to work in lived life (p. 15):

> It needs to make sense in one's everyday life, and it needs to be effective, to "work," in the sense of accomplishing some desired end (such as healing, improving one's relationship with a loved one, or harvesting enough food to last the winter).

Based upon her approach to lived religion McGuire (2008) presented a number of case studies with interviewees and their lived religions of embodied practices such as gardening (which for one of the interviewees became a valuable spiritual discipline requiring patience, hope and nurturing love), social activism for peace and social justice (which to another was the core of his spirituality and lived religion), and even food preparation which became a valued religious practice for an interviewee.

The third avenue of interpretation in this project is implicit religion, a term which "refers not only to a reality, but one which is distinct both from religiosity (in the conventional sense) and from secularity" (Bailey, 1990, p. 483). It is suggested that implicit religion refers to phenomena that are not ostensibly religious, for example, commitment in a public house or the local community (Bailey, 1990). It denotes phenomena which can be included in a more conventional understanding of religion but do not obviously belong there, since they do not resemble religion nor understand themselves to be religion (Hamilton, 2001). Luckmann's (1967) concept of invisible religion which neither resembles mainstream religion nor may include a self-understanding of being religious is in that sense closely related to implicit religion (cf. Ganzevoort, 2011b). Bailey (1990, 1997) defined implicit religion somewhat broadly as a commitment to the human and/or the local community, or as "integrating foci" (Bailey, 1990, p. 490). An integrating focus among individual members of a community could, for example, be the sense of community that they experience. Bailey (1990) suggested that a commitment to the human is a form of experience comparable with that which has been described as a sense of the sacred by students of small-scale societies (cf. Pargament, 2008, 2011). Explicit religion may or may not be the vehicle for implicit religion. In this case implicit religion is employed because of its usefulness in interpreting the analysis through an alternate lens which provides this study with interpretations which would otherwise not likely be seen. The useful-

31

ness of implicit religion is also denoted in other empirical research in practical theology, for example, in ordinary theology (Astley, 2002).

2.3.1 Definitions of religion and spirituality

As already testified, several paradigms or methodologies of describing and understanding religion as lived and implicit are present in this study and used on different levels in regards to the narratives of the participants. For example, when ordinary theology (Astley, 2002) is used as the vehicle for considering explicit *God-talk* and the participants' articulations of their religious understandings and beliefs, then the religious methodology is more attuned to James' (1902) definition of religion as: "the feelings, acts, and experiences, of individual men in their solitude, so far as they apprehend themselves to stand in relation to whatever they may consider the divine" (p. 21b). Pargament (2011), however, suggested that "many contemporary psychologists would likely be comfortable" with James' classic definition of religion as "a definition of spirituality" (p. 30). Pargament (1999, 2011), on the other hand, defined spirituality as a search for the sacred. The relationship between religion and spirituality through the divine or the sacred moves the elaboration further towards the paradigm of lived religion and a definition of religion formulated by Ganzevoort (2009, p. 3) as:

> [T]he transcending patterns of action and meaning embedded in and contributing to the relation with the sacred. This is primarily a functional definition, aiming at maximum pliability so that we can account for new and different forms of religion. The core of the definition, however, is the relation with the sacred, which is not an endlessly open concept. Without going too deep into those waters, for me the notion of the sacred at least implies that it is a center around which one's life gravitates and a presence that evokes awe and passion. Often this is determined by the cultural context in which one lives and modeled by a religious tradition. In individual cases it may be something idiosyncratic that most people would not consider religious.

The sacred can, on the one hand, be understood in a more traditional sense as God, higher powers or divine beings, as well as other aspects of life that take on divine character and significance by virtue of their association with, or representation of, divinity (Mahoney & Pargament, 2002). From the outlook of the psychology of religion, the sacred can on the other hand be conceptualized in a broader sense as, "one that encompasses any variety of objects, from mountains, music, and marriage to vegetarianism, virtues, and visions" (Pargament, 2011, p. 32). Both the definitions of James (1902) and Ganzevoort (2009) may be used in re-

32

gards to a more traditional understanding of religion, through the divine or the sacred, in a collectivistic and/or individual manner but also invite a more open and lived interpretation of religion and spirituality. In this study there is no attempt to polarize religion and spirituality; these are rather viewed as closely related. Lived religion is understood as resonating to the depth of an individual and thus providing him or her with energy, power, passion, joy, peace, awe, and humility with which to sustain his or her spiritual existence. To lose such a lived religion would not only have an existential impact, it would also be a threat to the spiritual existence of the individual, to "man's spiritual self-affirmation" (Tillich, 2014, p. 39).[5]

Ganzevoort's definition (2009) also allows for a potential union with the broader paradigm of implicit religion (Bailey, 1990, 1997) by widening the understanding of an individual's potential lived religion with relevance for the spiritual life. This is a particularly useful combination of methodological lenses to adopt (i.e., lived and implicit) which presents an interpretation of the analysis which would otherwise not likely be seen. For example, a service member may experience that military communal life and service provide him or her with a higher purpose in life which includes sacrifice made in the interest of protecting the autonomy of the nation, freedom, human rights, and political ideas such as feminism. The structure of protecting this entity is embodied by the Armed Forces; the military community is devoted to the task of protection. The values, meanings, and practices embedded in such military communal life and service transcend the self in ways that most people would not consider religious in a traditional sense. The Armed Forces and the military community may be considered a "center" around which the service member's life gravitates including a presence that evokes awe, passion, joy, and meaning (Ganzevoort, 2009, p. 3). The nation and the military structure may be considered to be sacred and could potentially be violated which then would provoke powerful reactions, counter-actions, or even retaliations. This sacred entity with its military structure may ultimately be worth dying for (Lunde, 2009). However, by employing the paradigms of lived religion and implicit religion we could consider this as a type of lived and implicit religion with relevance for a service member's spiritual existence. Yet still, for the sake of clarity, instead of suggesting that this lived and implicit religion revolves around the sacred, the concept of a *military spiritual depth of life* will be employed and developed in this dissertation. The transcending patterns of action and meaning embedded in military communal life and service may contribute to the relation with a military spiritual depth of life which resonates deeply in the self and sustains the spiritual existence of an individual (Tillich, 2014). Such

---

[5] *The Courage To Be* was originally published in 1952.

spiritual depths of life may also be found in other contexts, and the theological theory on transition from military to civilian life in chapter 9 is built around the idea of such spiritual depths of life.

2.4 Correlational and critical theology

The introduced practical theological approach to the study of praxis locates stories of ordinary people as a central methodological resource which is ripe for collection when striving to compile knowledge with which to construct a theological theory (Ganzevoort & Bouwer, 2007; McGuire, 2008; van den Brand, Hermans, Scherer-Rath & Verschuren, 2014). Personal stories of activities and storied experiences allow reflection upon how people construct meaning with relevance for questions of life such as life, death, trauma, dreams, desires, and identities (Ganzevoort, 1993, 2008, 2014). Within this study the exploration revolved around how the interviewees constructed and reconstructed identities in meaningful ways across time during transitional processes after leaving full-time military service. The theological theory construction across this dissertation is built upon these prerequisites of lived religion, ordinary theology, and implicit religion, and is partly designated to speak or resonate to the participants who have contributed to the project over time by sharing their narratives of experiences. As such, this practical theological approach has much in common with narrative psychology, which characteristically explores everyday social and cultural practices of ordinary people (Clandinin, 2013; Clandinin & Connelly, 2000; Crossley, 2000; McAdams, Josselson & Lieblich, 2006; Mishler, 2004; Scherer-Rath, 2014).

This relationship between narrative accounts of practices, storied experiences, and the actual theological theory building, particularly in chapter 9, is also understood as a type of correlational theological method wherein an empirical understanding of a transitional process and existential questions therein are given theological answers (Tillich, 1957). In this method both independence and interdependence of existential questions and theological answers exist. From one perspective the questions and answers are independent from each other since the theological answers to humans' existential concerns are not found in humans themselves but instead drawn from other sources. However, the correlational approach implicates that there is a mutual dependence of the questions and answers which could be called a "theological circle", illustrated as an ellipse with two points: existential questions and theological answers (Tillich, 1957, p. 14). Tillich's (1957) idea of a correlational theological method serves as a source of inspiration, but is not stretched so far as to postulate upon generic existential predicaments of the current Swedish, or for that matter global, military society. There is not just one existential question and one theological answer, but rather many questions and many potential theological answers, and this theory is just one among those. This theological theory building primarily focuses on the transition from military to civilian life as rooted in the empirical accounts of the participants, but it also hopes to lead to a further outgrowth to widen its service, as much as possible, to a broader military audience.

The introduction of a critical correlational method, via the revisionist model for contemporary theology, serves as a theological answer to Tillich's correlational model. This revisionist model was proposed by Tracy (1975), partly because Tillich's method did not call for a critical correlation of the results of one's own investigation of a situation with the theological answers to it. Tracy's (1975) critical approach champions that the answers, as well as the questions, must be critically investigated. The analysis which spans across chapters 5, 6, 7, and 8 of this thesis represents the investigation of the participants' situations (or storied experiences) during transition, and the theological interpretation of this analysis across the dissertation, which culminates in chapter 9, includes the implication that such an answer shall be critically tested by consideration of other answers to transition from military to civilian life. It is suggested that those who present other answers to transition from military to civilian life, or make use of such answers, explore this theory building critically.

2.4.2 Self-reflection
The theological theory building hopes to heighten and assist a personal and critical self-reflection by the participants (and a military audience) upon the many layers and experiences in military transition to civilian life. The critical perspective in the theological elaborations functions to widen and potentially strengthen the approach to the theory building with theological material and Christian texts that articulate alternative questions which are worthy of reflection (Tracy, 1975). These questions are not explicitly formulated as limited little questions, but rather seen as an invitation to sow seeds which may grow and develop, any time and any place. Even though the theological theory construction is preliminary and locally built upon a limited number of participants and their experiences, it may have the capacity to assist other service members, as well as those who have already transitioned or will transition in the future, during the personal and critical self-reflection upon the many layers and experiences in the process. The idea of reaching a broader military audience includes an invitation for other research endeavors which consider this theory building and can widen the content beyond the

empirical accounts of the participants. How well the theological elaboration may work and/or assist the presented audiences (e.g., people who work in the field, participants, and a military audience) is in fact an empirical question.

2.5 Defining the existential features of the study

Theological and psychological existential paradigms have served as influential sources from which inspiration has been derived throughout this project, and this section will expound upon existential features of this study. The theologian Tillich serves as an inspiring source for a theological approach which intends to describe individuals' existential concerns in life through different modes of anxiety. In Tillich's existential theology as presented in *The Courage To Be* (2014), which was originally published in 1952, individuals' anxieties are frequently used when referring to the idea of nonbeing. Three sources of anxiety are highlighted as threatening being with nonbeing. Death as nonbeing threatens being by the annihilation of the bodily existence. Meaninglessness and emptiness of nonbeing threatens the spiritual existence of being or an individual's spiritual self-affirmation. Thirdly, the moral responsibility of being in the world as life requires an answer from the individual, the individual is required to answer, is eternally threatened by nonbeing via a risk of failing to find an answer to life. Thereby, a transition from military to civilian life is considered to be a potential threat to both the spiritual existence and the moral responsibility of being. A firm military identity, a salient experience of contributing to something larger in life, and a sense of meaning in life, may be temporarily or permanently lost in a transition from military to civilian life and this may encumber an individual with a sense of meaninglessness, emptiness, and identity loss which may pose a threat to the spiritual existence. This threat of nonbeing may be accentuated if an individual stumbles during the identity reconstruction and actualization of what he or she potentially is in the new life as a civilian and suddenly finds himself or herself in a situation with no direction, identity, purpose, and/or destiny. Nonbeing threatens the moral self-affirmation, and an individual may experience the anxiety of self-condemnation. Tillich (2014) suggests that courage is self-affirmation "in spite of that which tends to prevent the self from affirming itself" such as a transition which to its character deprives the individual of the old being in the world and thus requires an answer from the individual to a new situation (p. 31). Tillich's theological understanding of existential concerns has influenced the theological-existential features of this study, particularly in the theological theory building on transition from military to civilian life in chapter 9.

Other inspiring accounts for the existential features of this study are derived from psychological paradigms with an emphasis upon existential concerns with theoretical relevance to self-identity work. Of importance is the psychologist Yalom (1980) who carved out four major existential human concerns including death, freedom, isolation and meaninglessness. Such existential concerns implicated a secular or non-religious world view wherein humans needed to deal with fundamental emptiness, nothingness equating an absolute freedom or authorship. This condition of being in the world challenged the meaning of human existence, not in the least from an existential psychological perspective. The concerns were grouped into four categories, the first of which was a psychological need to cope with death and the definite end of life. The second focused upon freedom, which equated with the responsibility and authorship for one's life. The third concerned isolation, which was itself subcategorized into three spheres: intrapersonal (e.g., sacrifice of one's own potential or whishes), interpersonal (e.g., loneliness, isolation from other individuals) and existential isolation (e.g., an unbridgeable gulf between one's self and other beings, a separation between the individual and the world). The fourth category revolved around perceptions of meaninglessness of existence and how these contrasted against the inborn human desire and need for meaning. Death, freedom, isolation and meaninglessness implicated a need for people to cope with a sense of being alone, yet still the self had a responsibility to construct meaning and purpose for his or her existence and life within this world. One lens through which to reflect upon such existential concerns in regards to freedom could be through a consideration of human willingness to escape from the challenges of freedom by submission to authoritative leadership and world views (Fromm, 1947). In regards to experiences of meaninglessness, Frankl (2006) suggested that man's ultimate quest was the search for meaning in life. Independent of the outlook chosen for the perception of life, life demands, or alternately requests, some type of answer from humans (Tillich, 2014). People need to instill or create meaning in life and to attribute meaning onto experiences throughout life in order to sustain a life worth living. This also includes experiences of military service and transitions to civilian life, particularly if deployment to conflict areas has exposed service members to combat, death, suffering, or left them witness to assault and war crimes (Larner & Blow, 2010; Schok, 2009). An emerging perspective on recovery from moral injury after war with a focus upon soul repair stresses the need for societal support at different levels (e.g., institutions, civilians, significant others, and spiritual caregivers) to aid and assist former service members in the process of repairing their souls (Brock & Lettini, 2012). The self and the cultures in which it navigates are highly involved in such processes of creating and attributing meaning onto experiences of life. Identity construction and reconstruction are meaning making processes which continue throughout life and wherein the self plays a key role in collaboration with other people and cultural influences and guidelines (Neimeyer, 2012). Self-identity work in a transition from military service to civilian life is subject to personal, social and cultural meaning making processes. In recognition of the self's authorship, Koole, Greenberg & Pyszczynsk (2006) suggested that the self should be added to Yalom's (1980) concept of death, freedom, isolation and meaninglessness as a crucial corner-stone to the existential themes of life. A question such as *who I am* implicated a potential life-long existential driver for a person as he or she addresses who I am, who I am supposed to be and how I may fit in the world and life over time. Such questions of life may be of profound concern for a person, especially amid a transitional process with an emphasis on identity re-construction (Scherer-Rath, 2014).

CHAPTER 3

Narrative Identity and a Dialogical Self

3.1 Meaning through a narrative thought mode

This introductory section to the chapter serves to describe humans as narrative agents, who make and create meaning out of experiences in lived life through the processes of telling and retelling stories. Narratives operate as mediums through which experiences, identities, selves, others, and lives are both individually and collectively given meanings which are mediated and negotiated throughout stories (Bruner, 1986; Clandinin & Connelly, 2000; McAdams, 1988, 1997, 2013; McAdams, Josselson & Lieblich, 2006; Mishler, 2004; Polkinghorne, 1988). Throughout this chapter, and dissertation, narrative and story will be used interchangeably. It has been suggested that humans use a narrative principle when we think, perceive, imagine and make moral choices (Sarbin, 1986). These narratives are so ingrained in our inherent modes of action such that these narratives become an organizing principle for our lives (Polkinghorne, 1988). The narrative structures we live by will influence us in both conscious and unconscious ways. Already as children narratives are assembled from one's surroundings, and a variety of channels of distribution will help to construct a certain disposition of the self. It could be said that the software of the self is built-up through cultural and subcultural narratives within society. Such narratives will closely intertwine in the very shaping of a self which is conceived of a repertoire of culturally influenced yet personal voices with different stories (Crites, 1986; Crossley, 2000; Hermans et al., 1992; Ricoeur, 1998a; Scheibe, 1986; Webster & Mertova, 2007). Cultural narratives which speak within the self are to some extent personal appropriations and adaptations of narratives from society, and thus the individual is a composite of, yet in a way also an original author of, his or her composition. In line with this emphasis on humans as narrative agents, it has been suggested that the construction of a story follows a specific type of thought mode, which Bruner (1986) would describe as a narrative mode of thought. The contrasting or opposing mode of thought is the paradigmatic or logico-scientific one, which "attempts to fulfil the ideal of a formal, mathematical system of description and explanation" (Bruner, 1986, p. 12). In Bruner's original postulation, narrative mode leads instead to good stories, gripping drama, and believable historical accounts as it gravitates around human-like intention and action and the outcomes which ensue.

Polkinghorne (1988) suggests that narration is one of the operations of the realm of meaning which helps us understand our experiences of life. The construction of meaning is an activity shaped in the narratives told by each and every one of us. A story is a meaning structure, and this implies that to tell a story is to engage in a form of a meaning making process driven by the self. Meaning is always present in a story, explicitly or implicitly, on a personal as well as a cultural level. As life is lived stories will be told and retold, and changes in social and personal life call for narrative construction and reconstruction. These types of changes may result from different events such as the loss of a significant other, tragedy, a life-threatening operation, economic recession, transitions due to job loss or relocation to another place, divorce of parents, or divorce on a personal level to name only a few. All of these situations are to some level already instilled with meaning inherited from the cultural traditions within which they are located. However, at the same time a person as an agent of meaning has the potential, through a narrative thought mode, to interpret and retell another type of story, which may or may not intersect with or draw from a cultural tradition of meaning in regards to such events. By suggesting that telling and retelling stories is indeed a vital aspect, on a personal and cultural level, when constructing meaning from experiences in lived life, a significant assumption for a narrative approach has been displayed. Thereby the next section will explore the relevance of narrative approaches to identity and self.

3.2 A narrative approach to identity and self

Clandinin (2013), an early driver in the field of narrative inquiry, stated some years ago that since the time of her and colleagues' explicit interest in narrative inquiry as a research approach in the early 1990's "there has been an explosion of interest in narrative inquiry" (p. 10). However, even though we have witnessed a highly increased interest on narrative approaches to identity and self throughout the last three or four decades, it has much deeper roots. Already in the 1890's when Freud explored and developed what he described as a scientific practice of psychoanalysis, he almost exclusively worked with narrative accounts made by his patients (Alcorn, 2008). Freud would, as many psychologists or therapists of today may indeed recognize, aid his patients by working together through anxieties and assist patients to write new narrative accounts of their lives. New transformative life stories thus include an emotional reformulation of memory. With Freud as the starting point for the theoretical narrative journey in this section, two metaphors, told by researchers about one hundred years later, appear particularly useful to illuminate the interrelatedness of narrative approaches to identity and self throughout the rest of this chapter. The first metaphorical suggestion was made by Sarbin (1986) as he proposed that the narrative is a root metaphor for psychology. This implies that a narrative approach is a root avenue to human psychology. The access to the per-

40

ception of experiences in lived life is embedded in narrative accounts. Moreover, self-identity is expressed through narrative accounts. The second metaphor is derived from Hermans & Hermans-Jansen (1995) as they underscored that the basic metaphor underlying the approach to the self is that each person is a motivated storyteller. This suggests that by asking a person to tell a story of him- or herself, one likely invites a motivated storyteller who will tell her or his story with great self-interest (McAdams, 2013). In summary, these two metaphorical positions are easily recognized in Freud's work; his chosen methods seem to indicate that the access to the psychology of humans was situated in the narratives told by his patients who in turn were motivated storytellers. Suggestively, these two insights on narrative approaches to identity and self have been entertained by psychologists, therapists, counsellors, psychiatrists, researchers and others as useful strategies at least since the end of 19th century.

Throughout the last decades a broad variety of approaches to narrative identity and self could be found within a range of disciplines employing myriad theoretical and methodological outlooks, including but not limited to psychology (Crossley, 2000; McAdams, 2001; Sarbin, 1986), sociology (Slocum-Bradley, 2010), education (Clandinin & Connelly, 2000), literary theory (White, 1990), practical theology (Ganzevoort, 1994, 2011a; Ganzevoort & Bouwer, 2007), ethics (Hauerwas, 1980; MacIntyre, 2007) and philosophy (Ricoeur, 1991, 1992). Even though there are commonalities it would indeed be difficult to describe the research field on narrative identity as a homogenous field which upheld one theory on narrative identity; such a generalization would impose the risk of losing many of the rich nuances. The research field on narrative identity and self may rather be viewed as a field consisting of an array of narrative approaches or theories about identity which share some common threads. Amid methodological differences within the field of narrative research, many researchers assert that personal narrative, identity and self are closely related. Mishler (2004) formulates this by stating that "We express, display, make claims for who we are – and who we would like to be – in the stories we tell and how we tell them" (p. 19). In line with such a postulate there is an informal agreement that every story told is some type of a self-representation, which in turn equates a personal narrative to a kind of claim of identity (Clandinin, 2013; Ganzevoort, 1993, 2008; Mancuso, 1986; McAdams, 2013; Mishler, 1986; Sarbin, 1986). Additionally, such conclusions infer that a narrative approach is a productive and qualitative lens to use when narrowing in on empirical issues of identity in lived life (Clandinin & Rosiek, 2007; McAdams, Josselson & Lieblich, 2006, 2002; Polkinghorne, 1988).

Narrative analyses of storied identity claims can be conducted in many ways such as through themes and characters (McAdams, 1988, 1997), models including emplotment, perspective, tone, role assignment, relational positioning and justification for an audience (Ganzevoort, 1998, 2011a), development of stories (Gergen & Gergen, 1986), core narratives (Mishler, 2004; Riessman, 1993), long term field studies which take into account several oral and written and other sources (Clandinin & Connelly, 2000), and life story approaches (Birren & Cochran, 2001; McAdams, 1997, 2013), just to name a few. Some of these analytical approaches will be applied in different chapters of this dissertation. However, narrated characters in the stories told hold a particular relevance for the dialogical approach of this dissertation. By making specific claims of identities, through the stories of who we are, narrated characters will appear based on fragments from cultural and subcultural narratives (e.g., I as a father, I as a mother, I as a warrior). These cultural and subcultural characters are appropriated, perhaps further equipped and/or stripped, by the self in the construction of identities. It has been suggested by Sarbin (1986) and others, such as Mancuso (1986) and Crites (1986), that the author of these narrative characters in the story of who I am is *I* of the self. Formulated in another way, "I" construct a character of "Me" which the self then presents in the personal story of who I am (Sarbin, 1986, p. 18). The narrative construction of characters, with different features, has been suggested as a possible definition of narrative identity by Slocum-Bradley (2010). This implicates that narrative identity consists of two aspects: the character as such (e.g., I as a service member, I as a brother, I as a husband) and the specific features of these characters (e.g., competent, focused, efficient, loving, caring). Additionally, from a dialogical perspective, it is important to add the articulation or relationship between characters or voices, the potential dialogue between characters of the story (Hermans, 1996a, 1996b). The challenge of several characters of the self is narratively resolved through the distinction between character and story. "The many are the main characters; the one is the story within which the characters are given form, function, and voice" (McAdams, 1997, p. 118). This implies a set of I-positions that author a set of characters who become united, likely with tension and multiple plotlines or story lines, through a personal story of who I am (Grimell, 2016a).

3.3 The development of a self as a dialogical narrator

A further development of the idea made in 1986 by Sarbin and others was proposed in 1992 by Hermans, Kempen & van Loon as they offered a progressive translation of the I-Me distinction through the self as a dialogical narrator. The self as a dialogical narrator holds several

I-positions, and depending on time, situation, and audience, these I-positions author different characters of the self in the personal narrative (e.g., I as a service member, I as a brother). However, there have been several early contributors, located in the tradition of American pragmatism such as James (1890) and Mead (1934), to the development of dialogical approaches to the self. James serves as one important forerunner to the development of the conceptualization of a dialogical self as a narrator of characters (Hermans, Kempen & van Loon, 1992). James (1890) made use of the distinction between the self-as-knower (the I) and the self-as-known (the Me). The I, which equates as the self-as-knower, acts on experiences of lived life in a subjective manner. The Me, on the other hand, is the self-as-known, or the empirical self that is composed of all things that the person can call his or her own in a broad sense. This suggests that, for example, not only my body, but also my father, my wife, my car, my job, and even my antagonist(s) are part of myself as extended to the society. The other is not outside of the self, but rather an intrinsic part of it. Moreover, James (1890) described three aspects of the I. The first is identity which equates sameness over time, second there are distinctness from others, and third volition which refers to rejection and appropriation of thoughts. Somewhat later, Mead (1934) added further components to the development of the self as a dialogical narrator through the awareness of how selves are expected to conform to existing institutional structures yet are simultaneously able to innovate them. Mead's distinction between I and Me have both similarities and differences when compared with James'; they shared the agentic perspective on the I, but Mead emphasized even more strongly the influence and significance of others on the self. Innovation is a part of the I, meanwhile Me according to Mead answers to the organized attitudes, rules and regulations of the generalized others. In summary it could be stated that James' theory is rather individualistic, whilst Mead's approach is more fundamentally relational as the relation precedes the self.

Bakhtin (1973), rooted in the Russian dialogical school, serves as another source of inspiration for the development of a dialogical self schools of thought. All of the characters that belong to James' self are more explicitly elaborated in Bakhtin's (1973) metaphor of the polyphonic novel presented in his book *Problems of Dostoevsky's Poetics*. The metaphor of a polyphonic novel acknowledges the position that in these works of Dostoevsky there is not a single author at work, but rather several authors and thinkers represented by the different characters. There are a number of characters which function as a plurality of consciousness. The polyphonic approach suggests the existence of a multiplicity of voices that have the capacity to accompany or oppose each other in a dialogical manner. This has a vital importance for a dialogical self, as this dialogical construction makes the spatial dimension utterly integral from a narrative point of view. This should be understood in the light of narrative approaches wherein, generally speaking, the temporal dimension (time) often holds a particular importance. However, in a dialogical approach space, due to the gallery of autonomous characters who tell stories that are temporally dispersed, becomes simultaneously essential; space is equally as important as time. Everything coexists and lives side by side, as if both space and time are crucial for a dialogical self. One of the classic definitions of a dialogical self (Hermans et al., 1992, p. 28) particularly emphasizes the dimension of space:

> The I has possibility to move, as in a space, from one position to the other in accordance with changes in situation and time. The I fluctuates among different and even opposed positions. The I has the capacity to imaginatively endow each position with a voice so that dialogical relations between positions can be established.

Building upon the works of these forerunners, including James (1890), Mead (1934), Bahktin (1973), and others such as Buber (1970), who emphasized the significance of considering the other, the idea of a dialogical self has been developed further during the last decades and continues to evolve through the Dialogical Self Theory (Hermans, 2001a; Hermans & Hermans-Konopka, 2010; Hermans & Gieser, 2012). This enterprise has been, and continues to be, pursued and cultivated by many researchers worldwide.

3.4 Dialogical Self Theory

The concept of a dialogical self is tightly integrated into Dialogical Self Theory (DST), which combines what Hermans and Hermans-Konopka (2010) conceptualize as traditional, modern, and postmodern understandings of the self (see Hermans & Hermans-Konopka, 2010, p. 82–119, for a full review). The theory is described as "a *bridging theory* in which a larger diversity of theories, research traditions and practices meet, or will meet, in order to create new and unexpected linkages" (Hermans & Gieser, 2012, p. 1). DST is so broad and complex, and is formulated in such an open way, so that different, separated or even contradictory conceptual systems can be found within DST, and this very diversity can better enable interaction with other theories, traditions and practices.

The dialogical self theory postulates a self which is described as an extension to its society; this self is viewed as a "society of the mind" which is built upon and borrowed from the surrounding society so that even this exterior society also becomes an intrinsic part of the self

(Hermans, 2002, p. 147). This implies that the self harbours similar types of tensions, conflicting ideas and potentials for dialogue as the surroundings (Hermans, 2003, 2004). Additionally, this constructs a self with multiple I-positions which make up the position repertoire of the self (Hermans, 2001a, 2001b). The notion of an I-position is a key concept in DST as well as for a dialogical self. It has been suggested that there are two types of I-positions of the self: those I-positions linked to the internal (otherness-in-the-self) and those to the external (others-in-the-self) domain of the self. I-positions related to the internal domain of the self are located inside of a person (e.g., I as ambitious, I as disciplined). External I-positions are extended to the external domain of the self (e.g., my colleagues, my wife) but are nonetheless an integral part of the self. It is important to underscore that, given this basic assumption of the extended self, the other is not outside of the self but rather an intrinsic part of it (Hermans, 2001a, 2008; Day & Jesus, 2013).[6] The aggregation of these I-positions thus becomes the position repertoire of the multiplicity of the self (Hermans, 2001b). Unity is, however, still a central concept (Hermans & Hermans-Konopka, 2010). Unity and continuity are narrated by attributing I, me, or mine to positions, and even if they are contradictory, they nonetheless belong to the composite self.

I-positions of the composite self may have conflicting desires which result in expected decentring (disorganizing and destabilizing) movements, or conversely similar desires which lead to centring (organizing and stabilizing) movements of the self. This movement may be viewed as a dynamic process of positioning, repositioning and counter-positioning as I fluctuate in time and space over existing, new and possible positions. The multiple self promotes integration between such movements of the self (Hermans & Dimaggio, 2007). As external or internal I-positions diverge further or even come into conflict, the composite self may act to reintegrate such positions (Hermans & Hermans-Konopka, 2010; Nir, 2012). The dialogical capacity of the self may differ from person to person; it may be flexible or un-flexible (i.e., locked under a dominant I-position). The dialogical capacity of the self is tightly linked to society, and a lack of dialogue in a society may have a corresponding effect on the capacity of the dialogical self (Hermans & Dimaggio, 2007; Hermans, 2004). The dialogue of the self may be conducted between different I-positions such as between two internal I-positions (e.g., I as impatient agrees with I as restless), between internal and external or extended I-positions (e.g., I as restless gets frustrated to work with my lazy colleagues) or even between two exter-

---

[6] Also see Raggatt (2012) for an overview. Raggatt (2012, p. 31) suggested that an internal position is an I-position with a distinctive inner voice and a personal history, while an external position is an other-in-the self, for example the voice of a teacher, a parent, or a partner.

nal I-positions (e.g., my wife enjoys interacting with my colleagues and their wives and that helps me to interact better with my colleagues). This implies that I-positions within the multiplicity of the self give voice to different characters of the individual who thusly become united through a complex personal narrative (Hermans, 1997). The personal narrative, which consists of many characters or I-positions, is the empirical composite term of the theoretical idea of a dialogical self. The variety of voices can be discerned and "function like interacting characters in a story, involved in a process of question and answer, agreement and disagreement" (Hermans, 1999, p. 72).

3.5 Some key concepts of a dialogical self

As already introduced, the concept of an I-position presupposes the multiplicity of the self. The I, due to changes in time and space, is constantly involved in a process of positioning over a variety of existing, new and possible positions which implicate potential decentring movements of the self. The I accepts and even appropriates some of these I-positions while denying or even rejecting other positions as it attempts to centre the self. As a broad range of I-positions of the self are constructed by the culture at large (e.g., man, women, teacher, student, doctor, nurse) social dominance and power will be reflected or transferred into such positions (Hermans & Hermans-Konopka, 2010; Hermans, 2013). A collective voice of a social group may speak through a story of an individual just as a collective voice of an institution may speak through the mouth of an individual (Buitelaar, 2014; Hermans, 2012a, 2003). The social language of a social group is incorporated, to a higher or a lower degree, into the I-positions of the self. But a collective voice may be influenced by an agentic character of the self, which of course has its own intentions and may be assisted by other I- positions. For example, I speak as an officer (with a collective voice of a militaristic institution) in a particular military situation, but at the same time I very likely to some degree express my personal opinions as a father with children who is relatively similar in age to the other young service members. Suggestively, military culture may be represented on an individual level by a collective voice that emphasizes camaraderie, loyalty, discipline, obedience, and endurance across the ranks, but this collective voice is not likely to speak without first being influenced to some degree by the internal and external I-positions of the self.

As life is lived, the dialogical process between I-positions may experience friction. Conflicting positions may blatantly clash due to divergent desires and needs. Such a situation may radically decrease or even disconnect the dialogical process. For example, a service member in transition may experience great difficulties when the student and officer I-positions attempt to converse. The content within cultural constructions of positions may be too divergent to see eye to eye and move forward together. However, the development of a third position, for example as a reserve officer, may bridge such divergence or conflicts between the student and military I-positions (Grimell, 2015, 2017a). A third position has the potential to unify two conflicting positions without denying or removing their differences (Hermans, 2013; Raggatt, 2012). Such a development may result in a powerful third position which derives psychological energy from two dominant I-positions while simultaneously reactivating the dialogical capacity within the individual.

An individual may also have the capacity to assume a meta-position (or meta-cognitive activity), which enables the self to transcend specific I-positions and move above its self. The self would rise to a bird's-eye perspective to consider different positions simultaneously (Hermans & Hermans-Konopka, 2010; Hermans & Gieser, 2012). From a meta-position one can "take a broader array of specific I-positions into account and have an important executive function in the process of decision making" (Hermans, 2013, p. 86). The ability to take a meta-position or bird's-eye view facilitates the continuity, coherence, and organization of the self from a spatial view point.

Another way to assist and aid coherence and organization of the self from a temporal outlook are through promoter positions. The self may require reorganization or innovation as new situations in life are encountered. This may be made possible by promotor positions, innovators of the self par excellence. Promoter positions produce and organize different I-positions on a temporal level in order to allow innovation of the self as a whole. Real, remembered, anticipated, or imaginary significant others may function as promoters, and promoters may be located within the internal and/or external domain (Hermans & Hermans-Konopka, 2010). Promoter positions such as significant others (e.g., father, mother, teacher, team leader, or spouse) may exert long-lasting influence as promoters of an individual's development. Inspiring promoter positions, such as a teacher or parent, imply openness towards the future of the self as innovators of the self (Hermans-Konopka, 2012). For example, a service member may feel compelled to terminate a stressful identity reconstruction in transition, but upon thinking of an inspiring commander manage to pull through by focusing on the thought: *I am as a ranger trained by my highly respected Captain to never give up even if the mountain seems unclimbable. I don't want to fail my Captain who would not expect anything else of me right now than to go on and endure this transition.* As a result a new I-position may evolve on a

47

temporal level and thus support reorganization and innovation of the self as a whole by bringing a new empowering identity to a person. According to Valsiner (2004, 2005), promoter positions can be recognized by a number of characteristics such as openness towards the future and a potential to produce specialized and qualitatively different positions in the future self. Through this openness they host the capacity to integrate new and already existing positions. Promoter positions have a central place in the position repertoire which includes the capacity to reorganize the self towards a higher level of development. Moreover, they function in the service of continuity of the self, but in the same time give room for discontinuity. Continuity is served by their capacity to link the past, present and the future of the self, and discontinuity to a certain degree results from the fact that they serve as a source of new positions.

The last concept with relevance for this dissertation is the capacity to cooperate. A dialogical self has the potential to engage a coalition of positions, which may work together to assist and support each other (Nir, 2012). Depending on a specific life event and its impact on the self, a coalition may form and cooperatively act due to the shared desires, motives and interests of these I-positions. Such a coalition may become dominant and could potentially decrease the capacity for dialogue, or it could promote innovation of the self due to the necessity of addressing change. An emerging coalition of positions can serve as a powerful force that sustains a person on a path and direction in life that would not otherwise be traversable.

3.6 Transition: A crisis or a process of adaption

3.6.1 Crisis as disorganization of the self
A transition may or may not lead to crisis; however, a crisis and a transition have rather different impacts on the self from a dialogical outlook. Presented elsewhere (Grimell, 2016a) it has been suggested that as life is lived, unexpected and traumatic changes may result in a crisis. A crisis of the self is understood as a disorganization of the self in which one or more core-positions lose their function. A position is considered a core position when a large number of other positions are dependent on its functioning. When a core position loses its organizing function over the position repertoire, then those other positions are likewise eroded in a cascading manner, and disorganization of the self is very likely to manifest. This can begin an avalanche where many other positions are consequentially affected and undermined. This equates that the narrative structure of who I am is literally impacted, possibly to the degree

that it is shattered and fragmented (Ganzevoort, 1993, 1994, 2008; Janoff-Bulman, 1992). The main overarching story, and thus stories of various I-positions, of who I am are compromised and threatened. This disorganization implies a regressive movement of the self, but can however lead to a positive outcome. Depending upon "the number and quality of the promoter positions that are available and accessible in the internal and external domain of the self" a disorganization could actually be a step toward a positive and progressive result (Hermans & Hermans-Konopka, 2010, p. 243).

Two types of conflicts are commonly recognized amid crisis (Hermans & Hermans-Konopka, 2010). A uni-level conflict refers to a conflict between two I-positions at the same level of integration of the self. For example, an ethical person may have learned important moral guidelines but at some point in life exercised a type of behaviour resulting from another I-position at the same level of integration which violates such moral standards. This leads to a conflict in the self in which one position (e.g., I as an ethical and moral person) is experienced as clashing with the other (e.g., I as a service member engaged in combat and perhaps killing other humans). There can also be a multi-level conflict wherein a position located on a higher level of integration (i.e., more developed) finds itself in conflict with a position on a lower level of integration (i.e., less developed). For a rather mild but clearly multi-level example of conflict, a recently born but increasingly dominant position as a committed researcher is in conflict with a long and deeply integrated position of a believer, spanning from childhood to mid-life, who wishes to attend sermons and congregational life more regularly but is frequently overruled by the researcher who strives to use each hour as rationally as possible and feels that research should take precedence. It is not always an easy methodological task to interpret which I-positions are at the same level of integration of the self and which are on different levels. But empirical time (e.g., how old or new a position is) and narrative features of themes (e.g., how something is expressed, how often it is said, attached emotions) within a story considered amid other clues which help to gauge the relative power and importance of different I-positions may serve as guidelines in such an interpretative task.

In sum, as life goes on, the story of who I am may remain more or less intact, which reflects an integrated, organized, and centred self which can gracefully engage in expected dynamics of positioning and counter-positioning between I-positions or characters. Traumatic changes in life may disrupt this story and impair or even disconnect the dialogue of the self (Hermans & Dimaggio, 2007). Crisis may fragment and shatter the assumptions of the story and the self (Haynie & Shepherd, 2011; McMackin, Newman, Fogler & Keane, 2012). The self is deeply affected by such a crisis and may become disintegrated, disorganized, and excessively decen-tred (Hermans & Hermans-Konopka, 2010). Integration and reorganization may be enabled by promoter positions, which are innovators of the self par excellence. A coalition of posi-tions could also promote innovation of the self to restore integration of positions and dialogue among them, and from a narrative perspective to reconstruct the story of who I am.

3.6.2 Transition as adaption of the self

As new situations in life are encountered the self will likely need to adjust its organization of positions. "In the case of a transition, the self is confronted with a new, unfamiliar or even threatening situation that requires an adaption or reorganization of the self" (Hermans & Hermans-Konopka, 2010, p. 239). However, a transition does not necessitate the deconstruc-tion of core positions but rather instigates the adaption or reorganization of I-positions due to a new situation. From a narrative perspective the stories of who I am still exist but need to be reorganized and retold. Thus an internal reorganization of positions equates to an empirical reorganization of stories. Such a transitional situation may become a challenge for a dialogical self as it may result in decentring movements of the self (Grimell, 2015, 2016a, 2017a). These movements, more or less, disrupt the existing integration and organization of positions. If the dialogical self senses that it is losing ground faster than it is gaining, that forward traction has been lost, especially over an extended period of time, then this regressive movement may en-tail significant and looming risk of crisis, chaos, and fragmentation. Such a back-slide begs for re-direction.

In a transitional movement I-positions may experience increased friction or even conflict dur-ing the process due to differing desires. Both the transition itself and any resultant conflict can affect the dialogical processes, which may deteriorate or eventually become disconnected. But transition also entails the possibility for centring movements that work in directions of unity and integration. Such progressive movements may restore or reorganize positions of the self in the process of adjustment to a new situation in life. Core positions may continue to exist, and even thrive, amid adaptation due to transition.

A variety of strategies may be used by the self in the process of adaption. One example is the capacity to engage a coalition of positions built around shared desires, interests, and motives. Coalitions may work together for cooperation and support a dialogical approach of the self. Such a blend of I-positions engaging in a coalition may nurture adaptation or innovation of the self amid the necessity of addressing change (Hermans, 2008). Nonetheless, the converse may also prove true; a dominant coalition may decrease the dialogical capacity.

The discovery and creation of a third position may potentially bridge such conflicts and restore dialogue (Hermans, 2013, 2003). A third position has the capacity to unify two conflicting positions without denying or removing their differences, and thus a third position can lead a dialogical self to find consolation and even resolution amid conflict. "At the same time, the third position has the advantage that the energy, originally invested in the resolution of the conflict, can be used in the service of the development of a third position" (Hermans & Hermans-Konopka, 2010, p. 156). Finally, promoter positions may also assist the self in transition and even dire crisis, and promoter positions can give rise, on a temporal level, to new narrative identities.

3.7 A narrative methodology embedded within the dialogical framework

Dialogical Self Theory characteristically includes an application of narrative approaches since embedded in the theory is the self as a dialogical narrator with I-positions, characters, or Me's which the I can use when positioning and counter-positioning amid the interactions with individuals, institutions, cultures, and the encounters of situations in life (Hermans et al., 1992; Hermans, 1996a, 2001a, 2001b; Hermans & Hermans-Konopka, 2010). Through each I-position the self is enabled to experience things somewhat differently since, for example, two internal I-positions have distinct inner voices and personal histories (e.g., I as ambitious in comparison to I as shy), and this suggests that situations in life may be experienced in alternate ways using alternate I-positions as lenses. Additionally, when voices from a military commander, teacher, partner, father, mother, or child, i.e. "others-in-the-self", are taken into dialogical consideration situations may also be experienced in new and varied ways (Raggatt, 2012, p. 31). The concept of experiences is important from a narrative point of view. Clandinin & Rosiek (2007) suggested some time ago, inspired by the pragmatic tradition of Dewey and others, that experience "does not refer to some precognitive, precultural ground on which our conceptions of the world rest. Instead, it is a changing stream that is characterized by continuous interaction of human thought with our personal, social, and material environment" (p. 39). This understanding of the concept of experience implies two consequences. First, narrative analysis is concerned not only with exclusively personal experiences but also with the investigation of social, cultural, and institutional voices that speak through and influence an individual's experiences to different degrees, as a human is partly constituted, shaped, and

51

expressed by these voices. Such voices could, by employing a dialogical terminology, be described as collective voices (Hermans & Hermans-Konopka, 2010). This implies that experiences are layered and include both personal and more collective layers. Second, a continuous interaction between the self, others, and the world introduced the idea that experiences grow out of other experiences, and experiences lead to further experiences as a result of a person's interaction with the self, other humans, communities, and the world (Clandinin & Connelly, 2000). Taking this a step further, a narrated experience may likely change across time as a result of the continuous interaction with the self, others, and the world which from a dialogical point of view involves a continuous flow of positioning and counter-positioning, appropriation and rejection. Additionally, Clandinin (2013) understands continuity from an ontological perspective as experiences are continuous, and ultimately the only base upon which humans can ground the understanding amid the stream of personal, social, and material interactions. Clandinin & Rosiek (2007) argued "what you see (and hear, feel, think, love, taste, despise, fear, etc.) is what you get. That is all we ultimately have in which to ground our understanding. And that is all we need" (p. 41). A pragmatic-inspired and narrative understanding of experience inferred that narrative analysis is a methodology which investigates experiences as storied (Connelly & Clandinin, 2006). This suggests that in narrative analysis there is no direct access to experiences but rather to narratives about experiences or storied experiences. Such narratives about experiences are also dependent upon the dialogical narrator or more precisely upon which I-position tells the story about the experiences (e.g., service member, son, daughter, partner, man, women). Experiences among Swedish military personnel in transition from military to civilian life were therefore understood as narratives about experiences or storied experiences, experienced from and told by different I-positions.

3.7.1 Narrative identity construction and reconstruction during transition

Narrative approaches within a dialogical framework are frequently used among researchers, psychologists, therapists, counselors, and theologians who utilize the Dialogical Self Theory. Narrative approaches are embedded within a Dialogical Self Theory framework since the many stories of tension, opposition, conflict, disagreement, negotiation, cooperation, and dialogue which may make up the structure of a narratively complex self may be understood as storied characters, voices, or I-positions which populate a narrative self. However, within a dialogical framework there is no single formalized and accepted narrative approach which demands universal application but rather several approaches which exist in parallel and share a focus on utilizing I-positions or voices as tools to help understand a dialogical self from the outlooks of, for example, psychology, therapy, counseling, and empirical theology. Narrative reconstruction wherein actors, or voices, which stem from I-positions of the self reshape or reformulate the self-narrative across time has been investigated in psychological and therapeutic research on narrative processes of innovation and stability within a dialogical self (Dimaggio, Salvatore, Azzara & Catania, 2003; Gonçalves & Ribeiro, 2012; Hermans, 1999, 2003; Neimeyer, 2012; Nir, 2012; Raggatt, 2012; Rowan, 2012). The narrative approach employed in this dissertation is understood as a type of narrative approach emerging from and located within a dialogical framework. From this narrative outlook, identity construction and reconstruction refers to how preexisting and new I-positions shape the identity claims in the interview narratives during transition, and how these narrative claims changed the stories of who I am across time. From a dialogical framework it was assumed that storied characters of the self (e.g., military, student, employee and other civilian identities) held corresponding I-positions in the self. Moreover, predefined positions such as a third position, promoter position, meta-position, and other positions were, if they existed, likely to manifest as narrative characters or point of views in the self-identity work across the transition. The first interview narrative with the participants marked the empirical starting point for the investigation of the process of narrative identity construction (and a potential commenced reconstruction) in this research project. In order to render such an analysis robust and transparent in regards to the characters the following methodology was applied.

Explicit self-description made by the interviewees in the narratives were considered to be identity claims made by the characters of the self (Clandinin, 2013; McAdams, 1988, 1997, 2013; Mishler, 1986, 2004; Sarbin, 1986). Even though an interviewee did not always explicitly said, *this is my specific I-position as a service member*, the military character in the military story represented a specific point of view (Riceour, 1998b) in the self which equated an I-position (Grimell, 2015, 2016a, 2017a, 2017b). This applied for the rest of the characters as well.

The interviewee was encouraged to identify a character or voice explicitly. For instance, as a result of such a request, an interviewee may have stated, *this is the service member in me speaking*. This represents a declaration of a specific I-position. The researcher occasionally failed to ask for such identification by the interviewee, yet identified a specific character of the story in later analysis. When any identification was deemed potentially ambiguous the analytical observation was followed by an email to the interviewee who included a description of the analysis and proposed I-position. The interviewee then confirmed whether this observation actually represented the interviewee's self (Grimell, 2017a).

Added to this methodology was a narrative element borrowed from another narrative paradigm or methodology presented by Ganzevoort (2011a) which emphasized the tone of the narratives, which in this case is linked to storied emotional experiences of characters. Since the transition equated storied experiences of emotional issues for the participants it was helpful to address such issues as the tones of the characters. The self-identity work could therefore be linked to the evolution of preexisting and new tones, narrated through old or new characters, in the interviews narratives. As already stated, there is no single narrative approach which has emerged from a dialogical framework but rather several ones designed to serve different research purposes.

The element of relational positioning (Ganzevoort, 2011a) was likewise added and in this case refers to how the characters related to audiences in the construction and reconstruction of personal stories over the period of investigation. Relational positioning becomes particularly interesting in an investigation wherein participants transition from one dominate military culture, including the identity claims thereof, to another culture with new identity claims. Storied forms of relational positioning towards military and/or civilian audiences are particularly helpful in the quest to understand the self-identity work and the evolution of preexisting or new characters. For example, if military audiences systematically are left out across time or if a participant distances himself or herself from such audiences and instead is relationally positioning towards a new civilian audience, then this is suggested to demonstrate a potential growth of a certain new I-position or character of the self.

Finally, a longitudinal design with repeated interviews created the possibility of a triangulation (Patton, 1990; Polkinghorne, 2005; Verschuren & Doorewaard, 2010) between each interviewee's narrative accounts, wherein preexisting and new characters of I-positions evolved over time and were compared within a storied landscape of the self, and it was this evolution which was understood as potential narrative identity reconstruction. Within this design the perceived rearrangement, movement, conflict or dialogue between narrative characters of the self, expressed in the storied accounts, was the potential self-identity work (Hermans, 1996a, 1997, 1999, 2001a, 2003).

3.8 Assessment of DST's application to this chapter

Dialogical Self Theory has contributed to the endeavors to map and grid narrative self-identity work in transition from military to civilian life throughout this project through its capacity to suggest connections between narrative characters or points of view and I-positions in the self. Such connections have advanced the understanding between conflicting self-narratives and internal conflicts within the self which often tend to manifest within a transition from military to civilian life. Positioning, re-positioning, and counter-positioning have been transferred into the narratives through the diverging or even conflicting identity claims made by the inter-viewees. DST has provided the interpretation of the processes among the interviewees with a promising framework to understand and describe the movements within the self (Grimell, 2015, 2016a, 2017a, 2017b, 2017d, 2017e, 2017f).

Yet there are also challenges within the DST model by Hermans & Hermans-Konopka (2010) which deserve to be articulated. This model is complicated and complex with its many socie-tal, cultural, and personal layers of I-positions which ultimately, collectively imply that the self is populated by an endless number of I-positions or voices. A question which may be posed is how far one can stretch the model's claim and elasticity of I-positions in the self both in theory and in practice? A number of preexisting and new characters or points of view were demonstrated to populate the self-narratives of the interviewees over the project, but given such a consideration of the model these would only have illustrated a fraction of the psycho-logical topographical map at the moment of the interview. In practice, the model may chal-lenge the empirical findings by implying that there may be shadow positions and numerous other positions which may influence the self in unknown ways. The model acknowledges, by proposing a potentially endless number of positions within the self, an eternal potential to evolve in complex and un-anticipated ways throughout life.

Another related and interesting question is what the binding factor of self is? From the out-look of DST it could be suggested that the composite dialogical self serves to unite I-positions, that the composite self works in the service of integration and dialogue (Hermans & Hermans-Konopka, 2010). A logical question which follows is: what is the binding factor of the composite self? With the DST model in mind it is crucial to separate between a hard and a soft version of the multiplicity of the self. The hard version implies that parts (or positions) of the self function in autonomous ways and hold capacities for making direct relationships which do not require mediation of any integrating agency. The soft version, on the other hand, suggests that positions or voices need the assistance of some agency to link them together and hence create and further unity and continuity. Hermans & Hermans-Konopka (2010) prefer the soft version of the multiplicity of the self which proposes that the I itself can work as this agent to guard a certain degree of unity and continuity in the self, or sameness using James' (1890) words.[7] The I has an agentic function and the capacity of appropriating and rejecting activities and positions. Additionally, the I can operate on different levels: being purely engaged in a position, reflecting on this position, and/or taking a broader number of positions into consideration. In summary, this suggests that a binding factor of the self is the I.[8] The DST model of the I, however, does not extensively discuss the foundation of the I nor inborn elements in the I of the self which for each and every individual could host the potential to create a certain disposition, drive, or desire of the I. This chapter will conclude by suggesting that the I is not solely a social construction but may include inherent elements which have the potential to shape the foundation of the I in unique ways for each and every individual.

---

[7] James (1890) described three parts of the I: sameness, distinctness from others, and volition.

[8] From a narrative point of view it could be proposed that the binding factor of the self is the story, that the self is a story (McAdams, 1997; Mishler, 2004; Polkinghorne, 1988), and that the foundation of the I is the authorship (Sarbin, 1986). From a spiritual perspective it could be suggested that the foundation of the I is the spirit of the self, the true self, the essential binding core of the self which propels the self forward (Pargament & Sweeney, 2011).

CHAPTER 4

Method

4.1 Purpose, relevance, and research question

As mentioned in the first chapter, the overarching purpose of this research project is to describe the role of existential and/or religious dimensions in identity reconstruction among Swedish military personnel during the process of becoming civilians. The purpose of the project, with a reference to the process of self-identity work with its layers, called for a qualitative and longitudinal study design with repeated interviews with the participants over time as they transition and integrate into civilian life and population. The relevance of the purpose unfolds on several levels. To start, it serves to cover a general gap in the research field on transition from military to civilian life in regards to (a) existential and religious dimensions, (b) in identity reconstruction (c) over time in a specific context. The combination of longitudinal and qualitative approaches is seldom present in military empirical research on self-identity work in transition to civilian life, and such work is especially rare within a Swedish context. Additionally such a combination of a longitudinal and a qualitative approach as in this study may help to highlight that military and civilian cultures shape different narrative characters with corresponding but diverse I-positions which the self needs to centre and integrate. The participants of this study provide unique insights into self-identity work among adults as they transition from one dominant military culture to another. Therefore, from an academic standpoint, the purpose of the project holds relevance as it attempts to illuminate a seldom explored realm which should be more fully addressed empirically and theoretically. Moreover, the theoretical and qualitative lens of a dialogical self, which is rarely employed in the understanding of self-identity work in transition from military to civilian life, holds academic relevance as well. Within disciplines such as psychology or sociology, which to a large extent dominate the research on transition from military to civilian life, the longitudinal and dialogical approach to self-identity work is seldom found, and this implies that the purpose of the project holds particular relevance for such academic disciplines. In addition, as existential and religious dimensions seldom accompany studies on self-identity work in transition from military to civilian life, this focus may too provide the research field on transition to civilian life with potentially novel insights which could then be further built upon. For practical theology, the purpose illustrates relevance since few theological empirical and/or theoretical studies have approached transition from military to civilian life from such an angle (e.g., longitudinal, qualitative, contextual, dialogical). The purpose of the project, which includes the combination of a longitudinal and qualitative design, can serve all of the academic disciplines of theology, psychology, and sociology with potentially new and/or alternate findings. Finally, it is suggested that the research purpose has social relevance since transition from military to civilian life affects a large number of military personnel. The ways in which service members deal with identity issues in transition will impact their social environments such as partners, families, friends, new potential employers, and colleagues, as well as global social systems via, for instance, public health questions (Grimell, 2017b).

The central research question which was derived from the purpose of the project was: what is the role of existential and/or religious dimensions in identity reconstruction among Swedish military personnel in the process of becoming civilians?

In the subsequent step, the research question was then reformulated and divided into three minor subquestions which in turn would return three subanswers to aid in answering the research question. Three subquestions were then formulated and abstracted through such a process:

- What are the experiences of Swedish military personnel in the process of becoming civilians?
- How is the identity constructed and reconstructed in the transition from a service member's to a civilian's narrative?
- What are the existential and/or religious elements in this process?

These subquestions were essential for answering the research question and fulfilling the purpose of the project in systematic ways. The function of the three subquestions was to structure the analysis of investigation into three interrelated blocks: experiences, identity work and existential/religious elements. These subquestions were then utilized to organize the following three main empirical chapters.

- Chapter 5: What are the experiences of Swedish military personnel in the process of becoming civilians?
- Chapter 6: How is the identity constructed and reconstructed in the transition from a service member's to a civilian's narrative?
- Chapter 7: What are the existential and/or religious elements in this process?

Chapter 8 will share the reflections from the participants which were gathered in the evaluation letters, which also provide further context and data for the continuation of the theological reflection upon the empirical research which follows in Chapter 9, wherein a theological theory on transition from military to civilian life will be developed.

4.2 A qualitative, narrative, and longitudinal approach

A qualitative method appeared to be a suitable approach since the study aimed to describe subtle self-identity work in narrative identity reconstruction processes on an individual level across time (Kvale & Brinkmann, 2009). "A primary purpose of qualitative research is to describe and clarify experience as it is lived and constituted in awareness" (Polkinghorne, 2005, p. 138). Therefore, qualitative research has, by delving into the nuances in experiences of lived life, a particular advancement compared with quantitative research when addressing storied issues of self-identity work in transition. In order to meet the purpose and main research question, the project has collected a type of qualitative oral data through an interview design. Additionally, this qualitative data-gathering approached its subjects with an interpretative orientation whereupon the emphasis was steered towards content and the process of meaning making or the construction of meaning in the lived lives of people (Crotty, 1998; Gorman & Clayton, 2005; Kvale, 2007). Within such a qualitative approach was embedded the assumption that a productive way to understand lived experiences in life was to focus on personal perceptions and interpretations of one's self via, for example, interviews in their natural settings (Flick, 2002; Liamputtong & Ezzy, 2005; Merriam, 2002, 1998; Verschuren & Doorewaard, 2010). In previous research on transition from military to civilian life with an emphasis of identity issues, a qualitative approach has been opted for as the best methodological fit to explore the research topic since it offers a method of inquiry into the meaning that individuals ascribe to the human problem of life transition (Brunger et al., 2013; Burkhart & Hogan, 2015; Savion, 2009; Yanos, 2004). Experiences and processes, like self-identity work in transition, can only be understood through the eyes and words of the people who are or have experienced that particular situation. This suggested that qualitative research was conducted in the natural world within a specific context; it was emergent rather than strongly prefigured and predefined, and it was fundamentally interpretative (Rossman & Rallis, 2003). With such a qualitative approach the aim was to suggestively build theory as well as portraits of existential and religious dimensions in longitudinal self-identity work by inductive analysis of content and processes with each participant.

It has been suggested that qualitative research "is an umbrella term under which a variety of research methods that use language data are clustered" (Polkinghorne, 2005, p. 137). As already extensively introduced through the theoretical framework of analysis in chapter 3, a narrative approach appeared to be particularly useful in the enterprise of understanding experiences and identity processes in lived life (Clandinin & Rosiek, 2007; McAdams, 2001; McAdams et al., 2006; Raggatt, 2006, 2002, 1998). A transition implied a disruption of a story that created voids in a personal narrative into which new characters may progressively emerge and grow (Hermans, 2001a). Meanwhile preexisting characters continue to act. One of the basic premises of Dialogical Self Theory was that different I-positions produced different narratives (Hermans, 1996a). A narrative analysis was tailored to be an inductive inquiry built around the interviews (Clandinin & Connelly, 2000; Clandinin, 2013; McAdams, 1988, 1997, 2013; Mishler, 2004). Additionally, a qualitative inquiry addressing self-identity work in transitional movement would benefit from a narrative approach wherein the development across interview narratives could be studied over time. This equated that the longitudinal focus was significant in order to describe the narrative identity reconstruction as an ongoing process. Such an analysis included content as well as the very processing of narrative accounts. Recurring annual interviews over time were vital to capture the content and the evolution of each individual's identity reconstruction process throughout the transition from military to civilian life. The longitudinal approach, together with existential and religious dimensions in self-identity work, rendered this project a novel contribution to the field of research that addressed transition from military to civilian life.

4.2.1 The joint production of knowledge

The narrative analysis of this study was built around the interviews. The interview situation - which included the briefing prior to the interview, the actual interview and the discussion afterwards - was understood as a relational and dialogical process which included a "complex sequence of exchanges through which interviewer and interviewee negotiate some degree of agreement on what they will talk about, and how" (Mishler, 2004, p. 110). The participant's accounts of their life experiences was situated in that context and may therefore be viewed as co-produced. An interviewer's presence and involvement was integral to the interviewee's account (Ganzevoort, 1998). Therefore, Mishler (1986) suggested that a "story" is a joint production (p. 82). The participant's stories were influenced by a number of things such as their physical location, the interactions and the relationships established throughout the situation. The knowledge was therefore co-constructed during the ongoing dialogue between the interviewer and the interviewee (Clandinin & Connelly, 2000; Crossley, 2000; Kvale & Brink-mann, 2009; Riessman, 1993). From such an epistemological outlook there was no intention as an interviewer to put on a neutral mask and follow a tightly directed standardized protocol in order to carve out some objective truth inside of participants who were perceived as objects. This would rather obstruct the process, and quite possibly render the participant uncomfortable and unsecure. Instead, the interviews were conducted by a committed researcher striving to establish a tone and climate of cooperative exploration of identity experiences of military personnel in the process of becoming civilians wherein the participant was the expert on his or her own experiences (Clandinin, 2013; Mishler, 2004; Polkinghorne, 1988). Additionally, Polkinghorne (2005) suggested that "to obtain interview data with sufficient quality to produce worthwhile findings, researchers need to engage with participants more than a one-shot, 1-hr session; they need to attend to establishing a trusting, open relationship with the participant and to focus on the meaning of the participant's life experiences rather than on the accuracy of his or her recall" (p. 142). Such an approach was even more significant from a military cultural perspective. There are natural power contrasts between a researcher and research subjects, and likewise between elder and younger peers. When the power contrast between different military ranks was added to this mix, then it quite plausibly becomes even more crucial to have and clearly express this focus on cooperative respect for different life experiences, in contrast to cultural hierarchies (Mishler, 1986; Riessman, 1993).

For many participants, however, it was a significant connection throughout the study that the researcher has been a military officer who has also transitioned into civilian life. This is not a particularly new insight, and already some decades ago the narrative researcher Mishler (1986) postulated that from an interviewee's perspective it is important that the interviewer shares the idea of what constitutes an appreciated identity in the shared culture (see also Clandinin, 2013). Moreover, Brunger, Serrato & Ogden (2015) addressed the challenge of researchers who were unfamiliar with military culture and therefore do not share the knowledge and appreciation, something which may impact upon a researchers ability to elicit more detailed responses. Brunger and Serrato, who acknowledged their own lack of previous military knowledge and experience, felt that some participants were reluctant to engage with them as interviewers on a deeper, more emotional level. The idea of *researcher acceptance* "is therefore of principle importance when attempting to facilitate dialogue and insightful research" (p. 97). This suggested that military cultural values, military identities and the full range of transitional experiences were more likely expressed in these narratives gathered by an interviewer with similar military experiences. Additionally, some participants have participated with an explicit therapeutic goal of engaging in some kind of self-identity work. Others have expressed altruistic motives of sharing more knowledge about military transition to civilian life. Taken altogether, the interviewees in this qualitative interview study were understood as "motivated storytellers" who in many regards demonstrated cooperation and willingness to share and tell their storied experiences of identity and meaning, good and bad, throughout transition from military to civilian life (Hermans & Hermans-Jansen, 1995, p. 27). These suggestively strengthened the validity (i.e., to measure what is intended to be measured) of the study (Ganzevoort, 1998; Mishler, 1991): to investigate existential and religious dimensions in self-identity work during transition from military to civilian life.[9] The longitudinal design may have deepened the trust between the researcher and some participants since details were narrated in later interviews which were left out in earlier ones (in some evaluation letters this design was recounted as aiding engagement; however, one participant also dropped out of the study due to his limitations in regards to time).

In summary, from this epistemological outlook, no storied interview account was perceived to be complete, and the participants "include only a small sample of their life experiences, selecting what they seemed appropriate in the context of the interview and appropriate to the course it took" (Mishler, 2004, p. 110). However, the willingness to share experiences facilitated the exploration of the process under investigation, but these storied accounts did not speak for themselves, or provided direct access to other times, places or situations. These narrative accounts were interpretative and, in turn, require interpretation.

4.3 The researcher's positions

This section serves to present the researcher's position as transparently as possible because every researcher likely has stories that will influence, among a number of things, the specific research field and dedication of scholarly interest (Clandinin & Connelly, 2000; Hermans, 2012b). In my case I am a former officer in the Swedish Armed Forces. I served altogether for about ten years and obtained the rank of a Lieutenant. After serving as a platoon commander I began my own process of transition and identity reconstruction as I left full-time service to become a civilian via university studies. That was not an easy transition, far from a linear process of identity reconstruction. The story of who I am was interrupted, and at times lost, as was the related meaning in life. Realization of a new meaningful reformulation of a story of

---

[9] The topic of validity will be further discussed in the end of this chapter.

identity was quite a challenge. After almost two years in psychology studies, I decided to study to become a minister in the Church of Sweden; however, after another three years at the university and fulfilment of the academic studies to become a minister, I decided to re-enroll for full-time service because my identity and related meaning still resonated stronger in the I-position of an officer. But after one more year of training soldiers, a coalition of the family oriented, minister and academic I-positions within me made the complicated and difficult decision to leave active service and finalize the ordination as a minister. So I did. Somewhere in that process this project was designed and approved; meanwhile I kept both a formal and a voiced I-position as a reserve officer in the Armed Forces.

The motivation for designing and conducting this research on self-identity in transition grew from a combination of factors rooted in my own experiences, primarily the lack of research on the subject matter that could assist me in understanding self-identity work during the transitional process, and a sense of responsibility to make a contribution to both former service members who had endured this transition but who still had questions about it and to active service members who at some point in the future will transition to a civilian life.

Today my narrative identity reconstruction rests primarily upon three important narrative characters with specific stories of who I am; an officer, a minister and a researcher. These narrative characters and their related stories have three significant I-positions within myself, shaped by rather different cultural contexts such as the Armed Forces, Church of Sweden, and the university settings in primarily Sweden (Umeå University) and the Netherlands (Vrije Universiteit, Amsterdam). The characters were presented linearly from a temporal perspective, first the officer, followed by the minister and then the researcher. However, as for space and dialogical positioning, the researcher would appear to be the stronger, followed by the officer and the minister. Still, they all have their different voices and contribute to the dialogical routes of myself in specific ways different days.

Moreover, there are other important I-positions of myself which produce other narrative characters and stories of who I am (e.g., I as a father, I as a husband, I as a son, I as an outdoor person, I as a music lover). At times, a healthy dialogue among I-positions resonates onto the narrative characters in the story of who I am. Sometimes tension and conflict among the narrative characters is symptomatic of tension and conflict among I-positions of myself (Hermans, 1999). Although populated by one particularly salient narrative character and I-

63

position, the researcher, this project has been a collaboration of these I-positions and many more.

In addition to the fact that I conducted the interviews as a researcher with a stated purpose, the participants also knew that I was a former military officer. In the eyes of the participants I am a person who has served, and we shared a common military background which established a sense of basic trust throughout the interviews (Mishler, 1986, 2004). As real humans, there in reality was no such thing as a perfectly neutral and objective approach to research in general, or to an interactive qualitative and longitudinal research enterprise such as this (Clandinin & Connelly, 2000; Clandinin, 2013; Ganzevoort, 1998). As I repeatedly accompanied the participants during their potentially most vulnerable years of transition, I learned to know them, but most of all their interview stories very well. I read their transcripts and listened to their digitally recorded interviews over and over again. Even though the development of the relationships were asymmetrical, wherein I as the researcher kept asking the questions, relationships have indeed been established where I feel and care for the participants' situations and processes even as I strove to not interfere, which was of course in and of itself impossible because there clearly must be some effect upon the participants from asking such deep and profound questions which most probably led to introspection, and possibly further repercussions (Scherer-Rath, 2014).[10] This assumption was later confirmed by the evaluation letters which were given to the participants after concluding the interviews and which revealed that the questions influenced the participants' self-reflection (presented in chapter 8). Although my own former experiences were not explicitly invited into the interviews and were almost never shared with the interviewees, my own existential and religious dimensions in identity reconstruction in transition to civilian life were mirrored by their lived life experiences on the transition (Kvale & Brinkmann, 2009). My lived experiences of transition were useful and assisted me in asking relevant processual questions which than result in even more content.

As it was important to recognize my own transition, tension, conflict, self-identity work, and other experiences throughout my transition, I was driven to formalize my own stories which identified influential I-positions of myself prior to this research project. This was done by reflecting upon how my own most influential preexisting and new internal and external I-

---

[10] Someone may raise a question how the reliability was influenced by the fact that I feel and care for the participants; I suggest that it is important to approach an interview with commitment and authenticity in order establish trust. To feel and care for the participants' situations and processes, yet without losing the professional interview-guided direction throughout the interviews, is part of such trust-building authenticity as a researcher and a human.

positions and storied characters which had shaped my transition were themselves shaped by the transition and then writing these reflections down on paper. The aim of this self-reflection was not to create a complete and final account of my own transition, tension, conflict and self-identity work, but rather to advance growing awareness of my personal story. This was intended to safeguard the interviewees' stories of transition from any bias that could be introduced in the analysis of their processes of transition by isolating their stories as much as possible from my own transition; it was an effort to limit the variables (Clandinin & Connelly, 2000). Still, a story perceived as a story passed does change in how it was and is perceived and recounted by a self which is naturally continually enriched with an ever growing body of knowledge and experience, and thus my stories were likely affected by all of the narrative accounts that have been told and retold by the interviewees throughout the project (Clandinin, 2013). Just as for the participants during the longitudinal project, my stories have changed, too, throughout the years of the project.

4.4 Methodology of the project: Sampling, participants, and interview design

4.4.1 Sampling

In order to learn about the issues that were of fundamental importance to the purpose of the study, the term purposive sampling was significant. Since the qualitative approach of the central research question was not focused on how much or how many, random sampling was not optimal for this study. Merriam (2002, p. 12) gave the following advice:

> Instead, since qualitative inquiry seeks to understand the meaning of a phenomenon from the perspectives of the participants, it is important to select a sample from which most could be learned. This is called a purposive or purposeful sampling.

By purposeful sampling it was identified, in the early phase of the project, that it would be beneficial to cooperate with regiments in order to recruit participants in the process of leaving full-time service. As the researcher was a former officer, and currently a reserve officer, the access to the military organization was facilitated in some regards (e.g., the researcher had cultural awareness of the organization, knew how to navigate within the system, and was known by at least one regiment). Contacts were made on a local level with two Swedish regiments (through the veterans' coordinators) for assistance in recruitment of participants. The request was approved. But the regiments wanted to control the process and distributed the letters of information about the project via local officers on different units. Approximately

65

fifty copies of the letters were sent to each of the regiments. From one of the regiments (i.e., Norrbotten Regiment) two participants volunteered rather directly, but then, no additional volunteers stepped forward. The reasons for this were probably manifold, and were impossible to know with certainty since there was no access to the local exchange of information in the final communications with the service members in the units. Some suggestable motives for the absence of volunteers during the autumn could be the length of the study, the theological approach of the study, and that the fact the exit of service was somewhat seasonal due to the start of educational programs on universities; this study was launched during the autumn which suggests stability in the ranks.

The paucity of volunteers early on coupled with the longitudinal design of the project created a dire risk of severely prolonging the already anticipated long data gathering phase of the study. However, since the longitudinal design was critical for the study focus across temporally long transitional processes, a decision was made to accelerate the process by both widening the criterion for participation in the project relative to exit point in addition to employing a snowball sampling strategy which involved querying a number of people who had access to potential participants. The criteria, after the revision of exit time, became:

- Willingness to participate in a longitudinal study
- Employed by the Swedish Armed Forces as a service member
- Served for approximately two years or more
- Presently grappling with the processes of transition and self-identity work and plausible or identified existential and/or religious dimensions
- The elapsed time between exit and the first interview could range from 0 to 2.5 years (the only change in the criteria, which previously required that the initial interview promptly followed or even preceded exit)

This change enabled recruitment of the rest of the sample, and fortuitously a rather diverse sample, as desired. However, this process required approximately nine months purposeful recruitment as the sample of participants, and therefore the interviews, were far-flung across Sweden. Roughly thirty days per year have been consumed solely by travel and interviews. Meanwhile, some volunteers who did not fit the criteria in regards to exit time were not included in the project. The first interview cycle (Time 1) began in August of 2013 and spanned throughout the entire following year, and then immediately continued with Time 2 (T2) throughout the following year, and Time 3 (T3) the year after so that sampling was completed in August of 2016. Each individual was interviewed at approximately the same time of year each round. As the sample was enlarged it could be concluded that a much longer time frame of transition, spanning zero to four and half years, would now comprise the data set. The extension of the time criterion expanded the insights in regards to transitional processes thanks to a broader time frame. In summary this was perceived as a positive outcome of the necessitated change.

The subsequent eighteen participants volunteered through the snowball sampling method (Noy, 2008; Polkinghorne, 2005). Calls were sent out via participants in the project, full-time serving officers and transitioned colleagues via email, Facebook, telephone, and in the flesh. All participants were informed about the study by a letter of information (presented in Appendix I). The letter of information presented the background of the project (i.e., a need to gain knowledge about the process of transition with a specific focus on meaning and identity), and described the purpose of the project, the number of interviews, the research ethics and the anonymity and other formalities. Prior to the actual distribution of the letters, a group of active and transitioned service members (both male and female) assisted the researcher in refining the content and tone in the letter. The reference group was satisfied with the final version. The first two participants received their letters face to face from their officers on the Norrbotten Regiment, whereas the rest of the letters of information were distributed by email or post as the participants volunteered. In all cases the participants had to complete a response letter and return it. This also served as a preliminary informed consent agreement until the interviews, during which the participants were properly informed about the study face to face, given opportunities to ask questions, and thereafter were provided with a formal informed consent agreement to sign (presented in Appendix II). In the response letter the participants were required to suggest a time and place to conduct the interviews. The response letter also included a small questionnaire which yielded the information which made it possible to make decisions regarding the purposeful sampling of potential participants for the study.

The very deliberate decision was made to exclude from the criteria for participation any confessional requirements such as *I see myself as Christian/religious/spiritual*. The goal was to absolutely not narrow the scope or exclude, and thus the letter of information was framed more around *identity* and *meaning* in the process of transition. It could be suggested that this more open set of criteria make the sample more recognizable and applicable to the wider military population. Sweden is well known as one of the most secular nations in the world (Ahmadi, 2006, 2015; Ahmadi & Ahmadi, 2015; Wikström, 1993), and the nuanced definitions of spirituality and existentialism in a land where angst towards organized religion is not un-known, so the goal was to be as open as positive in search of each individual's deeper mean-ings.

4.4.2 Participants

The sample consists of service members in transition to a civilian life, heterogeneous in terms of age, rank, branches, mission experiences and total years of service. The majority of the sample included service members aged between twenty-three to thirty-five years old. Four service members were around sixty years old and thus their transition was actually the process of retirement. Since they have served for such a long time, they appeared to stand out in a particular way that may jeopardize their anonymity when details of their service were present-ed (Kvale & Brinkmann, 2009). Therefore, in order to avoid such a risk all of the retirees were ascribed *36 years of service or more* in this dissertation even if they have served for a much longer period of time, and in some cases their position was also slightly altered. Three service members were female. The majority of the sample included Caucasian males and fe-males, while one was of Asian descent. A guideline for qualitative research is to derive a wide range of qualitative information-rich cases, and this was met through the illustrated diversity (McCracken, 1988; Patton, 1990). In order to get an overview, the details of the participants are presented below. All of the participants were given fictitious names throughout this study. The participants did not participate in the production of fictitious names. Since all of the par-ticipants had Swedish rather frequently used names they were given Swedish rather frequently used fictitious names. It may also be added that the positions are very general so as to not re-veal too many specific details that may ultimately, together with the narrative accounts and portraits, risk jeopardizing the anonymity of the participants.

Table 1. Details of the nineteen participants at the time of the first interview (T1)

Name	Age	Sex	Rank	Code[11]	Position	Service time	Branch
Adam	21	M	Private First Class	Other ranks 2 (OR-2)	Signaller	2 yrs	Army
Mattias	25	M	Private First Class	Other ranks 2 (OR-2)	Sharp shooter	2 yrs	Army
David	23	M	Sergeant	Other ranks 5 (OR-5)	Squad commander	3.5 yrs	Army
Emma	24	F	Sergeant	Other ranks 5 (OR-5)	Analyst	4 yrs	Marine
Helen	24	F	Sergeant	Other ranks 5 (OR-5)	Interpreter	2 yrs	Marine
Erik	25	M	Sergeant	Other ranks 5 (OR-5)	Technician	5 yrs	Marine
Gustaf	27	M	Sergeant	Other ranks 5 (OR-5)	Staff member	5 yrs	Army
Jonas	33	M	Sergeant	Other ranks 5 (OR-5)	Staff member	5 yrs	Air Force
Lars	25	M	Sergeant First Class	Other ranks 6 (OR-6)	Intelligence analyst	5.1 yrs	Army
Oskar	26	M	Sergeant First Class	Other ranks 6 (OR-6)	Intelligence analyst	4.5 yrs	Army

[11] Since the ranks may differ slightly between the different branches of the Armed Forces the NATO-codes are presented in order to relate each rank to the unifying NATO-system.

Andreas	28	M	Colour Sergeant	Other ranks 7 (OR-7)	Patrol commander	8.5 yrs	Air Force
Karl	26	M	Second Lieutenant	Officers 1 (OF-1)	Quartermaster	5 yrs	Marine
John	26	M	Lieutenant	Officers 1 (OF-1)	Platoon commander	7 yrs	Marine
Peter	28	M	Lieutenant	Officers 1 (OF-1)	Platoon commander	8 yrs	Marine
Maria	32	F	Lieutenant	Officers 1 (OF-1)	Platoon commander	11 yrs	Army
Roger	62	M	Captain	Officers 2 (OF-2)	Technician	36 yrs	Army
Lennart	61	M	Captain	Officers 2 (OF-2)	Instructor	36 yrs	Army
Stig	61	M	Major	Officers 3 (OF-3)	Chief of staff	36 yrs	Army
Tore	62	M	Major	Officers 3 (OF-3)	Staff officer	36 yrs	Army

4.4.3 Interview design

Based on the widened criterion in regards to the time elapsed between exit from service and entrance into the study, the participants were organized into three groups, roughly equal in size, depending upon the amount of time elapsed between the exit and the first interview. The use of time as the organizing principle of the sample was perceived to be a meaningful way forward in regards to the emphasis of a longitudinal and processual inquiry. As for the distribution of participants, the groups were developed rather intuitively based upon the amount of time which had passed between exit and the first interview in combination with the aspiration for equally sized groups. The sample groupings according to time are presented below in the interview design. The possible combinations to compare group differences are colored in the same ways in the columns of the interview design.

Table 2. Interview design of groups based upon the amount of time (T) elapsed between exit and first interview

Group	Participant	First interview/exit	T1 (2013-2014)	T2 (2014-2015)	T3 (2015-2016)
1	Roger	-1 month	One month previous to one month post exit	~1 year post exit	~2 years post exit
	Stig	-1 month			
	Adam	0 month			
	David	0 month			
	Emma	1 month			
	Lennart	1 month			
2	Erik	3 months	3-9 months post exit	~1.5 years post exit	~2.5 years post exit
	Andreas	3 months			
	John	4 months			
	Oskar	6 months			
	Peter	6 months			
	Lars	7 months			
3	Maria	13 months	~1.5 to 2.5 years post exit	2.5-3.5 years post exit	3.5-4.5 years post exit
	Tore	17 months			
	Gustaf	17 months			
	Karl	24 months			
	Jonas	24 months			
	Mattias	28 months			
	Helen	30 months			

However, the interview design of the project was challenged as the second interview cycle began; it then was revealed that several participants within different groups had actually conducted some types of military services following their initial interviews (T1). In one occasion an officer had actually reenlisted to full-time service, while others were scheduled for deployment on international missions. This equated that the transition had been interrupted, postponed, or even wholly aborted, by the decision to reengage in military service. The methodological and theoretical question which logically ensued was whether this should impact the interview design and reset these individuals' exit dates, which would then necessitate a reorganization of the participants within the groups. But instead of reorganizing the participants within the groups, this was understood as a part of the self-identity work in transition, and these dynamics were perceived as included amongst the dialogical processes of transition from military to civilian life. The I of the participant's self could easily be expected to act and fluctuate between military and other positions by positioning and counter-positioning as different I-positions of a dialogical self were reorganized throughout a process of transition or reenlistment (Hermans & Hermans-Konopka, 2010).

4.5 Interview Methodology

4.5.1 Interview structure, transcribing, and development across time

The interviews were based on a semi-structured design in order to cover topics relevant to the purpose of the project, central research question, and subquestions (Kvale, 2007; Seidman, 2006; van den Brand et al., 2014). Open questions were designed to allow the participants to construct answers in ways that they found meaningful (Bruner, 1990; Riessman, 1993; Webster & Mertova, 2007). The interviews started with the question, "If you think for a while, in what way would you describe your life or service as a service member?" Through this approach, the participants were encouraged to tell their own stories in their own way (Clandinin & Connelly, 2000; Crossley, 2000; Ganzevoort, 1998; Kvale & Brinkmann, 2009). The topics covered were: Military Story, Transition, Relationships, Identity, and Existential Concerns. The interviews generally lasted between one hour to one hour and thirty minutes, in some occasions longer (more than two hours) and in some shorter (in a few separate instances about thirty minutes depending on delayed bus/train connections or a tight schedule for the participant, but on the other hand in each instance this only happened once to any individual and his other interviews were unrestrained). The same interview-guide (presented in Appendix III) has been used throughout all of the interviews to enable comparison of the narrative process across time. The semi-structured design also allowed for improvised follow up questions, in regards to either content or processes, depending on what the interviewee formulated in his or her narrative accounts. The actual interview intervention consisted of three blocks or phases.

First, prior to the actual interview, the researcher presented a general briefing about the project; followed by an opportunity for the interviewees to inquire about the project and its developments. The actual interview followed and constituted the second phase. After the interview, there was always an opportunity for the participants to again ask questions, and it was common for interesting conversations to emerge as the digital recorder was shut off. The researcher always took observational notes or memos of the conversations afterwards, and in those circumstances where something profoundly useful emerged felt the obligation to ask the interviewee for permission prior to using those data in this dissertation.

The interviews were completely transcribed so that the spoken word has been transferred into written text, as this gave an authentic sense of the interview; however, "not fully equivalent to talk" (Bell, 1988, p. 102). This was such a time consuming aspect of the pre-analysis methodology, due to the longitudinal interview design in combination with the length of the interviews, that this service was provided by two medical secretaries (both were informed of the confidentiality of the participants and were willing to safeguard the anonymity of the interviewees).

Each participant selected the location (e.g., café, library, home) where he/she preferred to conduct each interview. Throughout the first interview cycle (T1) basically all of the interviews were conducted in public places; however, from the second interview cycle (T2) forward the majority of the interviews were conducted in the homes of the interviewees. This movement from public, rather neutral settings to such private and personal settings as homes could be subject for interpretation as an indication of the growth of trust between interviewee and interviewer.

4.5.2 Translating Swedish narrative accounts into English

The process of translating Swedish narrative accounts into English narrative accounts to use in the dissertation's empirical chapters (and in various articles, too) was a challenge in order to adequately transfer what has been said in one language into another. In cases where there were uncertainties, these matters were presented to a bi-lingual consultant who has English as the first language and Swedish as the second language. In the narrative accounts square brackets are used to explain military expressions, clarify ambiguity, or to shorten a narrative account wherein the participant said things which are irrelevant for the meaning as such in regards to a theme or issue. Constant repetitions made by the participant such as *I, I, I* were shortened to just one word, and other sounds like *ah, eh, oh, ah* and such were not presented in the examples of the narrative accounts.

4.6 Material of analysis

The material of analysis in the project included several empirical sources. The main foundation of material for analysis was, of course, built upon the interview design which included three interviews, conducted on an annual basis, for each interviewee. The longitudinal interview design generated a total summation of sixty-seven hours and thirty minutes of audio digitally recorded interviews. Moreover, the interviews were completely transcribed to written text as this gave an authentic sense of the interview. Needless to say, the transcripts of the interviews have grown into a comprehensive mass of data. All transcripts were incorporated into a hermeneutical unit in the qualitative analytical software program Atlas.ti (version 7.5.16) in order to organize the narrative data. The distribution of the total sums of digitally recorded interview times is presented below.

First interview cycle (T1)	22 hours and 14 minutes
Second interview cycle (T2)	20 hours and 30 minutes
Third interview cycle (T3)	24 hours and 46 minutes

When the third interview cycle was conducted each and every participant received, face to face, an evaluation letter (presented in Appendix IV) which they were encouraged to respond to after the interview and return to the researcher. The purpose of the evaluation letter was to investigate how the participation in the study had affected their experiences of transition regarding self-identity work and meaning, the relevance of the interview questions, and in what way(s) the interviews may have affected the participants. Every single participant responded, and this totally unexpected outpouring of positive and introspective evaluation letters served as an unanticipated but meaningful tool to understand how the interviews indeed affected the participants' self-identity work. The evaluation letter was not included in the original research project proposal but instead added into the design as the project entered the last interview cycle (T3), primarily due to an interest to learn if and how the interviews may have affected the participants amid their personal reflections post-interview. This was an interesting and in retrospect crucial subinvestigation; participants often revealed both in the end of the interviews and as we parted that they ruminated a lot about what they had said during the interviews and reflected upon who they were and their decisions in their lives. All of the returned evaluation letters were also scanned into pdf-documents and transferred into the hermeneutical unit of Atlas.ti. The results of the participants' answers in regards to how the interviews affected the

72

self-identity work are presented in chapter 8 and will be brought into the discussion during the last part of the dissertation.

4.7 The process of analysis

Chapters 2 and 3 fleshed out both a theological, religious, and existential conceptualization and narrative identity and a dialogical self framework so as to provide a comprehensive introduction of the theories, concepts, and the narrative methodology employed in the analysis of the interview narratives. This section serves to present how the analysis was conducted in a number of steps.

4.7.1 Overview of the narrative interviews: Hand and pencil analysis

As already mentioned, the process of narrative analysis was an inductive inquiry built around the interview. As an early step in the analytical process transcripts were used in close re-reading to summarize the content and abstract plot(s) or story lines, theme(s) and tone(s) of the interviews (Clandinin, 2013; Clandinin & Connelly, 2000; McAdams, 1988, 1997). This was in correspondence to what Ganzevoort (1998) would have described as global reading which serves as the first step "to get a general picture of the text" (p. 28). Global reading was then followed by discerning the story lines, whereupon the tentative meaning of the central themes was partly developed, however without the quantitative technique described by Ganzevoort (1998). Through such a process every transcript was reduced into a short story, but also tailored to briefly investigate the subquestions of the main research question to get an idea of what was going on. Such an initial analysis provided the researcher with an overview of the interview narratives. This analysis was made with hand and pencil on the paper transcripts, and the results were transferred into computer files.[12]

4.7.2 Moving deeper into the material: Qualitative data analysis program

The subsequent step revolved around transferring the digital versions of the transcripts into a qualitative data analysis program. This was important in order to keep track of the vast amount of material gathered throughout the project. Atlas.ti functions as an organizer wherein the material was coded in different ways to investigate content and processes. This qualitative data analysis program was chosen as a powerful tool to help analyze the mass of data in more detail and depth. The questions used as the interview guide were converted into fifteen indi-

---

[12] To ensure academic integrity, the initial analysis of the paper transcripts and the short stories are preserved for future reference.

vidual codes which are presented below. Thereby, to present an example, was the personal military story coded as a personal claim of a military identity (or character), the civilian story of a student as a claim of a student identity (or character), and so on. The intent behind holding so close to the interview guide in coding was to preserve to the narrative idea of having open questions that served to invite the interviewees to tell stories and make their own claims of narrative identities (or storied characters). In order to keep the codes personal and inductive semi-colons were used after each code (i.e., military identity; emphasis of competence, always willing to solve the task, loyalty). Thereby each and every code becomes individually applicable; this was the purpose in order to track individual changes in content and processes.

- Military identity; inductive description
- Military culture; inductive description
- Camaraderie; inductive description
- Motive for enlisting; inductive description
- Motives for leaving; inductive description
- Transitional experiences; inductive description
- Civilian culture; inductive description
- Civilian relationships; inductive description
- Military relationships; inductive description
- Identity; inductive description
- Student identity; inductive description
- New civilian identity; inductive description
- Existential and/or religious concerns; inductive description
- Direction in life; inductive description
- Reflections about the interview; inductive description

In order to enable comparison of group differences or similarities across time, and to make use of the design in a broader sense, fifteen code families were developed. Code families facilitate the organization of all of the individual codes into group data. By doing so nuances on an individual level were lost, but nuances on a group level could instead be illuminated. However, this was not a narrative interpretative tool. Atlas.ti coded in this way could only present differences or similarities between families, but in order to investigate what was happening the researcher had to return to the transcripts and try to grasp and interpret what was occurring. Atlas.ti could not do that job, but it helped the researcher, depending on what was coded, to display patterns between or within groups.

4.7.3 Analyzing experiences of Swedish military personnel in the process of becoming civilians

The first step in the analysis of the first subquestion was inductive and individually tailored, made by the hand and pencil model described earlier to get an overview of the content of transitional experiences in the transcripts. This involved adding comments and reflections to the paper transcripts and initial insights of the transitional experiences and stimulated further analytical ideas and proceedings. The subsequent step was to work with the transcripts in the hermeneutical unit within Atlas.ti, thus organizing and developing the transitional experiences with codes over time. Once the inductive experiences were coded, five overarching organizing themes were developed in close relationship to the experiences. Within the five common themes, a number of transitional experiences were titled as issues or subthemes to organize the experiences within the overarching themes. The hermeneutical principle for the development of these themes was that the issues or subthemes could be understood in reference to the overarching theme and vice versa. This suggested a reciprocity between overarching themes and locally emergent parts of the interview narratives as the overarching and common themes contributed to the interpretation of the local parts, and then the local parts contributed to the interpretation of the whole theme as such (Ricoeur, 1998c). For example, Sergeant David narrated transitional experiences in the first interview: "I carry with me some kind of failure, some anxiety, some vibes of depression; it actually goes up and down." This was described as two subthemes of transitional experiences: *feelings of anxiety* and *feelings depression,* which in turn were located within the overarching theme of *emotional issues*. This was the hermeneutical principle which suggests a mutual relationship between a storied experience, a subtheme, and an overarching theme. The overarching themes made it possible to organize the transitional experiences in a meaningful way, as it otherwise would have been quite a challenge due to the longitudinal design of the project to meaningfully describe the experiences among Swedish military personnel during the process of becoming civilians.

The five overarching common themes which emerged as a result of analysis and organized the storied experiences were:

- Identity issues
- A pro-militaristic position in the self
- Emotional issues
- Satisfaction

- The importance of significant others

4.7.4 Analyzing identity construction and reconstruction in the transition

Identity construction and reconstruction referred to how preexisting and new I-positions shaped the identity claims in the interview narratives during transition, and how these narrative claims changed their stories of who I am across time. This evolution was understood as narrative identity reconstruction and self-identity work. Over time the interview narratives were populated by different characters (or I-positions) of the participants and coded accordingly (e.g., military, student, partner, employee, and other civilian identities). Such different characters vocalized contrasting positions in the self which created tension and conflict, but also potentials for cooperation and dialogue and growth. The comparison between characters constructed in military cultures (with specific values, meanings, and practices) and characters constructed in civilian cultures (with specific values, meanings, and practices) discerned opposing narrative characteristics. In fact, preexisting and new emerging civilian characters showed counter features compared to military characters. Additionally, the narrative element of tone and relational positioning accompanied military and civilian characters in opposing ways which were important tools in order to understand narrative identity reconstruction and self-identity work in relation to experiences of transition, significant others, and audiences.

4.7.5 Analyzing existential and religious elements in the process

The concept of existential elements in the analysis opted for an inductive approach to articulated questions of life in the self-identity work. It was assumed that questions of life in the process of identity reconstruction were significant for the lived life of a person and as such could be understood as existential elements. The method included asking life questions which explored the lived life of the participants in the present process of transition, but also reflections upon personal stories within the interview narratives which had major (past) or may have significant (future) impact on the participant's life. Existential elements referred to storied experiences with relevance for the questions of life in the transitional process. *Existential concerns* was used as an open analytical code with the potential to address such storied experiences in the self-identity work and organize these inductively. Through the inductive narrative analysis six common existential themes or elements could be developed across the sample with relevance for the self-identity processes as presented below:

- Identities
- Meaningful employment and/or life styles

- Significant others
- Beliefs and values
- Sacrifices imposed upon significant others and/or the self
- Temporary departure from society to instead envelope one's self in the natural world

The concept of religious elements was chosen within this dissertation to refer to narrated experiences of relevance for the participants' questions of life connected to some type of belief in or experience of God and angels, i.e. transcendent or higher powers (Astley, 2002; Hermans, 2015) and spiritual emotions such as uplift, awe, humility, mystery, gratitude, joy, peace, and serenity (Pargament, 2011; Pargament et al., 2014). The method included asking question in regards to the beliefs and experiences, but also considered personal stories within the interview narratives which have had or may have religious/spiritual influence on a participant's life. *Religious concerns* was used as an open analytical code with the potential to address storied experiences with relevance for the questions of life tailored to explicit religious elements. Again, there were no confessional requirements to participate in the study, yet with time five participants described under their own ambition themselves as believing in God, angels, or experienced a religious/spiritual dimension in the Swedish nature or in church during musical events. Amid quite disparate religious experiences, only one theme was discovered which was related to the significance of nature for the self.

4.8 Criteria to assess research

4.8.1 Transparency
In general it has been suggested that the integrity and honesty of research can only be upheld through transparency (Lincoln & Cuba, 1985; Mishler, 2004; Polkinghorne, 1988; Riessman, 1993; Webster & Mertova, 2007). Transparency in this case included, but was not limited to, systematically building the dissertation chapter by chapter wherein background, theory, method, narrative analysis, and discussion were thoroughly presented and related to existing research via references. Moreover, the transparency of this project, in a wider sense, includes nine published articles in international peer-reviewed journals, eight of which made use of material derived from this project. Eight of the articles made use of the specific narrative and dialogical approach. Completion and submission of these articles served as a means of learning how to conduct qualitative research rooted in interviews, formulate analyses, build theo-

ries, and then coordinate submission, revision, acceptance, and publication, all in all long processes with many checks and interactions which hopefully and theoretically operate to safeguard the integrity and honesty of the research (Kvale & Brinkmann, 2009).

4.8.2 A qualitative approach to validity and reliability

A qualitative, narrative, and longitudinal research project such as this does not prioritize identifying generalizable and repeatable events or truths, but instead aspires to describe individual processes of transition from a narrative point of view (Ganzevoort, 1998). Therefore, concepts such as validity and reliability, which are often used to assess and guide traditional (quantitative) research, require some rethinking from the outlook of this project. This dissertation was inspired by Polkinghorne's (1988) understanding of validity which posed that, from a narrative perspective, validity is more closely related to meaningful analysis. Thus, if a narrative analysis includes an important finding, even as an individual occurrence, this can be described as a significant result since it offers qualitative insights. Additionally, Ganzevoort (1998), in reference to Mishler (1991), suggested that narrative research may score higher on validity (i.e., to measure what it is intended to measure) depending on the quality of data collection. This implicates asking interview questions which address the topic of investigation in adequate ways. On the other hand, reliability in terms of replication may be more difficult to capture within a narrative study.

The strength of narrative analysis, and the trustworthiness of the data, should not be a matter of theoretical argumentation due to analytical protocols, but rather presented via narrative analysis and the narrative accounts made by a participant to the reader (Clandinin & Connelly, 2000; Crossley, 2000). The published articles and the dissertation serve to bring those analyses, findings, and theory building to the surface in transparent ways. The narrative data should be accessible for researchers and participants as long as case sensitive information and the anonymity of the participants are protected (Clandinin, 2013; Polkinghorne, 1988).[13] One participant requested his own transcripts in the interest of self-analysis and has already received all of his narrative data. Upon the initiation of the research project in the spring of 2013 the researcher also started to write a diary wherein the research process and project has been described. This served not only as a story of the study, it also served to safeguard the integrity of the project by honestly helping the researcher recount and introspect upon the ups and downs, dead ends and promising avenues throughout the project (Hermans, 2012b).

---

[13] All of the material (e.g., interview recordings, transcripts, short stories, analyses, notes) is preserved in the interest of academic integrity.

The idea of reliability as the trustworthiness of the transcripts (Polkinghorne, 1988) was also vital for any narrative enterprise this included. But since the transcription process transfers the oral interview to a written text, it goes one step further from the actual digital recording (Riessman, 1993). It must be emphasized that the most rich source was the interview itself, and on one hand the interviewer actually could see and feel myriad cues and body language and channels of communication beyond just what was audible, whereas on the other hand the human mind is always subject to perception and recollection whereas the recorded word does not change, even after many years and other experiences. But relative to both of these, some nuance and detail was unavoidably lost during the transcription process, as with each subsequent step which led further from the interview. There must be a close mutual relationship between re-reading of each transcript and re-listening to each recorded interview to minimize the loss of details such as shifts in tone, pauses, bodily utterances, intensifiers, changes in the voice, or the exchange between interviewer and interviewee. Since a large number of the transcripts in this project have been transcribed by two medical secretaries, they highlighted as instructed any uncertainty in the transcripts, and these sections were subsequently deliberately checked by the researcher. Meanwhile the frequent re-listening to the recordings by the researcher (who also conducted all of the interviews) throughout the analysis in combination with the reading and rereading of the transcripts acts as an additional control. Fifty seven interviews were conducted throughout the project, and due to variables such as wind and background noise some naturally have lower sound quality than others, and this affected transcription. Some words and even sentences were lost due to the noise in a café, for example. The transcribers have missed some words in the process of transcription, and the researcher may have missed some words, too, in the process of control. The most important lessons learned were that the actual interviews and transcripts must live in a mutually supportive relationship throughout analysis, and that there was a compromise to be made in allowing interviewees to select comfortable locations where they may share more profound information, but may also be more difficult to hear.

4.8.3 Relocating storied real life experiences into the dissertation

The kind of narrative data required to study existential and religious dimensions in identity reconstruction among Swedish military personnel in the process of becoming civilians needed to be collected from the lived experiences of the personal lives of the participants (Polkinghorne, 2005). The quality of the data was tightly connected to the purposeful sampling of the participants, which in turn equates that the experiences and perspectives of the participants

79

must be present in the dissertation (Merriam, 2002). This was a challenge in many respects. First, there were extensive amounts of narrative material from the interviews which were utterly impossible to present with all of their detail and nuances in a dissertation due to the limited space given in such a format. Thus voices do need to be presented directly from the interviews, but space allows for only a small amount relative to the total body. The selection of a limited amount of storied experiences and perspectives among the participants inferred an inbuilt challenge: how to select storied accounts from such a rich data set. The criteria for selection included the goal that every participant should be voiced in the dissertation, and that this should be done in a balanced way relative to the three subquestions of the analysis, to avoid becoming tendentious. However, some voices may be presented as representative of a particular group in order to be able to present cases of narrative data more comprehensively (Grimell, 2016b).

4.8.4 Confidentiality

The next challenge in the process of selecting narrative accounts to populate the dissertation with the participants' experiences and perspectives was the protection of their anonymity (Clandinin & Connelly, 2000; Clandinin, 2013; Riessman, 1993). Some of the most personal and interesting stories may through their detail consequently compromise a participant's anonymity. In order to protect the confidentiality of the participants some details have been slightly altered or omitted in the explicit parts of the interviewee's narrative accounts in the dissertation or in published articles. This does not change the meaning of the content as such, it does change what has been said but a criteria for inclusion in the dissertation was that if the meaning was lost then the story was not worthy of inclusion. Several instances necessitated email discussions between the researcher and the participants regarding how to reformulate an episode or make a description in a relevant way that safeguards confidentiality. Some episodes or details were left out simply because the participants did not wish for those to be published. Moreover, a cultural awareness as a former officer informed decisions over which types of details or episodes should be omitted because these could potentially jeopardize simultaneously both an participant's identity and his or her future chances to serve; fully three years or more after active duty it was rather common among this set of interviewees to continue with military service in some way. The participants' real life names were replaced by fictitious names in the dissertation and published articles.

CHAPTER 5

Experiences of Swedish Military Personnel in Transition to Civilian Life

This chapter of the dissertation serves to present the results of the analysis in regards to the first subquestion which addresses the experiences of Swedish military personnel in the process of becoming civilians. This entails that the content of the storied transitional experiences, but also the development of transition upon three evolutionary paths in regards to time, are highlighted in the chapter. The methodology of the analysis was first and foremost built upon storied experiences of the interviewees in the process of becoming civilians. The interview guide explicitly addressed the motives in regards to the decision to leave service and the emotions and experiences throughout the process of becoming a civilian in each and every interview. Additionally, specific answers in the interview situation have resulted in a variety of follow-up questions in regards to the experiences in the transitions. Moreover, experiences of transition appeared throughout the whole interview narratives, for example in questions which addressed relationships with significant others, identities or more existential concerns. The results of the analysis, in regards to the experiences of becoming civilians among the interviewees, are presented in a number of steps which provide insights into the content of the transitional experiences as well as the discovery of three evolutionary paths of transition within the sample. The experiences among the interviewees in regards to the process of becoming civilians were seen as part of the self-identity work, and thus part of the reconstruction of new (meaningful) identities. The divergence down different paths suggests that transitional experiences influenced the participants' self-identity work in different ways. The processual development down one of the three transitional paths was part of the narrative reformulation of who I am.

The chapter takes its starting point in the results of the content analyses which serve to present common themes of transitional experiences among the sample. The goal in presenting such broader themes as an organizing principle of experiences from the interview narratives is to provide a distinct overview of the results of the content analysis of experiences as generated by transition in this sample. Each and every theme is amplified with examples of storied experiences from the participants to provide vocalized details to share what was behind the common themes and to be transparent about how the researcher has worked with the material.

The steps of chapter 5 are:

- Presentation of common themes for leaving (including content analysis which leads to the development of analytical themes)
- Presentation of common themes found within transitional experiences (including content analysis which leads to the development of analytical themes) which is illustrated in regards to the common themes using the narrative accounts of transitional experiences
- Mapping of the transitional paths throughout the process of becoming civilians (process analysis resulting in three developmental schemes among the sample)

5.1 Common themes for leaving

The perceived motives or reasons to leave full-time service influenced the process of becoming a civilian since, for example, a medical release due to PTSD may bring medical and psychiatric conditions to the process which severely affect the experiences of transition and reintegration into a civilian life and population. Therefore, it should be noted that all nineteen participants within the research project were voluntarily released as they decided to end their employment under their own fruition, or reached the date for retirement or the conclusion of time-limited employment contracts. Throughout the analysis of the interviews, four common themes were developed in close relationship with the narrated motives experienced by the interviewees as their reasons to leave full-time service. The hermeneutical principle for the development of overarching themes was that the subthemes could be understood in reference to the common themes and vice versa. The common themes are given below.

- Disappointment in the employer
- Stagnation of professional and/or personal development
- Curiosity to explore new avenues in life
- Retirement/expiration of employment contract

The two common themes of disappointment in the employer and stagnation of development, which were sometimes themselves interrelated, appeared to dominate among the motives within the decisional process to leave full-time service. Disappointment in the employer included the inability of the Swedish Armed Forces as employers, with their representatives on different organizational levels, to handle the participants' needs and desires efficiently and properly, but also disappointment in the military cultures with perceived shortcomings such as difficulties for female service members to be fully accepted by their male peers. Disappointment in the Armed Forces included the implications of the extensive reduction of the Swedish Armed Forces in combination with a change in the way in which the Armed Forces filled their ranks: in this instance going from a conscription system to a professional employment system which implicated a more rigid system concomitant with reduced opportunities to serve.

Stagnation of professional and personal development included experiences of not being allowed to pursue new or higher career paths or sustain the development of skills and performance; instead service was experienced more as repetition instead of progress, innovation, and expansion. Meanwhile, in some instances a sense of stagnation came after having grown and peaked rather rapidly in skills and performance due to the intense Swedish campaign in Afghanistan, whereas a return to ordinary service life in Sweden marked a pertinent decline of development. Stagnation also referred to criticisms of a narrowmindedness within military cultures which interfered with a wider and more open approach to life.

Curiosity to explore new avenues in life is another common theme articulated throughout the analysis which implies openness and a will to explore life beyond the military context.

Retirement and conclusion of employment contracts had more of a formal character in the process of leaving full-time service. However, even in the case of retirement, among the retirees in the sample it was not as final as it first sounds since the participants who retired in their early sixties have the legal right in Sweden to continue to serve up until the age of sixty seven. Similarly, upon the fulfillment of time-limited employment contracts there was and is always a possibility to reenlist again for un-occupied positions, albeit on lower ranks or less advanced positions. The distribution of the common themes among the sample is:

Group	Participant	Common themes for leaving
1	Roger	Retirement
	Stig	Retirement, disappointment
	Adam	Stagnation, disappointment, curiosity
	David	Stagnation
	Emma	Stagnation, disappointment
	Lennart	Retirement, curiosity
2	Erik	Conclusion of contract, disappointment
	Andreas	Disappointment, stagnation
	John	Stagnation
	Oskar	Stagnation, disappointment, curiosity
	Peter	Stagnation
	Lars	Stagnation, curiosity
3	Maria	Disappointment, stagnation, curiosity
	Tore	Retirement, disappointment
	Gustaf	Conclusion of contract, disappointment
	Karl	Stagnation, disappointment, curiosity
	Jonas	Conclusion of contract, disappointment
	Mattias	Stagnation, disappointment
	Helen	Conclusion of contract, disappointment

In order to give the common themes some voiced examples, narrative accounts are given from each group. These examples are neither outliers nor extremes but rather quite representative as for the common themes of disappointment in the employer, stagnation of development and curiosity to explore new avenues in life. The narrative accounts also reveal the degree of interrelation, for example between stagnation of development and disappointment in the employer.

5.1.1 Disappointment in the employer and stagnation of development

Sergeant Emma had been deployed to Afghanistan and was a military analyst who at the time worked in a staff section. She also had a civilian academic degree which equipped her particularly well for analyzing specific tasks. At the time of the first interview she was free from duty, one month post exit, and studying at a university to buy some time while looking for civilian employment. When asked why she left the Armed Forces, she replied:

> It is a certain frustration to discover that my civilian academic education is not appreciated. Just because I'm not an officer my word still counts in some contexts, but even if I have a Master's degree in the specific subject matter it is the Captain that will get up and the Sergeant will sit down. In one situation I was more or less told explicitly to my face by a superior "You realize that the only way out of this situation is to either become a reserve officer or an officer", and then I am thinking that the system is constructed in the wrong way if you don't utilize your personnel and the competence that exists, and then I feel that it is not my style, it is someone else's. I'm not going to settle down, I can't see the horizon cause I'm not in the right place to do it, I don't know if I'm the right person to do it at all. I experience that I have hit the wall, and that I am being limited.

5.1.2 Curiosity to explore new avenues in life and stagnation of development

Sergeant First Class Oskar was a specialist officer in the intelligence field who had been deployed to Afghanistan. At the time of the first interview, six months post exit, also studying as a university student, he responded to the same question posed to Emma with:

> I have always been interested to study on a higher academic level and in correspondence with the ambiguity in regards to careers of specialist officers, development of salary, and all of those aspects, in combination with my striving to study, it made me experience in the end that I should probably leave service. I have not left completely; instead I

keep a continuous contact with the unit which I like a lot, but after the decision I experience that it was the right one to make, and I would not want to go active again even though I liked it a lot. The turning point for me was some months prior to the actual decision when I sat and talked to a buddy in my section and asked how his development had been and if he had like a five year plan, and he had talked to his commander, and it didn't look too good, and then I thought he is seven years older than me, and he does basically exactly what I do.

5.1.3 Stagnation of development and disappointment in the employer

Private First Class Mattias had served as a sharp shooter, was twenty-eight months post exit, a university student, and replied in the first interview cycle to the same question as to why he left active service with:

I was employed under certain conditions; we were supposed to deploy then and then, but the longer the service kept going you realized that it won't happen, and, when it for the third time, when it failed the third time, what my employer had promised us, to deploy, and it didn't happen, then I realized that it could take many years before deployment. The reason why I joined the Army was foremost because I identified myself with the military. I felt that I could belong there; I like it when it is straight business, action, and the way it is in the military. I had a greater goal to go to places where help-organizations can't go, but where military organizations can. To serve was a path to get there, but when I realized that it wasn't going to happen I then felt that I don't want to do this anymore. [...] When I was serving, this was a disappointment.

5.1.4 Disappointment in the employer

Major Tore, seventeen moths post exit, had served in a staff section. Overall he had served *36 years or more* on a number of positions from company commander to positions on battalion level. He could have served further, but decided to retire when he had the chance due to a new administrative system called Prio, and during the first interview he stated:

During many years I was in charge of the economic system, and in the old system you had perfect control, but when Prio [the new administrative system in the Swedish Armed Forces] was introduced it became impossible. Before the introduction I had total control, and I don't know if it is that I don't understand the system or if it is too complex to be used in the most outer tentacle of the octopus. [...] Is it the idea that platoon

85

commanders shall sit 50% of their time and administer their soldiers, or are they not in command in order to be outdoors and exercise with their soldiers? And here somewhere I lost my feet on the ground.

An observation across time, since the same question about the motives for departure has been posed throughout all interview cycles, was that the participants kept close to their initial motives or reasons for leaving full-time service as expressed during the first interview cycle throughout the process of retelling the stories of transition in interview cycles two and three. However, in many cases the distinct emotional criticisms or critical points of view toward the Armed Forces tended to decrease and fade, particularly in the cases where during the first interview cycle these were most strongly articulated. This change of tone can be understood in at least two ways. Many participants, as will be described later, returned to service in a variety of ways, which implied that new, perhaps more positive, experiences were gained and incorporated into their military stories. Among those who traversed upon a full return to civilian life, the most emotionally laden tones, as articulated in the first interview cycle, tended to fade across time as a type of narrative smoothing wherein the more positive aspects of serving tended to be preserved, instead of the negative ones, in the stories of service (Spence, 1986). Another interesting observation in the first interview cycle when compared with the following interview cycles was that some participants were convinced that the motives and decision to leave were perfectly right in this early phase of transition. However, this affirmative and positive experience of the motives of departure and the decision to leave full-time service in the initial phase changed across time for some. This was likely related to a self-identity work wherein the military sense of who they were accentuated over time (for a further description see Grimell, 2016b, 2017d, 2017f).

5.2 Common themes found within transitional experiences

As the analyses proceeded on an inductive individual level in regards to the experiences of the interviewees in the process of becoming civilians, five broader and overarching themes were subsequently developed as a result of the analysis based upon the content of the experiences among the participants in transition across time.

Common and overarching themes of transitional experiences as results of analysis:

- Identity issues
- A pro-militaristic position in self

- Emotional issues
- Satisfaction
- The importance of significant others

These overarching and common themes served to beset or host a large variety of experiences, which are presented below as issues or subthemes in transition to civilian life which are complemented by examples of narrative accounts which vocalize the subthemes.

5.2.1 Identity issues

As for identity issues, these were experienced by almost all of the participants at some point throughout the process of becoming civilians; the only exception was the retiree Lennart. The common theme of identity issues contains seven subthemes or issues that were more or less articulated among the participants (Grimell, 2016b). Suggestively, a collective voice was discerned among the participants in regards to military community and camaraderie. All of the participants, across generations, articulated the depth of camaraderie during military service, and thereby echoed a cultural militaristic voice throughout the interview narratives of the participants. Yet while every participant articulated the value of camaraderie in service, the majority but not entirely expressed the issue of losing extraordinary community and camaraderie in transition.

Identity issues included experiences of seven subthemes:

- Asymmetry between military-veteran identities and new civilian identities, where military-veteran identities keep a dominant position in the self, and where the perception is filtered through a military-veteran lens
- A clear sense of a military "me"
- Adjustment problems to new settings
- A slow process of reconstructing a new meaningful story of who I am as a civilian
- Difficulties to find meaning and/or motivation in a new civilian life, which implies difficulties of reconstructing the story of who I am to become as a civilian
- Loss of extraordinary community and camaraderie
- Dichotomy between military and civilian worlds/relationships

Examples of narrative accounts of the seven subthemes within identity issues:

Lieutenant John had served seven years at the time of the first interview, most recently as a platoon commander. His case presents an articulated asymmetry between military-veteran identities and new civilian identities where military-veteran identities maintain a dominant position in the self, and where the perception was filtered through a military-veteran lens. John described his experiences of being a university student, four months post exit, in the first interview, such as:

> The institution [academic] I belong to, they are very critical, oriented much towards the left [politically] and maybe even more than so, because they are really critical against everything that is military, most of the entire west, western military powers. And it became like a huge collapse, it become extremely weird. Then I have severe difficulties of feeling any confidence at all for many of the people in the institution. [John recounted an extended real life example about a seminar where he and the people from the institution had entirely diametrical positions in regards to the UN in which John is positive and they are critical]. It became like a short circuit, I just get so frustrated. They can give really good arguments, but in the way it is narrated it becomes really emotion-laden; then it becomes a counterproductive discussion, so it testifies again to how I identify them in regards to myself. They really become the other.

Lieutenant Maria had served for eleven years, also as a platoon commander. For some time she had been employed by a civilian company to work with leadership development. Maria narrated a sense of a military "me" or a military mode in her, and even though she had a new narrative identity as a civilian employee, the old military self was still present thirteen months post exit. Maria said in regards to her military identity and new civilian identity in the first interview that:

> They touch each other somewhere in the middle, so there is an essence left, absolutely, this [civilian] working place consists of several consultants with military backgrounds who have adapted to a civilian context, however it is true that some stripes will never leave you. Results, to deliver results, responsibility, mission focus, leadership, are such things that no matter how much of a civilian I become, it will always be just to switch on that mode.

Colour Sergeant Andreas had served more than eight years and was a specialist officer. He had conducted one mission to Afghanistan and engaged in combat. During the first interview three months post exit while active as a university student, he described his difficulties adjusting to a civilian context as:

> I feel a greater sense of safety among people in uniform, you are naked but in the same time camouflaged, you all have the same filter, you interact with a shared code that everybody knows but no one says out loud. Then I think it is easier to make demands, both to myself and others, and battle buddies subscribe to that more than the civilians. You don't have to be afraid that anyone will be offended in the military context; instead you know that "yeah, I did wrong; I should have solved the task". I don't think that atmosphere is present in the civilian context. I'm more worried of getting on wrong terms with civilians than with service members.

Private First Class Mattias had served two years as a sharp shooter and had studied on university for a little more than two years, longer than he had served. He testified to a slow process of reconstructing a meaningful identity as he transitioned into the university context. Mattias described the difficulties of creating a new meaningful story of who he is by comparing his military with his civilian identity:

> I could identify myself with being a service member, and if I entered a room I felt that I was a soldier. Today when I enter a room I don't feel like I am an academic even though I am one. I have a harder time to identify who I am today than when I served. It may have several reasons, but I miss being able to identify myself and having such strong feelings for something.

Sergeant Erik had served for several years and was at the time three months post exit. He had made several missions in Afghanistan and elsewhere. He recounted difficulties finding purpose and motivation in the civilian life as he studied in the university context. In regards to Erik's studies he responded:

> "Why am I doing this?" is a question I sometimes ask myself. "What is the purpose and why?" And in the military context and from my military self I get a rather direct answer every time: "This is the purpose! Good, good, then I have a task, I have a goal, I have a why." But to write this essay about this and that, write about the development from the realism to the neo realism. "But why? What is the purpose? Who will read this? What I am going to use it for? Why? I can't see what I can use this text for?" It won't develop this area of research. As soon as it is examined by the teacher it is a dead mass, a dead

piece of paper. Nothing more. And then it is hard, too, it is what makes it so difficult to find motivation.

Lieutenant Peter had served for eight years, ultimately as a platoon commander. The loss of community was a salient issue throughout the first interview narrative. He was at the time a student, and responded in the first interview six months post exit in regards to his battle buddies:

> I still have contact with my squad commanders and old colleagues, and talk to them frequently. But I don't miss the tasks, I miss the service members and the community and those things. I haven't found that elsewhere, and I'm not against the idea to take a position in the Armed Forces again. [Peter narrated how weird and mixed it felt to not be a part of the Armed Forces and concluded by saying] At this point in time it feels like an emptiness since I no longer have the military community, but I don't miss the tasks.

Sergeant Helen had served for two years and been deployed in Afghanistan, and in the first interview, thirty months post exit, she described her experiences of being a university student from her military point of view wherein the dichotomy between the military and university cultures was distinct:

> You learn not to question things until utterly necessary, and when you encounter civilians, for example in civilian studies, there are a lot of stupid questions on the lessons, and I think you learn to not ask those rather well in the Armed Forces; you are silent and keep quiet up until it is necessary to say something. I think that is the thing I think about in regards to my military identity. Yes, and that I don't complain until it really hurts me badly, and you don't question anything until it is completely wrong. Some indoctrination is something I continue to appreciate among other people, too.

In summation, these experiences of identity issues were solved or dealt with in different ways across time due to the decision to traverse one of the three different paths which in turn shaped the evolution of personal stories.

5.2.2 A pro-militaristic position in self

Experiences of a pro-militaristic position in the self were narrated and emphasized a positive approach to military service on a personal level, a significant shared detail in the military I-positions and narrated military identities among all of the participants which never ceased to exist over the three interview cycles. The participants highly valued and esteemed their own service, camaraderie and military identities, yet simultaneously revealed disappointments in the Armed Forces as an organization or employer which, according to them, had failed in their professional interactions in either or both a narrow and/or a broad sense. All of the participants narrated one or more pro-militaristic experiences of service across time, and this led to the suggestion that each and every participant had a pro-militaristic position or voice in the self, even all of those who had chosen a full transition to civilian life. In fact, the pro-militaristic positions in the selves among the participants who fully transitioned to civilian life continued to narrate their respect and appreciation for the personal development gained via service. Such narrative accounts and claims of military identities persisted alongside new and meaningful civilian identities. This was suggestively another expression by a collective voice that stems from military culture which expressed itself through the stories of the interviewees.

A pro-militaristic position in the self included experiences of three subthemes:

- Pride of having served and positive emotions attach to the service
- Consideration of serving part-time or full-time
- Continuation of part-time service

Examples of narrative accounts of the three subthemes within a pro-militaristic position in the self:

Second Lieutenant Karl, who had served five years, nurtured a pride of having served and had positive emotions attached to service. Karl was at the time of the first interview narrative twenty-four months post exit and a university student, and he described his emotions:

> I have some type of pride which sits rather firm, and which I don't believe has changed across time. It is attached to some kind of self-confidence somehow, and inner-safety most of all.

Private First Class Adam, who had served for about two years including a mission in Afghanistan and recently begun university studies, described his positive emotions for continuing to serve part time in the first interview such as:

> Right now it feels good to cross over to part-time service because then I can do what I think is fun in service: join the field exercises; I'm a signaler, and I signal which is damn fun.

Major Tore had served *36 years or more* and had always felt at home in the military context until his recent administrative developments. He tried to explain what he liked within the military context during the first interview:

> I don't know whether I have some kind of inner predisposition for order, I want structure in things, even though it may be simplistic to say so, but something like that, it has been pretty scheduled if you can use that word. And to socialize, you were pretty molded in the same form, even if you were different you had basically the same values and experiences, with some nuances of course.

5.2.3 Emotional issues

Experiences of emotional issues served as an umbrella which hosted a variety of emotional experiences among the participants. Emotional experiences of emptiness, sadness, or grief as a result of the loss of an extraordinary community, camaraderie and meaning were common.

Emotional issues included experiences of eight subthemes:

- Feelings of emptiness
- Feelings of grief (or sadness)
- Feelings of bitterness
- Feelings of confusion and/or frustration
- Feelings of anxiety
- Feelings of depression
- Feelings of economic worries
- Feelings of other issues

Examples of narrative accounts of the eight subthemes within emotional issues:

Sergeant Jonas had made several deployments to Afghanistan and elsewhere on contracts of employment with specific time limits which added up to about five years of active service. At the time of the first interview, twenty-four months post exit, he was preparing to end a short time civilian employment. Jonas articulated salient emotional experiences, feelings of emptiness and indifference to his prior deployments in Afghanistan and elsewhere, and in regards to those experiences he said:

> The feeling of being deceived, to be deceived by something, but I can't really put the finger on what, and by whom, but it is a feeling of un-satisfaction that I personally be-

lieve I have transformed into some kind of indifference to what I have done. I repeat myself over and over again in regards to that feeling of emptiness, something is missing.

Lieutenant Maria, a former platoon commander, described in the first interview thirteen months post exit her experiences of grief which arose amid the loss of military identity and her connection to her troops as she said:

> Six months ago, my identity as an officer was so very strong that I still addressed myself as an officer, it felt weird not to address myself as an officer or not to serve in the Armed Forces, and like a grief not to have the troops anymore. Really weird. Like being without an identity.

Sergeant Helen had endured a demanding deployment to Afghanistan, partly because of a type of warrior culture that emerged among male service members within the Swedish unit; it did not accept female service members on the same prerequisites as the male service members, they questioned her capacity and performance. Meanwhile, frequent engagement in combat was itself very demanding, and later led her to meet with a psychologist to handle traumatic combat memories after her return to Sweden. Helen described feelings of bitterness at the time of the first interview about two years post exit:

> I think it is pretty demanding to return [to the memories and emotions], as we do today, and think about it and everything that was hard. But in the same time I have a lot of positive emotions, but it is very split, much nostalgia and in the same time rather bitter memories.

Lieutenant John encountered, as a university student, criticism toward military powers in general from his academic institution in seminars or via teachers and researches, and this generated distinct identity confusion; the transition was demanding for him. In regards to his struggle of transition from military to civilian life and a possible return to the Armed Forces John recounted feelings of confusion and frustration due to several dimensions as he was about to start the second term at university:

> It is fun to play with the idea to be back in the Armed Forces, and it is fun to play with the idea to get an employment outside, to start to earn some money, more than now when I am living on a very low level, and move back [to his hometown]and so on. But I try to somewhat downplay such thoughts, not to think about everything. Although I think about it a lot, but I try to take it in small steps because it was a really difficult

adaption, to relocate and start to study. It was damn tough. I didn't expect to have to study that much, and I had to restrain myself and think about the next step. Now I am focusing and preparing myself, it is damn obvious; I am in a planning-phase. It is damn obvious. I have started to read some articles and the course description. Then I will take it step by step. But the split is there, it really is, and it is damn tough. I think it would be great to have a civilian employment, but I know how much fun I have had in the Armed Forces.

Sergeant David had served for some years, but a back injury hindered his performance relative to his own expectations, so he made a personally taxing decision to leave. David described his mixed emotions in regards to the process of becoming a civilian, just days after he had left full-time service, in the first interview:

I carry with me some kind of failure, some anxiety, some vibes of depression; it actually goes up and down. Happy memories too, but like I said, it is mixed emotions.

Major Stig had served for *36 years or more* and was scheduled to serve one more month when first interviewed. Prior to his retirement he had been concerned with the economic impact of retirement and feelings of silence or emptiness:

Honestly I have been seriously worried about retirement and to discover what my pension will be like, and if you look at the house and start adding up all of the monthly costs and then the flexible costs you begin to think this won't work, but then you ask retired colleagues, and they say it will work. For a while it has been like "but what happens when I retire, in the middle of the winter, it's not fun to take a walk in minus 30 degrees when it snows. Will life stop then?" Because this is an occupation of camaraderie, colleagues; even if you don't socialize privately it is filled with buddies whom you interact with. And you think "will it become silent as death?"

Captain Roger had served for *36 years or more* and still had some months to serve prior to his retirement. He confided another type of issues, or feelings of issues, in the first interview related to retirement, aging and death:

One of the biggest concerns is that I could become passive: if I become passive I think I will die rather soon thereafter, and that is the biggest misgiving that I have, and I will oppose it by all means.

In summation, experiences of emotional issues described through the eight subthemes were related to the progress of identity reconstruction, which indicated that in the cases where the self-identity work did lead to a sustainable construction of a new meaningful identity of who I am, many of these negative experiences grew less painful or were even wholly ameliorated. On the other hand, in the cases where self-identity work did not lead to such a reconstruction, the interviewee was left dealing with emotional issues even years after the exit point, or simply returned to part-time or full-time service.

5.2.4 Satisfaction

Satisfaction implies positive experiences in regards to the transition amid experiences of identity or emotional issues. Satisfaction was related to the development of preexisting or new ways of life such as the development of identities, feelings of gratitude for positive effects which had been gained throughout service, but also feelings of relief of no longer being submitted to the military chain of command.

Satisfaction included experiences of three subthemes:

- Embracing preexisting or new ways of life (and identities)
- Feelings of gratefulness or gratitude for personal development, experiences and camaraderie
- A relief to be free from duties and obligations related to service

Examples of narrative accounts of the three subthemes within satisfaction:

Captain Lennart embraced the new way of living as a retiree. He had served for *36 years or more*, and one month post exit he reflected upon his service and retirement:

> I have concluded my employment, I have been serving in the Armed Forces, and now I am a retiree. I have time to do things which I didn't have time to do before. I feel good about my service in the Armed Forces; I am proud over that, and it feels good. Today I have no regular contact with the Armed Forces, except for some veterans clubs. Instead I can devote my time to things I didn't have time to do before. I don't have to get up 06:00 every morning; I can sleep a bit longer. I have my daily workout, and then I do things that I am interested in. To me that is gardening, flowers, music and workout, and then suddenly comes the evening, and the day is over.

First Class Sergeant Lars also embraced his new way of living in a big university city. He was both a former specialist officer in the intelligence field who had deployed in Afghanistan and elsewhere and a university student seven months post exit at the time of the first interview, and his experiences of transition were decidedly positive:

> I experience that I left military service at the right time; there was nothing more to get, not in comparison to the time I invest right now as a student. If I would have let the years pass by and kept serving perhaps I wouldn't have experienced these positive feelings because it wouldn't have brought the type of stimulation that I wanted. But thanks to the exit timing I feel exclusively positive emotions.

Sergeant Emma, who had been deployed to Afghanistan and recently was serving under the condition of being on call to potentially deploy again, described relief in the process of becoming a civilian during the first interview:

> When I think of the idea of not returning to the military, when I think about the idea that I'm planning to quit, there is a huge feeling of relief. Then the entire stress of deployment is now over.

In summary, the experience of satisfaction across time was dependent on the process of self-identity work and the evolution of lives and identities which could be perceived as meaningful. The two long evolving narrative accounts of David and Maria which follow were initially filled with identity and emotional struggles prior to and during the first years of transition, yet both interviewees ultimately found satisfaction, one via full transition and the other through full return.

Sergeant David gave up his military dream about three and half years into his service because of an injury that severely reduced his capacity to serve to the high standard of both his military unit which his own expectations. Merely days after departure from active service, David testified that he experienced identity and emotional issues prior to his decision to leave:

> I had pretty gloomy thoughts during the evenings, and I had a very difficult time to sleep after the working day because I had such bad anxiety over the injury in the back and not being able to serve properly. So it was a lot of those thoughts that I had, and what to do instead; I cannot do anything after this; I am worthless once I am out in the civilian life, and I had to try to remain somehow in the military, and it was such a terrible anxiety and depression over that then.

In the second interview David recounted a frustrating year of utter failure in trying to find any long-term employment, but at least he had a temporary job at the time of the interview. He still missed the military service and camaraderie profoundly. He testified once again, but in even more detail, about the inner turmoil leading up to the decision to leave active service one year prior:

> I started to drink a lot during the weekdays, and on the evenings too, although nothing which interfered with my working during the daytime, because I only drank during the evenings, and I was grappling with the meaning with life; I was so good at something, and suddenly I felt that I was not able to fully continue it […] I think that that question will be un-answered until I return to the Armed Forces somehow. That is how I perceive it, or until I find something which can fill that emptiness. Until then it remains un-answered.

During the third interview about two years after the transition from military to civilian life David's back had healed, and he had returned to full-time service two weeks prior to the in-terview. He showed up to the interview in his uniform after the workday. David was referring to the last three years, including the time of the injury, as a "dark period" of his life. David testified that he could not fully comprehend the wholly positive emotions he now experienced as he had fully recovered from the injury and returned to full-time service:

> It cannot really be described. As I said earlier, my life has gone up and down for such a long time, but during these most recent two weeks back in active service nothing like that has been experienced, instead it has been positive through and through. So it is dif-ficult to describe since I have not felt like this in a very long time. I can feel that it is a huge adjustment in a really positive way.

When David was asked to describe what is important in his life at this point and looking for-ward prospectively he recounted:

> My job [as a Sergeant and instructor in the Armed Forces], and it may sound wrong to say it this way, but it really is my life, this is who I am. This is the only thing that mat-ters, it is my first priority, end of discussion. This is a fact. And also, of course, my mili-tary colleagues.

Lieutenant Maria wrestled with identity issues and emotional issues during her transition from military to civilian after eleven years of service. In the first interview thirteen months post exit she had just recently found long-term employed at a civilian company working with leadership development. Over the transition she had experienced that she did not understand the nuances and layers within a civilian working place and culture and stated:

> In this civilian working place there are things you do and things you don't which everybody understands, but I don't. That has been taxing to me, and like the deprogramming. It has been like a displacement of the identity, the repackaging of who I am if I am not an officer. Because, as I said, it is not just a professional identity or an employment, it is more like I serve as an officer; I am an officer.

In the second interview her identity issues and emotional issues were less salient, and she had strengthened her identity as a civilian worker even as, from time to time, she encountered occasions when she longed back to military service and colleagues. Maria's claim of her new identity and life was emphasized:

> I am not particularly sad that I have transitioned, and I am extremely satisfied with my current employment. I have kind of transitioned from the best job in the world to another best job in the world. So all and all I am very happy with how things have evolved.

In the third and final interview Maria's self-identity work had led her to new deeper insights which were important to follow in order to sustain satisfaction of life:

> What is really important in reality may differ, but for me it has more and more become a life balance. I am not interested in working myself to death, which I had tendencies to do before since I liked to work extremely much. Now I don't because it is important with balance […] I worked extremely much in the Armed Forces, and when I left it was not just leaving any kind of employment where you say "good luck", and then you go home. I did not experience myself to be working as an officer, but I was an officer. So it was huge to leave. I am happy that I have done that, I wouldn't like to change that, but I will never repeat that part again where my employment becomes who I am. So now I work instead, and that feels incredibly nice. […] When I work I want to do things which I enjoy but not to identity myself with my profession.

5.2.5 The importance of significant others

The importance of significant others included narrated experiences of the importance of social support in the process of becoming civilian. This could span from a wife/husband or co-habiting partner to wider family and friends. However, not all participants expressed or seemed to have the support of significant others in this process.

The importance of significant others included three subthemes:

- Partner
- Family
- Others

Examples of narrative accounts of the three subthemes included in the importance of significant others:

Sergeant Gustaf was seventeen months post exit and had been deployed in Afghanistan and elsewhere and had served in staff sections. He described a phase of confusion existing simultaneously as the guiding influence of a girlfriend some time ago when he returned to Sweden after his deployment:

> I studied some university courses, and I felt that I was somewhat in an existential vacuum. I had just been deployed to Afghanistan when I was quite brutally dumped by my girlfriend, and I had no time to reflect upon that before I returned home. It was first when I returned that I begin to think "what the fuck am I doing, what is this?" The precipitating factor was that I returned home and could switch on my brain again and begin to reflect upon other things than just military service. It was summer, and I tried to find the structure, and to manage to study a couple of courses, but I didn't find it and just felt adrift.

As I asked how he managed to get a grip upon life, he replied:

> It was when I met my [current] girlfriend, so that was like a factor which led me to become more structured, and then I started to complete the exams in different subjects. I found my energy again.

Sergeant David, who had been serving for about three and half years, testified for the importance of family and friends in his transition to civilian life. It is suggested that he, at the time of the first interview, was located in the very beginning of a similar type of vacuum as the one which Gustaf recounted above. In the first interview with David, just days after he had exited military service, he highlighted what was important to him:

99

The most important thing for me is to feel that I still have my friends [civilian] remaining here, that they haven't disappeared, and they have not, so that was damn nice to feel when I returned. And with family, they have supported me, of course they think it is good that I have left, no normal mother or father wants their kids to stay in the Armed Forces and keep busy with rifles and such, so they have supported me in the decision to come home, so it has been important that they are here too. Then those things with jobs, that type of stuff is not important for me now actually. Eventually one needs to have an income, but I feel that it is more important with the private life with family and friends, that is the most important focus right now.

An important driver for Second Lieutenant Karl to transition from military to civilian life was curiosity about the civilian world in contrast to feelings of stagnation and disappointment over his military prospects, and within this curiosity was the idea that service did not lend itself to an intimate relation with a girlfriend, especially when considering international deployments. This perception has followed Karl since then, and Karl's ultimate concern is the importance of an intimate relationship. He testified in the first interview that:

Maybe the biggest life question to me is my approach to an intimate relationship with my girlfriend in regards to my choice of school, how I think of my career and everything else.

Lieutenant Maria testified for the practical and emotional support she received from her family when she transitioned from eleven years of military service to civilian life:

They have been a support. To share thoughts and wonderings in life but also practically, no one except me has served in the Armed Forces, so I have turned to them and received much support in how to express myself, how to write my CV and how to perform on job-interviews and what kind of impression I make, so it has been a safety, a significant resource and support, so it has not entirely felt like walking around in a bottomless swamp, instead I have been surrounded by wonderful people who have supported me.

Once again it must be said that in those cases wherein identity reconstruction led participants to meaningful identities significant others played an important role in such an evolution over time of personal stories.[14]

---

[14] For more details about the importance of significant others also read the case study of Sergeant Erik, who had made multiple deployments in Afghanistan and elsewhere, and who was literally physically assisted by his sister

However, significant others not only assisted the participants in transition from military to civilian life but also from civilian life back to military service. Military buddies and colleagues played an important role for several participants who returned to part-time or full-time service. For example, Major Stig, who had served *36 years or more* but as he retired kept a foot in the military via a position in the Home Guard as a company commander. Stig dedicated much more time to the company than he was actually payed for by the Armed Forces, and he recounted in the second interview:

> Yes, but it depends on how engaged I become with those I serve with, so the company becomes like a family, and then I can contribute so it becomes good for them, so that they reach their goals and everything. The more I engage with the service members to reach these goals the harder it becomes to step down.

Lieutenant John returned to full-time service as a platoon commander after a year of university studies and claimed the importance of camaraderie as a significant factor for that return:

> That is what makes it different compared with other working places I believe. The general idea of the Armed Forces, a little bit romanticized, but you serve and live together all of the time. That is the point of reference. That is what I had in mind when I returned to the Armed Forces, as I returned I encountered colleagues who will stand by my side whatever happens in life and death, those are the ones I will hold on to. That camaraderie can be found on the lower level [...], but I miss that true sense of a family on the company level.

5.3 The transitional paths encountered across time

Now that common themes in transition, including more specific issues or subthemes with narrative accounts, have been presented, this final section of the chapter will describe a discovery of developmental schemes in regards to the civilian/military routes taken by the participants throughout transition. Keep in mind that throughout transition a chain of experiences and choices eventually lead the participants to choose and use different paths in regards to self-identity work. This section serves to provide an overview of the three types of paths in military transition to civilian life which were discerned within the groups, and thereby also as an introduction to chapter 6 which specifically elaborates the self-identity work among the par-

---

to take the taxing first step to unpack his suitcase quite some time after his return to Sweden and transition from military to civilian life (Grimell, 2015).

ticipants which is built upon these findings. The common themes of identity issues, a pro-militaristic position in the self, emotional issues, satisfaction and the support of significant others influenced the path followed: either a *full transition* to civilian life (which eliminates a relationship with the Armed Forces), a *hybrid outcome* of a civilian/military path (which alongside the civilian life at some point sustains a more formal or informal relationship with the Armed Forces), or a *full return* to military service (which at some point aborts the civilian transition). The roles of identity issues, a pro-militaristic position in the self, emotional issues, satisfaction and the support of significant others illustrate the complexities of the self-identity work in transition from military to civilian life and how the outcomes of such challenges for the self led a participant upon one of the three paths. The paths are understood as the evolution of three potential ways of dealing with tension, conflict, contradiction and dialogue, but also deeper meanings in life, during self-identity work in transition among the participants. The transitions affected the participants' self-identity work in different, even opposing ways, and the paths were an answer to such experiences. A full transition from military to civilian life included the construction of a new I-position which gradually grew, as did the story of who I am, and related meaning, to finally take the lead in the self. A hybrid outcome illustrated a more flexible process of positioning and re-positioning between military and civilian I-positions, stories and related meaning and significant others in military and civilian contexts. In a full return to military service an evolution was demonstrated wherein the persistence of a military I-position was overwhelming, and so was related meaning and the influence from battle buddies, which finally took precedence over the process and steered a participant back to full-time service.

Beginning with a description of the types of formal employments by the Armed Forces found among the participants upon the initial interview cycle, two participants had maintained a type of formal employment in the Armed Forces, including part-time service, while leaving active service: Private First Class Adam and the retiree Major Stig, who continued as a Company Commander in the Home Guard. Throughout a year the service of each totaled approximately three to seven weeks depending upon the needs of their units. This was their way of keeping one foot on the familiar military terrain, at least from time to time, while also keeping the other foot firmly planted on civilian ground. Two other participants, Sergeant First Class Oskar and Lars, were reserve officers and thus could serve when they wished. However, this was an open arrangement with no specific obligations (aside from the very small chance that the Armed Forces would order them to service amid crisis). Sergeant Emma, Lieutenant John and

Colour Sergeant Andreas were wholly free from duty due to university studies, but they were technically still employed by the Armed Forces even if they had no formal day to day interaction with their employer. Finally, Sergeant Gustaf had begun studying to become a reserve officer some months prior to the first interview but had not yet been appointed as a reserve officer. The remainder of the participants, totaling eleven, had no formal employment contract with the Armed Forces, and technically neither did Gustaf until he completed his training.

The civilian and military occupational status among the participants during the first interview cycle is presented below.

Group	Participant	Civilian occupation (T1)	Formal military employment (T1)
1	Roger	Retiree	
	Stig	Retiree	Tactical officer (part-time service)
	Adam	Student	Private First Class (part-time service)
	David	Unemployed	
	Emma	Student	Sergeant free from duty
	Lennart	Retiree	
2	Erik	Student	
	Andreas	Student	Specialist officer free from duty
	John	Student	Tactical officer free from duty
	Oskar	Student	Reserve officer
	Peter	Student	
	Lars	Student	Reserve officer
3	Maria	Employed	
	Tore	Retiree	
	Gustaf	Employed	
	Karl	Student	
	Jonas	Employed	
	Mattias	Student	
	Helen	Student	

Across time, as already discussed in chapter 4, this landscape of civilian and military occupational statuses and service within the Armed Forces indeed changed. The processing of experiences in regards to self-identity work laid the ground for the three different paths which made a significant distinction within the sample. The full transition to civilian life was perhaps what typically came to mind when one anticipated a military transition to civilian life, as illustrated below.

However, a transitional journey down such a path appeared within this sample to be less common than a voyage down the other two alternate paths: the hybrid outcome of a civilian/military path, or a full return upon a military path of full-time service as given below.

Full return to military service

The subsequent section will present a positioning of each participant upon one of the three discovered paths.

5.3.1 The developmental scheme of the full transition on a civilian path (six participants)

Simply stated, the participants following the full transitionary path to civilian life have kept their feet outside of any type of military service since their exit point, at least as long as the empirical research phase continued. In the illustration below each participant is positioned somewhere above the time arrow relative to the time elapsed post departure for that individual at the time of participation in the first interview.

Full transition from military to civilian life (six participants):

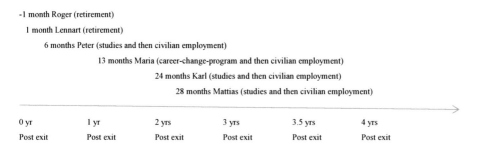

5.3.2 The developmental scheme of the hybrid outcome on a civilian/military path (nine participants)

The hybrid outcome of a civilian/military path was the path most followed by interviewees during this study as they transitioned into civilian life. In the illustration below the time for reentrance into military service is presented somewhere above the time arrow and prior to the participant's name, which followed by a short description of the designation. After the initial reentrance several additional part-time service duties were performed; however those are not presented here since the interest is in the selection of path instead of the frequency of part-time service. Private First Class Adam and Major Stig already were formally employed in part-time service as they left full-time service and transitioned to civilian life. In the case of Sergeant First Class Lars and Sergeant Helen their international deployments referred to longer international missions (approximately ten months) to a serious area of conflict elsewhere in the world. Meanwhile Major Tore and Sergeant Emma did not have any formal employment contract with the Armed Forces yet did on occasion, as they themselves chose, assist military units and personnel in training, hence their fit within the hybrid civilian/military path model rather than the linear civilian path.

The hybrid outcome of a civilian/military path (nine participants):

~2 months: Emma (part-time service in the Army)

~3 months: Stig (part-time service in the Home Guard)

~3 months: Tore (part-time service in the Army)

~ 5 months: Adam (part-time service in the Army)

~10 months: Andreas (part-time service in the Air Force)

~12 months: Oskar (part-time service in the Army)

~16 months: Lars (international deployment in the Army)

~2 years: Erik (begin reserve officer's training in the Army)

~3.5 years: Helen (international deployment in the Army)

0 yr	1 yr	2 yrs	3 yrs	3.5 yrs	4 yrs
Post exit	Post exit	Post exit	Post exit	Post exit	Post exit

5.3.3 The developmental scheme of the full return to a military path (four participants)

In this trend the participants' experiences led them to turn around on the civilian path at some point and reenlist in full-time service. In the illustration below the time for reentrance into military service is presented somewhere above the time arrow and preceding the participant's name, which is then followed by a short description of the designation. Sergeant Gustaf began the reserve officer's training approximately thirteen months post exit, so during the first interview he was following the hybrid path, but by the time of the second interview he had returned to full-time service and crossed into the category of full return to a military path.

The full return to a military path (four participants):

5.3.4 A summary of the three transitional paths

Taking these developmental schemes into account, there appears to be a crucial period across the groups between two months to two years following the exit point. Spanning from approximately two months to two years (with two exceptions of approximately three and half years), four of the participants had aborted the transition as such and reenlisted to full-time service, while another nine participants had engaged in part-time service, reserve officer training, or deployed upon an international mission; thus a total sum of thirteen participants had formally or informally kept serving part-time or reenlisted in some way, shape or form.

The occupational status, formal military relationship and development of civilian, civilian/military or military paths evolved among the participants across the first interview cycle throughout the third interview cycle as presented below (please keep in mind that Major Tore and Sergeant Emma also served part-time but with no formal employment contracts).

Group	Participant	Civilian occupation (T3)	Formal military employment (T3)	Path-choice (T3)
1	Roger	Retiree		Full transition
	Stig	Retiree	Reserve officer (part-time service)	Hybrid outcome
	Adam	Student	Private First Class (part-time service)	Hybrid outcome
	David		Sergeant (full-time service)	Full return
	Emma	Employed		Hybrid outcome
	Lennart	Retiree		Full transition
2	Erik	Student	Reserve officer (part-time service)	Hybrid outcome
	Andreas	Student	Reserve officer (part-time service)	Hybrid outcome
	John		Tactical officer (full-time service)	Full return
	Oskar	Employed	Reserve officer (part-time service)	Hybrid outcome
	Peter	Employed		Full transition
	Lars	Student	Reserve officer (international mission)	Hybrid outcome
3	Maria	Employed		Full transition
	Tore	Retiree		Hybrid outcome
	Gustaf		Reserve officer (full-time service)	Full return
	Karl	Employed		Full transition
	Jonas		Military Academy (full-time service)	Full return
	Mattias	Employed		Full transition
	Helen	Student	Sergeant (international mission)	Hybrid outcome

The displayed paths across transition will lay the foundation for the storied evolution of the participants in chapter 6.

106

CHAPTER 6

How is Identity Constructed and Reconstructed in the Transition

This chapter serves to present the results of the analysis in regards to the second subquestion of the central research question which address how identity is constructed and reconstructed among Swedish military personnel in the process of becoming civilians. The content analysis of identity construction and reconstruction investigated how preexisting and new I-positions, via their corresponding narrative characters, shaped the identity claims in the interview narratives during transition, and how these narrative claims changed the stories of who I am across time. To recap, only six participants out of nineteen fully transitioned and reintegrated into an exclusively civilian life and population during the project. Thirteen participants followed paths in their transitions which either included part-time service or a return to full-time service. This was quite an interesting discovery which was not anticipated at the onset of the project. When first interviewed only two participants were scheduled to serve part-time according to their formal arrangements (one as a soldier and another as a Home Guard Company Commander), and when considered from a temporal perspective it was easy to anticipate these to be civilian lives accentuated by the part-time continuation of military service. Time was tailored to each individual's storied evolution and dependent upon his or her self-identity work upon the traversed path. This chapter is built on three detailed transitional portraits, one representing each path, which each address the evolution of transitional themes on both an individual and subgroup level. The presentation of one case per path enables a more rich exploration of the processual and detailed narrative data which thereby serve to more fully demonstrate the self-identity work. The selection of participants was made following the criteria to have as representative of a case as possible for each of the paths: the process of identity construction and reconstruction during a *full transition* to civilian life, a *hybrid outcome* of active engagement in both the civilian and the military, and a *full return* to active service. This was a difficult selection process since many cases did represent a given path well in regards to self-identity work, yet there were always small qualitative differences between the cases which make each and every case interesting. Voices from both male and female service members were crucial to highlight. It was moreover desired to encapsulate some variety in regards to exit time, but also total length of service, rank, engagement in international deployments and even to some extent age. Since some cases had already been presented and published in journals, it felt better to present new and fresh accounts of other individuals in this chapter and thereby bring new data into conversation with published accounts in theory building. Thus Lieutenant Peter was chosen to represent the path of a full transition from military to civilian life, Sergeant Emma to voice a hybrid outcome of a civilian/military path and Sergeant Gustaf to demonstrate the path of a full return to military service. These cases were perceived as representative examples of the processes. Each portrait will begin with a summarization and the specific storied evolution of each path, including a table of the outcomes of the self-identity work in each path in regards to the transitional experiences.

6.1 A case study portrait of identity reconstruction in a full transition to civilian life

The six participants upon this path varied strongly in terms of post exit time. All members of this path shared, to a varying degree, the transitional experiences of identity issues and a pro-militaristic position in the self, emotional issues, satisfaction and the importance of significant others as already presented in chapter 5. These were all significant experiences in the process of becoming a civilian across the transition. A specific type of storied evolution was discerned among these six participants and began with intense transitional experiences of identity and emotional issues, much as with the other participants. However, after enduring such intense transitional experiences, civilian promoter positions and inspiring jobs or other major aspirations in life assisted these participants in reformulating and sustaining new meaningful stories of who I am as a civilian. With time the new civilian identities grew strong and salient within the self, although from time to time minor tension was voiced by military I-positions.

The table below shows the content of identity reconstruction, in regards to the transitional experiences, as expressed throughout the interviews and finalized during the third and final interview cycle by these six participants.

Overarching themes	The content of identity reconstruction (T3)
Identities	• A reversed asymmetry between military/veteran identities and new civilian identities wherein the new civilian identities become more influential; a salient tendency is that new civilian characters tend to be constructed with counter features in relation to the military characters • A clear sense of a military "me" persists, but without particular adjustment problems • A richly developed reconstruction of a new meaningful story of who I am as a civilian wherein several civilian I-positions/characters appear to cooperate in pursuit of shared desires • A withdrawal from military community and camaraderie in favor of a salient relational positioning to civilian friends and life
A pro-militaristic position	• Pride of having served and positive emotions attach to it
Emotional issues	• Wholly ameliorated or at least not demonstrated
Satisfaction	• Embracement of a new way of life and identities
Significant others	• Preexisting and new civilian promoters are significant for the processes of reconstructing identities and lives

6.1.1 Background

Lieutenant Peter was in his early thirties and had served for about eight years, mostly as a platoon commander. His motives to leave full-time service consisted mainly of salient experiences of stagnation due to the new administrative system called Prio which relocated him inside the company office with a computer and a telephone, instead of outdoors leading and training the platoon. The administrative burden became so taxing that only some few hours per week could be spent with the platoon. Peter felt like an administrator, and eventually the discrepancy between his expectation and prior experience as a boots on the ground service member and later a platoon commander in contrast to the now actual life of a platoon commander was too great, so Peter decided to leave the Armed Forces. This was not an easy decision, and, as presented in chapter 5, Peter was ridden by experiences of emptiness in regards to the colleagues with whom he maintained close and frequent contact. Peter was constantly updated on matters in regards to his former platoon and knew with detail what was occurring within the platoon six months post exit.

6.1.2 The first interview: Student, emptiness, and a military audience

When we met for the first interview (T1), six months post exit, Peter had recently begun to study a nature and tourism program at a campus in the northern part of Sweden. The campus was located near mountainous areas which served Peter well since he was deeply committed to many kinds of outdoor activities; the outdoor character, which consisted of adventuristic features, was one salient I-position in his self. Peter's military character as a platoon commander was described as extremely task oriented, efficient, focused, and uncompromising. As a platoon commander Peter always got the job done, and this character of an officer was a deeply rooted identity in his self which was sustained by his military peers in his self, and Peter stated:

> This is eight years of my life which makes me who I am. Now when I have left the Armed Forces it is not exactly like my friends see me as another person, instead they still see me as an officer through and through. My squad commanders were about to laugh themselves to death because they are convinced that I will continue to drop to my knees in a shooting positing every time I shall check my map up here in the mountains, even in my civilian clothes.

The tone of the first interview narrative revolved around emptiness and loss in regards to his battle buddies, and as Peter was encouraged to describe the military relationships around which these transitional experiences revolved he replied:

> You are interacting so intimately with each other all day every day, so you become best friends with everyone, or better than that, what I have told my comrades I have not told my best friends in my private life, because you serve so intensively together all the time. And I don't think you can find that experience outside of the Armed Forces, not in the same way that you trust each other there, and the shared focus which drives service members to really strive towards the same goal, and that you have the same interests.

The tone was anchored in the loss of significant others, and at the same time this narrative account suggested that Peter was using his story to maintain his relationship to the military community, which appears to be the intended audience for his story. Moreover, Peter had no intention to fill that emptiness due to the loss of battle buddies with, for example, student peers, and he claimed:

> I don't see that I will fill that [emptiness] with something else up here, or that I want to create like a super good relationship with my class peers up here, or to build up something like that.

This account distanced him from his current real life audience in the campus context, and it also suggested that his character of a student was not particularly evolved at the time. These could very plausibly be related to a situation involving his peers upon the onset of their studies together. When Peter began the program at the campus the course mates were intended to better get to know each other during the first days of the week, and Peter recalled:

> We had some assignments to attend to in the class during the first three days, where you were supposed to write something in regards to each other, and I think that the whole class wrote that I was militaristic, whatever that may be.

As a student Peter was defined by the others as a service man, which further activated his position as an officer. The first term turned out to be quite a challenge in the everyday classroom context since Peter from the onset continued to let his military I-position lead his way of doing things. He continued to be in command and to take charge of group exercises and resolved group assignments according to his military mindset and experiences as an officer. However, he recalled a specific turning point when he changed his routine behavior and approach to the group assignments, which suggestively was the narrative birthmark of a more conscious new position and student identity in his self:

> One episode was when we were supposed to build a shelter from the rain as we were spending time outdoors. I know how to do that as quickly as possible. Then I thought "I can let go of everything and let them decide, and maybe it will not be exactly as I would have preferred, but it will not be so bad." So I took a step back, completely, and it felt really relaxing for me, and I listened and let them implement all their weird ideas which went just fine. It took much more time than if I would have done it. But I think it gave so much to the others in the group.

Six months post exit Peter had begun to experience that he was in the conscious process of creating a new civilian character in his self. This character was still new and evolving, but some of its features included the capacity to take a step back and to listen to others, and to be inefficient and to do things without any specific purpose. This developing character showed many counter features when compared with the military character's efficiency, concentration on results, task-focus, unwillingness to compromise, and purpose when engaging in activities, and Peter stated:

> My friends here say that I am pretty much the same person, but I experience that I have made major changes, and I believe that if I would meet with my military buddies now they would probably observe a huge change in my behavior. I personally think I have another point of view on a lot of things, therefore changing the identity in regards to that, but well, the stripes are still there, so it is. But just to do things because it is fun, and it doesn't have to be efficient, it is such a huge difference compared to what I am used to. And I think now that it is damn nice, hard in the start, but damn nice now.

Important promoters in Peter's context during the time of the first interview appeared to be his teachers, who gave him individual assignments that challenged his military ways of doing things and assisted the development of the student character in progress. Yet the most significant promoter appeared to be his girlfriend, and Peter declared:

> My girlfriend, she motivates me to everything I do here and brings up all kinds of strange ideas for outdoor activities that I like.

6.1.3 The second interview: Member in a ski and rescue patrol, civilian and military audiences

When we met twenty months post exit for the second interview (T2) Peter had graduated from the program some five months earlier and described a specific episode in regards to that:

> Close to the graduation, the class was given a leadership assignment in order to get to know oneself better, and we were supposed to write something about every person in the class. And personally I didn't think that I had changed that much during that year, but the rest of the class thought so. I wasn't the same when I graduated, I had become more harmonious, calmer; things don't have to go 100% in one direction, instead it can take some time if you have fun or as long as people enjoy things. You don't have to go to such extremes all of the time, so it was quite a huge change personally for myself. I have had a task-focus, but there are several ways of solving a task, and I think now that there are two sides of the coin when it comes to how to solve tasks or problems. That is quite a huge change of mindset that I have made.

Moreover, Peter's character as a student, described by his student peers, now found it much easier to connect with others and open up and share things, and approached aspects of life in harmonious ways. This account of the characteristics of Peter's new I-position also located the student peers as significant promoters in the self-identity work. Just as they had defined him as militaristic, they had the power to redefine him as a changed person, and on a temporal level influenced the final construction of a graduated student who could approach life in quite opposite manners than the military character.

Another progression in Peter's life was that after graduation he found employment as a member of a ski and rescue patrol in the north Swedish mountains. This was a positive development for Peter since it was relevant to his education, complementary to his outdoor interest and also to a degree utilized his military experience such as medical training. Peter described the working context such as:

> Right now we are six persons who work together on a daily basis, but you have fixed routines as with the previous job [in the Armed Forces]. You work like ten hour shifts and from time to time seven days per week, so you are really spending time together, and no tasks can be solved individually. Yesterday I helped a woman who had probably broken her neck while skiing downhill, then it was four of us, the first on scene becomes the leader as the rest of the team arrives on the scene. Yes, it becomes a really tight

group. When we do such a rescue we don't even need to talk to each other because everyone knows what to do, so everything just flows, and it demands both training and trust in one other. [...] It is real life all the time; it is something which triggers you and every one that you work with; we have a community and belonging in what we do. Every one of us cares very, very much about what we do.

The tone of the second interview narrative was set by Peter as he stated that:

Perhaps I don't think so much about the meaning of life, but I feel the joy of living, and that has significantly changed since I left the Armed Forces. Now I have everything that I previously paid for and took vacation time to do right outside my front door all of the time; every day is a celebration, even when I work I ski, which is my greatest interest.

This and the other accounts in this second interview which spoke of the student peers and the members in the ski and rescue patrol served to establish and maintain relationships with civilian audiences, which was a new narrative development. As I asked if the camaraderie in the patrol corresponded to what he had experienced in the Armed Forces, he replied:

Yes I think it is, you may not be as tight, but the camaraderie is the same. Well, I had a community [military] which I sort of missed when I studied, and I experience no emptiness now when I am working here, I think it fits me, it fits me very well, and it feels like I have no longing to the Armed Forces.

Even though Peter has a pro-militaristic position in the self, he stated in regards to military and civilian friends that:

I would not say that I have military friends who have greater importance than my civilian friends; when we hang out together no matter what background they have it is exactly the same, nothing extraordinary or so.

The dichotomy between military and civilian worlds and relationships had been bridged, and the importance of military camaraderie and community had declined. Peter's working buddies and the new community held another position as promoters in a temporal development of the new character as a member of the patrol. Peter's girlfriend was the most crucial person for him, and they really enjoyed the shared outdoor life in the mountains.

113

6.1.4 The third interview: Member in a ski and rescue patrol and a civilian audience

When we met thirty-two moths post exit for the final and third interview (T3) Peter had continued his career in the ski and rescue patrol and appeared to be drifting even further away from his military life. Peter continued to present his civilian characters (e.g., graduated student, member of the ski and rescue patrol) with their counter features compared with his military character. As a summary when Peter was encouraged to describe the features of his civilian self he stated:

> I would say more humble, more open to others' ideas, more open in general to listen to others. And how should I explain, more open to try new things, not just because it seems productive or reasonable, but because it is fun.

His military character still existed and was described as structured, efficient, focused, scheduled and uncompromising. Peter said that sometimes there may become a conflict between his preexisting military I-position and new positions, particularly when it concerned physical training. His military I-position never shirked a workout because of being tired or having worked late, however, his new character of a civilian would not hesitate at all to cancel, and thus this had and would become a conflict in Peter's self. The metaphor of a coin with two sides was used, as in the prior interview, to describe Peter's characters in his self.

The tone was set by Peter as he felt harmonious and enjoyed the adventurous life in the mountains with his girlfriend, who was a major promoter of his military deprogramming. Peter frequently worked to expand the distance between his civilian self and his old military self; as a result he elevated working in the rescue patrol compared to the service in the Armed Forces:

> In the Armed Forces it is very, very seldom you execute a task for real. You undergo medic training with simulated injuries for years with the soldiers, but up here you attend a medic course for two weeks, and then you care for people that are dying. And I like that part unbelievably much. You feel important all the time, you need to be alert and prepared, and it doesn't work like that in the Armed Forces. You get into exercise coma [military jargon for a person who after some time during an exercise becomes tired, inactive, in the worst case even apathetic and doesn't have the energy or spirit to do anything more than exist] and just know that it is an exercise. But here when they call and say that there has been an avalanche and you get there, it is full focus. No one will stop because they are tired or to question why they are doing it, you just keep going on!

114

The ski and rescue patrol served as a sufficient promoter in Peter's new civilian story of who he was.

6.1.5 Summation of the path of full transition from military to civilian life

In the narrative analysis of the characters it appears that the civilian characters, which were more fully developed among those who traversed a full civilian identity reconstruction, showed significant counter features in reference to the military characters, as recounted in the case of Peter. A possible interpretation of this observation suggests that different cultural pre-requisites for military and civilian characters equip them with contrasting features. This endows the participants in the path of full transition with polar characters and I-positions in the self, with "two sides of the coin" using Peter's own metaphor. The trend in the full transition implied that since the military characters no longer seem to function well in civilian contexts, then the civilian characters instead grow ever more salient in the narratives as well as in the selves. Time was critical, and the temporal dimension implied that the narrative accounts established and nurtured the relationships with civilian audiences while further distancing the military audiences.

6.2 A case study portrait of self-identity work on a path of hybrid outcome

The path of a hybrid outcome in transition from military to civilian life included nine participants who varied strongly in terms of post exit time. Nearly half of the sample went down this path, which made this path the path most traveled during transition and reintegration into civilian lives among this sample. The participants shared many transitional experiences in the process of becoming a civilian, but to varying degrees. The variety of transitional experiences in regards to self-identity work was higher within this path; however, the shared strategy was to at some point embark on a hybrid path during transition and reintegration to civilian population to sustain the needs of different I-positions within the self. The specific type of storied evolution could be presented as a type of story wherein civilian promoter positions and jobs or major activities in life were pivotal, but new meaning grew slowly in regards to new civilian identities and jobs. In the midst of toilsome growth of identities and meaning in a civilian life, meaningfulness was already present in military service and promoted by battle buddies. The solution to the situation and the transitional experiences, such as identity and emotional issues, eventually led to some type of military part-time service which sustained or reformulated the military story of who I am. The blend of a civilian/military complex in life may in some cases lean more on the military foot and in other cases more on the civilian foot. Tension was present among civilian and military I-positions.

The table below shows the content of identity maintenance and reconstruction, in regards to the transitional experiences, as expressed throughout the interviews and finalized during the third and final interview cycle by these nine participants.

Overarching themes	The content of identity maintenance and reconstruction (T3)
Identities	• Co-existence of military/veteran identities and new civilian identities, where military/veteran identities may maintain an influential position in the self, and where the perception from time to time may be filtered through a military/veteran lens; the new civilian characters tend to be tailored with different features than the military ones but not be as salient as in a linear path to civilian life; from time to time tension may exist between military and civilian I-positions • A clear sense of a military "me" but without particular adjustment problems • A growing reconstruction of a new meaningful story of who I am as a civilian wherein several civilian I-positions appear to cooperate in shared desires • A decline in regards to military community and camaraderie in favor for relational positioning to civilian friends and life
A pro-militaristic position	• Pride of having served and positive emotions attach to it • Reenlistment to part-time service
Emotional issues	• Grew less painful, even wholly ameliorated or at least were not demonstrated
Satisfaction	• Embracing both military and civilian life to varying degrees
Significant others	• Civilian promoter positions assist the transition to a civilian life while military others and battle buddies have significance for the maintenance of service and military identities

6.2.1 Background

Sergeant Emma was in her mid-twenties and had served for approximately four years. She had been deployed to Afghanistan and was serving as a military analyst when she decided to leave due to disappointment and stagnation as described in chapter 5. As she already had an academic degree and was accustomed to the university context, she reapplied for university studies and was approved by her employer to be free from duty. One of her motives for this solution was to buy some time in order to work out what to do with her life. During the first interview one month had elapsed post exit.

6.2.2 The first interview: Disappointment, confusion and civilian and military audiences

When we met for the first interview (T1) it became obvious that Emma had one salient internal I-position, *I who like challenges,* and in regards to her military character Emma stated:

> This need of new challenges, well, the Armed Forces have from that perspective been a place, actually the only place where I have felt that I can get the combination of physical and intellectual challenges.

Her military character consisted of both intellectual analytical features and physical needs. Emma enjoyed working out intensively, and that type of physical identity and practice which the Armed Forces provided fitted her perfectly. Her military character was characterized by competence, ambition, motivation, and a strong will to deliver results both intellectually and physically. This strong will within Emma served as another independent internal I-position, and she proclaimed:

> I am a person who has a very strong will, and I have difficulties to take shit for things which I experience as not being my fault or my responsibility.

The student character was not articulated in the interview narrative, maybe since it was partly a way of making space in order to apply for civilian jobs. But *I with an academic degree* had cooperated with her position as a military analyst. The tone of the interview narrative consisted of disappointment upon the employer and confusion as for the future, and Emma confided:

> I feel a bit confused in life, in regards to my occupation, so maybe I should stick to it right now since it provides me with meaning, but in the same time I believe that I should not be afraid of letting go of it either.

Emma also experienced emptiness from time to time; her narrative example was as she walked around in the grocery store and the biggest decision of the day was whether to buy oranges or apples. In order to establish some balance in life Emma planned to freelance as an instructor in the Armed Forces when opportunities arose. Her narrative accounts served to maintain a relationship with significant battle buddies. She described the width of interaction with a military female friend, as they enjoyed utilizing opposing positions and characters within their selves and felt as though the movement between these was quick and easy:

> I experience that we can alter pretty fast between, yeah, and we are often rather coordinated, it can be about a discussion in regards to her recent deployment to Afghanistan and what happened there, and types of combat experiences [I-position as a Sergeant], to discussing if I am going to paint my fingernails [I-position as a civilian cultural female]. And I think that, and we have talked about it too, that this contrast is really nice. It is really nice to unite those parts [I as a Sergeant and I as a female]. Both these parts are really huge parts of who I am.

But Emma also had significant civilian others, for example both her boyfriend and her family were rather stressed throughout her deployment in Afghanistan. In fact, due to her parents worries she decided to turn down voluntary offers to redeploy. The significant civilian others such as her boyfriend influenced her decision to transition to a civilian life, and Emma recounted:

> I am pretty restrictive to talk about the job with my boyfriend because of many reasons, but also because he is not really comfortable with the military part of who I am or something like that. He thinks it is a little bit, well I don't know what, he is not completely happy with it.

6.2.3 The second interview: A security analyst and civilian and military audiences

As we met for the second interview (T2) thirteen months post exit her military character still included the same characteristics of ambition, motivation, and a sustained focus on results throughout field exercises. As she had planned in the first interview, she had served as an instructor from time to time over some weekends when given the possibility to do so, and she stated:

> I think that if I didn't have this connection to the regiment I believe I would have missed it more and felt like, well, I would have missed it more and experienced more nostalgia around certain things, but via what I believe to be a balanced connection to serve on my terms, this process has evolved quite painlessly for me, which is very nice.

New to the situation was that Emma had been employed as a civilian security analyst in a governmental agency, a new character of herself which resonated well with the internal position *I who like challenges*. She was satisfied with the professional development which also set the tone for the narrative as she shared:

> It feels like I have managed to bite off a big piece this time, so it entails plenty of challenges; it will be great fun, and I talked with my mentor the other day, and she said like "well, you need to realize that it will take two years before you can do it all by yourself, so take it steady."

Emma's character as a security analyst corresponds to the character of a military analyst in some aspects, but the culture in the governmental agency was rather different and thereby influenced the construction of the character such that it was more lonely in the job due to less teamwork, a mixed context with both males and females, civilian clothes, an absence of military formalities and hierarchies, and so on. Nonetheless, there appeared to be a large amount of cooperation between these two I-positions. Yet sometimes in the civilian work context

118

when Emma became stressed or nervous, the military I-position rose to dominance and she explained:

> When I find myself in a situation where I am supposed to talk in front of a larger crowd, then I can experience that the Sergeant comes crawling, I poise myself [in the military posture and manner] and talk in a special kind of way, and then after a while I realize "oh, this is a little bit awkward", but anyway then I have already started and am on my way.

The narrative accounts of her military buddies whom she met within the regiment when she sporadically served meant much to her. These storied accounts maintained the relationship with them, but they also served as promoters for serving part-time. As for civilian significant others in her life Emma said:

> Most important is my co-habiting boyfriend; very much revolves around him. I have a close relationship to both of my parents; they are still very important even if I get older. […] A really huge reason to leave full-active service is that I don't want to go anymore due to that my parents have told me how bad they felt when I was deployed, and I feel that their mental wellbeing is more valuable than my experience of deploying once more.

In regards to her co-habiting boyfriend she replied:

> When we met last year [i.e., Emma and the interviewer], my boyfriend and I had had it a little bit rough, it had been rather, not tense, but you know a little bit of ups and downs, and now we have really somehow found our way back on track.

The recent development with her co-habiting boyfriend had promoted Emma to stay the civilian path. She had also recently fulfilled a dream and completed some courses to become a personal trainer, which was a new character, in a sports club wherein she had made many new friends; Emma recounted:

> I could not make time for that when I was on full-time service in the Armed Forces and had to serve during evenings and be out on exercises; then it was too difficult to be a personal trainer in a sports club every Thursday evening.

Altogether, a number of civilian promoter positions had assisted Emma in her transition to a civilian life while significant others in the military context had simultaneously supported her part-time service.

6.2.4 The third interview: A security analyst, tension and civilian and military audiences

As we met for the final and third interview twenty-four months post exit Emma had continued to serve as a military instructor some weekends, which sustained her military character. Her first interview answer in regards to military service revealed that she still harbored some ambivalence about her decision to leave full-time service as she stated:

> But I thought last night: "No, I am pretty satisfied with how it is, although I am still a little ambivalent." I have thought of coming back, but I haven't really left either, but I have more and more landed in the concept that I have left, and that may be good.

Emma said that the metaphor of landing referred to finding the meaningful civilian job which she enjoyed as a security analyst in a governmental agency. Even though her new job was meaningful, her military character appeared to miss some aspects of service as Emma longed to:

> Get away from the computer, and back to the camaraderie, and get away from all those hellish codes, and all the things that create a mess in the job situation, and that I always find myself in front of the computer. I obviously miss the physical parts of service, I also miss getting out on exercises and finding myself in unplanned situations, when I don't know how it's going to be or how it will develop.

Despite such counter-positioning by her military I-position in potential cooperation with *I as an adventurous person* in contrast to *I as a security analyst in a governmental agency*, which revealed some psychological tension, Emma had grown more deeply rooted in her civilian life with her co-habiting boyfriend, family and friends including those at the sports club and, last but not least, her job, which set the tone of the interview narrative as she stated:

> I am very comfortable with my new work, and particularly due to the large amount of responsibility that I have received and the confidence that is entrusted in me, and I become positively challenged in that way. It is a context that fits me very well. [...] I have entered another type of work context which also considers significant matters. I work with something I find extremely relevant, almost more relevant than the military service because then it was more about preparation prior to something else all of the time. I do

none of that today, every day centers on dire real life things. When I am part of something that leads to something significant I feel an utterly different kind of satisfaction, the sensation that I have contributed something to making the country more secure.

Several of Emma's I-positions (e.g., *I as a girlfriend, a daughter, a person who like challenges, a personal trainer, and I as a security analyst*) which stemmed from the civilian context appeared to cooperate in her due to shared motives of staying the civilian course. Meanwhile promoter positions assisted the development on a temporal level as Emma had reformulated a new meaningful story of who she was as a civilian. The military I-position of a Sergeant also had promoters among the service members in the regiment where Emma served from time to time. The military story of who she was also served as a meaningful and significant story of who she was. Within Emma's military story she established and maintained significant relationships, especially with a particular group of active and former female service members.

6.2.5 Summation of the path of hybrid outcome

The path of hybrid outcome, whereupon influential civilian and military I-positions both demonstrated to exist and act within the narratives and the selves, was the path most travelled to civilian life and reintegration into a civilian population among participants in this study. However, the construction of new civilian characters was not completely correspondent to the type of characters constructed among participants treading the path of full transition; instead the civilian characters on a hybrid outcome in general contained less salient counter features (as with Emma who worked as a civilian security analyst in a government agency). The interpretation of such milder civilian counter features of characters was suggestively dependent upon the continued movement across two contexts: a civilian and a military setting. I-positions in the self were assumed to be interacting in a more dialogical manner, and amid such dialogue it is suggested that excessive divergence could lead to overly decentering movements which may be too taxing for the self to handle. Even though these civilian and military positions were characteristically not radicalized, ambivalence or even tension within the self were narrated over time as in the case of Emma. In general, a positive narrative tone did not rule out a distinct process of positioning and counter positioning between I-positions in the self. Such ambivalence was not narrated by those travelling either the path of full transition or the path of full return to military service, plausibly since the new civilian characters or renewed military characters in those cases rose to primary influence in the self while the counter characters, whether military or civilian character, lost influence over time. Those following the hybrid outcome displayed more dialogical concerns, complexity and deliberation within a more diversely populated self than those participants who traversed either of the paths (for dialogical concerns on a hybrid outcome also see Grimell, 2015, 2017a, 2017b, 2017d).

6.3 A case study portrait of military identity renewal via full return to military service

The full return to a military path included four participants who varied strongly in terms of post exit time. The members of this path shared with the participants on the other paths many of the transitional experiences of becoming civilians, but differ in their decisions to reenlist to full-time service to sustain the need of military I-positions. A specific storied pattern evolved and was discovered among these four participants in regards to how the transitional experiences influenced the self-identity work and prevented a sufficiently meaningful reformulation of who I am as a civilian. The storied evolution could be described as a story wherein the absence of civilian promoter positions and meaningful civilian employment opportunities sustained or increased the negative transitional experiences of identity and emotional struggles. Amid such a development the military I-positions remained influential and continued to narrate the meaningfulness of military service, including the importance of military camaraderie and community. The solution to this situation was to eventually return to full-time service.

The table below shows the content of identity renewal, in regards to the transitional experiences, as expressed throughout the interviews and finalized during the third and final interview cycle by these four participants.

Overarching themes	The content of military identity renewal (T3)
Identities	• A distinct asymmetry between military/veteran identities and new civilian identities, where military/veteran identities maintain a dominant position in the self, and where the perception is filtered through a military/veteran lens • A clear sense of a military "me", and in some cases relatively minor adjustment problems in civilian life • Distinct difficulties to find meaning and/or motivation in a new civilian life, which implies difficulties of reconstructing the story of who I am within a civilian realm • Reunion with the extraordinary community and camaraderie • Dichotomy between military and civilian worlds/relationships
A pro-militaristic position	• Pride of having served and positive emotions attach to it • Reenlistment to full-time service
Emotional issues	• Grew less painful, even wholly ameliorated or in the least undemonstrated
Satisfaction	• Embracement of the return to a military way of life and identity
Significant others	• Military others and battle buddies have been significant for the return, while the lack of civilian promoter positions hindered the transition to a civilian life

6.3.1 Background

Sergeant Gustaf was in his late twenties and had served on time limited employment contracts in Afghanistan and elsewhere and, between deployments, as an instructor in the Armed Forces. He had served for about five years, most often in staff sections. Gustaf's deployments included both the loss of service members and severe injury of other military personnel. His motives for leaving full-time service included the expiration of a time limited employment contract, but also disappointment in regards to how the military organization had handled some problems during the deployment. When Gustaf returned from his last deployment seventeen months prior to the interview he had experienced a type of vacuum wherein he lost energy and focus, as described in more detail in chapter 5. However, through a promoter position of a girlfriend, he eventually rekindled his energy and drive and managed to finish his university exams. At the time of the first interview he was about to complete a temporary employment contract as a teacher at a school.

6.3.2 The first interview: Identity confusion and military audience

As we met for the first interview (T1) Gustaf perceived himself as a Sergeant who was precise, distinct, duty-willing, maintained the structure and was direct on target in regards to interaction with others when he worked in the staff context. But in the same time, in other civilian settings such as the university and elsewhere, the military background influenced the perception of who he was (as in the case of Peter in the first interview), and Gustaf said:

> I think in the same time that this can be a burden for me sometimes because I believe that some may experience that, yeah, because of my military background, that I become perceived as square. There are pros and cons with that. Meanwhile there is one advantage with people experiencing that because there is diligence in that, I always deliver on time, so there are positives and negatives in this.

Meanwhile, as Gustaf expected to soon finish the temporary contract as a teacher, he was also studying to become a reserve officer because he felt a security in having a formal relationship with the Armed Forces, and he clarified:

> I chose the path of a reserve officer in order to prepare for myself so that I will not be completely abandoned by the Armed Forces and left all alone as I experience that many other service members are. It may not matter so much now, but it may in a couple of

years, when I have a connection in a formal way it is a kind of preparation for proactively sustaining my mental health.

By endeavoring to become a reserve officer Gustaf said that he cemented his military identity. Gustaf also had earned an academic degree in economics, although he never had worked as an economist, and when he worked temporarily as a teacher it was in other subjects. In fact, not much was said about the character of a teacher. In regards to the circumstance that he was about to finish his contract as a teacher a tone of sadness due to the absence of military colleagues was present, as well as an expression of identity confusion in the interview narrative as he pondered:

> Well, it is not necessarily an identity crisis but still some "what shall I do now?" [...] So, yes, it feels like some kind of identity crisis, "shall I stick to something intimately related to the Armed Forces, or should I, since I am an economist, perhaps work for a while as one may expect?"

Through Gustaf's narrative accounts of military colleagues in regards to sadness, he suggestively aimed to maintain the relationships with the military community and buddies. No particular promoter position was articulated in the first interview narrative.

6.3.3 The second interview: Full-time serving reserve officer with an military audience

When we met once again for the second interview twenty-nine months post exit Gustav had completed his formal military education and been appointed as a reserve officer. Defining characteristics of Gustaf's military character, in this reserve officer context, were to be precise, distinct, duty-willing, to maintain order and be direct in his interactions with others in the staff context. However, new to the interview narrative was the proclamation that he had recently returned to full-time service in a staff section, even though he still experienced that the Armed Forces as an organization had an inbuilt incapacity to adjust to the current situation in the world. Using Gustaf's own words:

> Well, there is camaraderie in many ways in the military service and that is hard to define, and this implicates that even if you feel uncomfortable with the organization you still thrive with, and I often thrive with, the people.

One dimension in military camaraderie which Gustaf experienced as particularly appealing was illuminated:

I think that it is the capacity, which I experience that the vast majority of the service members in the Armed Forces have, to be able to subordinate one's own personal will to a higher purpose; I like that idea, "to be able to accomplish this we need to do this, and to do so we must sacrifice this and that in order to do that." That is hard to find obviously demonstrated in other contexts.

As I asked how it had turned out that he had reenlisted for full-time service Gustaf replied:

Well, it was not about the organization as such; in this case it was a good friend who asked me if I wanted to assist him in the unit, so it was based on personal reasons. I can walk to the job in ten minutes, so it is neat, and I wanted to reach out to an old friend, so it is more some type of loyalty than a longing back to the organization.

The tone of the interview narrative was articulated in the question regarding how he experienced his return to full-time service as Gustaf replied:

I must say more satisfied, than when we met last time, I had more, well, I had more uncertainties as for my plan moving ahead than I have now; now it feels more that I see rather big potentials.

A military promoter and the camaraderie had brought Gustaf back to full-time service, and he distinctly positioned himself relationally toward the military community via narrative accounts that maintained and reestablished the relationships with military significant others.

6.3.4 The third interview: I am an officer with a military audience

When we met for the third and last interview (T3) Gustaf was still serving full-time in the staff section as a reserve officer. In regards to the question of how he experienced that his military identity had evolved during this journey Gustaf replied:

Well, but I experience that it has grown deeper in myself, and that I probably, if I would get the question of who I am, as if I were asked to introduce myself, then I would actually say that I am an officer. That I would not have done two years ago, I would not have done that, and on the other hand I was not an officer then. But I was that one year ago, although I would not have introduced myself like that then, which I would have done now. I have really landed into what I do now, and I think it partly has to do with the trust in me which my commanders show and the potential they see in me. The plans

125

which they have drawn up for me make it feel natural to proceed. It is about my journey and how the unit has supported that journey.

Gustaf was a little bit surprised that he had actually become a full-time serving officer in comparison to how he had reasoned during the previous interviews to maybe serve in the future from time to time. Gustaf thought that his current career in the staff section was very important for Sweden. Overall Gustaf was happy, which set the tone (satisfaction) for the third interview narrative; for example Gustaf reveled:

> It is very good! I am much calmer and more confident than I was last year and two years ago. So I am much calmer.

His narrative accounts continued to establish and maintain good relationships with military comrades and commanders throughout the third interview narrative. He was actually considering converting from a full-time reserve officer to a full-time tactical officer so as to open up an opportunity for a career as a regular commander for a staff section. Gustaf had also met a new girlfriend, but did not elaborate on this development.

6.3.5 The path of full return to military service

In the narrative analysis of the civilian characters utilizing this path not much could be said other than the fact that they do not seem to sustain a transition amid a dearth of promoter positions and meaningful employment opportunities, whereas significant others and meaning within the military context could catalyze the decision to return. The renewed military characters showed significant counter features in comparison to the civilian characters of those participants who continued down the path of full transition from military to civilian life. In regards to the narrative distance to a civilian world and its relationships, the trend was reversed in its direction but similar in its degree and expansion over time between the paths. Those on the full transition to civilian life narrated a growing distance from the military world and relationships, while those who returned to full-time service narrated a similar widening expanse between themselves and the civilian world and relationships. On both paths the outcome was the decline of opposing characters and their counter features, which in turn centered and integrated the self. Once the identity reconstruction or military identity renewal was solidified among the participants satisfaction and joy of life were established and internal debates in the self were ameliorated.

126

6.4 The dynamics of transition from military cultures to alternate ones

Theories which elaborate on military cultures and worlds have most often emphasized their uniqueness compared to civilian cultures and worlds, and even the dichotomy between military and civilian worlds (Devries et al., 2012; Edström et al., 2009; French, 2005; Hall, 2012a, 2012b; Huntington, 1957; Strachan, 2006; Verrips, 2006; Wertsch, 1991; Wilson, 2008). It is however difficult to know how theories resonate to empirical studies and different contexts. The results of the analysis presented in chapters 5 and 6 are on the other hand understood as empirical and qualitative storied experiences of transition from influential and powerful military cultures to alternate civilian ones. In the light of this empirical study it has been demonstrated over and over again that there exists a narrated distinction between the experience of military and civilian cultures among the participants, for example, in regards to the communal life of service members and extraordinary camaraderie. Such features, and others, construct a significant part of the military identities among the participants, thereby shaping military characters which a certain emphasis upon the value of military community and camaraderie. The participants' experiences of identity issues and emotional issues in transition from military to civilian life are therefore suggested to revolve around military cultural identities which stand in contrast to the newly encountered civilian cultures and identities which are built around other "values, meanings, and practices unevenly distributed" and adopted by its members (Gregg, 2005, p. 5). Civilian cultures and identities tend to be shaped by values, meanings, and practices which are often not just different, but even opposed to military cultural values, meanings, and practices, and this may result in tension and conflict in transition from military service, as well as during military service. The sociologist Segal (1986) described such an ongoing conflict between the military and the family, two institutions which she described both as greedy institutions which are each demanding of the individual's time and exclusive and undivided loyalty. As for these two greedy institutions there are underlying tensions between the needs of the military and the family which are mirrored in the self through characters or I-positions with opposing needs. This is, for example, present in Sergeant Emma's narrative account of the partner and the parents who were not happy about her full-time service and deployment to Afghanistan, which in turn were powerful motivators for Emma to leave active service since she could not really unite those two greedy parts of her life (except through a hybrid outcome where most of her life was lived in the civilian domain). Military and civilian characters often narrate opposing ideas of values, meanings, and practices shaped by the cultures to which they belong. The case study of Sergeant Helen illustrates this (Grimell, 2017b). Helen was a student at the time of the first interview thirty months post exit. During the first interview she was reflecting from a meta-position upon her military position and civilian position during an episode which occurred once Helen had returned to Sweden from a combat intense deployment in Afghanistan (Grimell, 2017b, p. 10):

It seems like I want different things, the military thing, I have been very influenced by that, that you are supposed to be cool, which I had no need to be before. That is probably what is absolutely most new to my personality after the armed service, I have more of, I believe it is a need to be calm, secure and not become stressed by unnecessary stuff. I am thinking of a thing, when we had returned from deployment and were already in Sweden preparing to go home, we had psychological sessions, you had the possibility to get extra support, if you said you needed it. But I was drawn into some kind of competition to be mentally healthy; I mean from my civilian I: "free psychology support, that is what people pay a lot of money for, that is really good!" But my military I took over completely, and I just wanted to be declared mentally healthy. That I was cool and well and good, and then I will walk out of here and get notified that I don't need to see anyone. And I have reflected a lot over that, it was totally sick, but it was something which really influenced me, and I was declared healthy, but I fixed that later.

With the addition of "I fixed that later" Helen was referring to a reaction that she had about twenty months post deployment when she was supposed to talk about her deployment and combat experiences on a seminar. In the middle of the seminar, suddenly a number of repressed combat and post-combat memories fled over her, and she started to cry. Later, she called the Veterans Health and was scheduled for psychological support to process the repressed service and post-combat memories.

The cultural dynamics of two very different military and civilian perspectives are also transparent throughout Peter's reflections upon his first year of transition from military to civilian life as an extremely task-oriented, efficient, focused and uncompromising platoon commander who found himself in a campus setting. Peter had a hard time to adjust to new and opposing cultural ideas in regards to what he was used to and experienced emptiness as he longed for his military comrades. This feeling of emptiness suggestively became a temporary position in Peter's self (Hermans & Hermans-Konopka, 2010). Peter's military character was kept active in his self through a complex process of positioning by frequent contact with his military peers, but also thought how he narrated and imagined that these battle buddies were thinking of him in different situations. Moreover, he was positioned (in a passive way) by his student peers who defined him as militaristic. But slowly over time, and with significant support from his partner, the highly cherished outdoor life in the mountains, his teachers, and finally his student peers who redefined him a civilian student character was shaped, with counter features compared to the platoon commander, and this new character took precedence in his self. Peter's civilian student character was much more calm and harmonious, the character allowed for connection and sharing with others, it harbored openness to new ideas and had the capacity to relax and do things just for fun without any specific purpose. Additionally, as an outcome of the transitional evolution Peter now enjoyed two cultural perspectives to employ throughout lived life, or "two sides of the coin" as he preferred to say, instead of having just one cultural approach to living life (chapter 6, p. 113).

Lieutenant John experienced similar cultural tensions as he transitioned from a military culture to civilian student culture (Grimell, 2017b). John experienced salient identity crises in his self as his military character and mindset were expected to adapt to this new cultural context. The clash between cultures could not be avoided as John's student peers were as critical to his military cultural position as he was to theirs. The positions were sustained throughout his year in university. The civilian student peers, as well as John, were locked into their cultural characters and positions. John endured one year in the student context and then returned to the military community and camaraderie through full-time service. John's, as well as Peter's, experiences of transition from military to civilian university cultures are not new and resonate with previous research of military transition into university settings; universities characteristically encourage and nurture individuality, a critical point of view, free thinking, and openness (Elliott, Gonzalez & Larsen, 2011; Rumann, 2010; Rumann & Hamrick, 2010; Wheeler, 2012). Additionally, service members pursuing higher education are often much older than their peers, and potentially possess drastically different life experiences related to deployment or combat (Whiteman, Barry, Mroczek & MacDermid Wadsworth, 2013; Zinger & Cohen, 2010).

6.4.1 A transition as self-identity work involved in the dynamics of localization and globalization
It has been suggested that military cultures harbor a set of values, meanings, and practices specific for those cultures and upheld through a distinct hierarchy, rules, codes of conduct, and uniforms but also more informally developed among units and personnel (Edström et al., 2009; French, 2005; Huntington, 1957; Wertsch, 1991) Larger military cultures and smaller sub-cultures among specific units are reproduced in the shaping and performance of military

identities within military contexts (Thornborrow & Brown, 2009). Those military contexts could be described as gated communities which are not allowed to be explored or particularly influenced by outsiders or civilians. The development and maintenance of military life styles and the performance of military identities within the military contexts are therefore very local processes with limited influences from civilian cultures and people. Military life styles and identities may, from time to time, through military deployments in Afghanistan or elsewhere, have the potential of being influenced by globalization (e.g., new cultural values, meanings and practices). However, the prospect of expanding the self-identity may be quite small in such missions given the nature of the deployment (e.g., peace-keeping, force-protection, combat). Deployments may rather fuel the risk of strengthening the focus of the local and the familiar, while intensifying the emphasis of *us and them* (Zimbardo, 2008).

Transition from military to civilian life can thus be understood through the dynamics of localization and globalization wherein global, un-known and un-familiar values, meanings, and practices encounter the local, known, and familiar ones to enhance heterogeneity in the self and emphasize cultural differences and even oppositions in the self (Hermans & Dimaggio, 2007; Hermans & Hermans-Konopka, 2010). The process of appropriating and rejecting alternate values, meanings, and practices, or via a dialogical terminology the process of positioning and counter-positioning between positions in the self, are helpful in order to understand what goes on in a self who is exposed to the dynamics of localization (i.e., making claims of the familiar and known) and globalization (i.e., positioning oneself in alternate values, meanings, and practices). As the participants in this study left the local and familiar military life of service they encountered globalization and were exposed to alternate values, meanings, and practices within civilian cultures which in many cases were opposed to that which was familiar to the participants. Such encounters of globalization increased the heterogeneity in their selves, as in the case of Lieutenant John, Lieutenant Maria, Sergeant Emma and others, which resulted in identity confusion (Arnett, 2002). Deeply rooted military values, meanings, practices, and identities were thereby stressed or challenged by other cultural identities and ways of living meaningful lives outside of military contexts. Identity questions such as who I am, where I am going, and my place in the world were articulated by many participants in their processes of transition. Identity issues and emotional issues found among the participants in this study was suggestively a result of the dynamics of localization and globalization which implied that each participant had to process such identity confusion, appropriating or rejecting, positioning or counter-positioning themselves in the dynamics of meeting

130

alternate cultures, as a part of the self-identity work in transition from the local military life to a global and seemingly uncertain civilian life.

Arnett (2002) also suggests that high levels of uncertainty may stem from globalization, and by building on the concept of uncertainty Hermans & Hermans-Konokpa (2010) have presented four aspects or dimensions which are included in such uncertainties: complexity (i.e., a great number of parts which have a great variety of relations), ambiguity (i.e., suspension of clarity), deficit knowledge (i.e., no over-ruling structure that can resolve contradiction between parts), and unpredictability (i.e., the absence of control of the future progression). The three evolutionary paths which were discovered among the participants, and which varied strongly relative to exit time, are seen as answers to such uncertainties in self-identity work. The paths of *full transition*, *hybrid outcome*, and *full return* to military service are understood as three ways of dealing with the dynamics of localization and globalization. The developmental scheme of a full transition from military to civilian life works in the interest of appropriation of new values, meanings, and practices wherein the participants are positioning themselves in new civilian I-positions with varying characteristics. This path fits nicely with a quite recent theory on transition from military to civilian life by Castro & Kintzle (2014) which was also located in and derived from an American context. This theory described a progression through which military personnel transition out of the military culture and into the civilian culture including its repercussions on personal, social, and occupational levels. The theory postulated three interacting and overlapping phases. The first phase highlights personal, cultural, and transitional factors which created the base for the transitional movement. Considering the case of Lieutenant Peter it was foremost built upon the experience of stagnation as he perceived he had become an administrator as a platoon commander. The second phase, navigating the transition, referred to factors that impact the individual transition from a service member to a civilian, which in Peter's case included initially taxing self-identity work which progressed through support from significant others, a meaningful context which allowed for a progressive identity reconstruction and life style in the mountains, followed sometime later by meaningful employment. The combination of such factors assisted Peter in appropriating new values, meanings, and practices in the reconstructed story of who he is. Peter's I was more and more positioning in the new civilian identities which were shaped over time, and the military character of himself was seldom brought to the narrative surface. The final phase of the theory addressed the outcome of the transition, including work, family, health, general well-being, and community which in Peter's case were demonstrated by satisfaction. From a dialogical point of view it is suggested that the military voice was gradually moved to the periphery of the self among those who traversed upon full transition path. The narrative structure of the self in the interview narratives was of course complex, but over time Peter and these other participants were distancing themselves from making military claims of identities by promoting other cultural values, meanings and practices.

As for the hybrid outcome, the theory on transition from military to civilian life by Castro & Kintzle (2014) is less helpful. The hybrid outcome is rather understood in line with Arnett's (2002) suggestion of a bicultural identity, or a hybrid identity, of immigrants which implied that identity confusion and uncertainties going from one dominant culture to another were solved through a dialogue between one part of the self rooted in a local culture and another part of the self developed to fit a life and an identity in a new country with other values, meanings, and practices. In the case of Sergeant Emma she kept positioning and re-positioning between such civilian and military I-positions in her life post transition. She appropriated new values, meanings, and practices and expanded her repertoire with new characters. The dialogue between the characters in Emma's case, and among the participants traveling on this path, held a complex narrative structure in the interview narratives, yet was more balanced and refrained from excessively distancing the self from either military and civilian claims of identities.

As for the full return to military service the dynamics of localization and globalization resulted in identity confusion and uncertainties, as seen in the case of Lieutenant Gustaf and Lieutenant John, wherein the participants at some point rejected alternate values, meanings, and practices and counter-positioned to the well-known, familiar, and local military community, camaraderie, and thereby to making claims of military identities. In these cases the position of the military characters became influential over time in the interview narratives, which potentially mirrored their positions in the selves. Additionally, the interview narratives also demonstrated over time a growing absence of claiming alternate civilian cultures and identities as part of their renewed military stories of who they were.

6.4.2 Applying the concepts of implicit religion and lived religion to the processes
It may be helpful to address some layers within the military tailored paths through the lens of implicit religion and lived religion for a broader understanding of the appeal to maintain the connection with the military ways of life. Applying implicit religion and lived religion on the participants' storied experiences would enrich cultural psychological elaborations on transi-

tion from military to civilian life with helpful insights. Following in the steps of Bailey (1990) and Hamilton (2001) it may be suggested that the deeply ingrained military communal life including values, meanings, and practices can be labeled as implicit religious in regards to the dedication to the local community and the commitment to the human. Bailey (1990) suggested that commitment to the human was a form of experience that could be comparable to the sense of the sacred in contemporary societies. The strength and significance of the military community and the loyalty and commitment to battle buddies, *until death do us part*, have the potential to provide these bonds between battle buddies with a type of sacredness which cannot, nor should not, be violated in regards to the values, meanings, and practices which are wanted and necessary during military service. Not only in individual terms can the sacred be understood, but also in terms of relationships and communities. Humans have a basic and irreducible yearning for a relationship with something that transcends the self, and according to Pargament (2008) communities and communal life can take on a sacred character for their members. Such a proposition goes beyond explicit religious communities and includes non-religious military communities as well (Grimell, 2016b; Lunde, 2009). In related ways practical theologians such as Ganzevoort (2011b, 2009) and Ganzevoort & Roeland (2014) have suggested that existential and spiritual questions in life can be addressed and understood beyond organized, institutional, and official religious communal life as the lived religion of ordinary people in secular contexts. Individuals who may not necessarily define themselves as religious in a traditional sense and/or regularly participate in explicit religious communities may, on the other hand, employ different types of lived religion in their lives which, for example, could include gardening, outdoor life or activism which can provide its practitioner with a sufficient way to understand life and death; it may have spiritual relevance for its practitioners (McGuire, 2008). Values, beliefs, meanings, and practices which guide the lived life of those practitioners may not be understood as religious through the lens of organized, institutional, and official religion. However, from the perspectives of both implicit religion and lived religion a wider understanding is adopted in order to acknowledge the existential depth and significance of such life styles. A closer look at some of the narrative accounts from the participants who live in such a Swedish secular context, participants with no articulated belief in God or transcendence, but who returned to full-time military service or the hybrid model appear to fit this interpretation of implicit religion (Bailey, 1990, 1997).

Lieutenant Gustaf narrated a particular set of military values and beliefs which were of significance to him in regards to his full return (chapter 6, p. 126):

I think that it is the capacity, which I experience that the vast majority of the service members in the Armed Forces have, to be able to subordinate one's own personal will to a higher purpose; I like that idea, "to be able to accomplish this we need to do this, and to do so we must sacrifice this and that in order to do that." That is hard to find obviously demonstrated in other contexts.

This is an interesting narrative account because Gustaf makes a claim that the vast majority of the service members are able to subordinate the personal will to a higher purpose and in doing so make sacrifices. This type of value, meaning, and practice may be hard to find demonstrated in other contexts but is not uncommon within religious communities, for example Christian ones (Bonhoeffer, 1959). However, Gustaf was not present in such contexts. The belief in God implies subordination by an individual to transcendent powers, but it may also include subordination to the values, meanings, and practices of a certain tradition which requires different types of sacrifices such as professions, dreams, desires, celibacy, and gender roles to name but a few. Gustaf's declarations of values and beliefs within military community and life which were specifically appealing to him do not have anything to do with organized, institutional, and official religions since Gustaf did not have any belief in God, religious calling, or anything of the sort. However, his commitment to a higher purpose, which included sacrifices, and a community of battle buddies who acknowledged and lived by such standards, was implicitly religious. The values and beliefs that emerged from Gustaf's military way of life could not the considered as explicitly religious. But what Gustaf was describing was rather a type of lived religion which provided his life with subordination to a higher purpose of life, sacrifices, meaning, and satisfaction, a type of lived religion which has proved hard to find demonstrated in other contexts. It may seem radical to suggest that military community life and service may include implicit religious dimensions and moreover be described as lived religion, but lived religion is hardly neutral, and: "In order to understand individuals' religion-as-lived, we must avoid romanticizing certain embodied practices, while ignoring others we may deplore" (McGuire, 2008, p. 118).

Sergeant Erik's narrative account further broadens the discussion of implicit religion and lived religion (Grimell, 2015). Erik served for approximately five years and had made several deployments to Afghanistan and elsewhere, and during the first interview he described the experience of a purpose which was transcending his self during deployments (p. 143):

There are few times when I feel that I have done something as important as when I work in the Armed Forces because it means something, it matters what I do. Even if I eat or sleep, it has a purpose, it is something bigger than me. I just don't do it for myself, I do it for the Swedish nation, for the Afghans we are trying to help. It needs to mean something that has been important and it is important to why I continue.

This is also a narrative account which included a belief in a greater purpose behind military service in the Armed Forces which was larger than Sergeant Erik: military service for the Swedish nation and the Afghans who Erik and his battle buddies intended to help. From this perspective the Armed Forces are the structure which makes it possible to do something for the nation of Sweden and the Afghans, and this could be seen a sacred character. Lunde (2009) has also suggested that the Armed Forces could be included in such a structure with sacred connotations. Moreover, Erik described a type of lived religion, as did Gustaf, to which he subordinated himself and which in turn provided his life with meaning. This was, as in the case of Lieutenant Gustaf, difficult for several participants to find demonstrated in other contexts and thus a major reason for Erik and others to traverse a hybrid path and construct a hybrid identity. Additionally, Sergeant Erik's lived religion also included the sacrifice of a longterm relationship with a girlfriend. The relationship was strained by Erik's deployment, and his girlfriend wished for him to return, but Erik decided to continue his deployment in Afghanistan. As a consequence she concluded the relationship, and this loss was taxing for Erik. During the second interview he had recently met a new potential girlfriend, and he described existential concerns or issues in regards to life questions since he had a wish to deploy again. The potential danger of sacrifices in the lived religion of military service generated metacognitive activity in his self, and Erik described the dialogical process between temporary emotional positions in regards to the recently growing relationship (Grimell, 2017a, p. 263):

Well, do you dare to go all in? I was so burned last time because I deployed. I sacrificed something as I deployed. What if I wanna deploy again (laugh)? Is it worth it, the stress that it may be like that again, or is it not, or won't I go this time, and will I let go of someone I want? It is like a lot of those thoughts, too. What if I become a dad, will I go then, no, I don't know.

A third case also highlights the significance in military service which transcends the self: Sergeant First Class Oskar (Grimell, 2017d). Oskar had served for approximately four and half years and recounted his experience of meaning during a deployment in Afghanistan six months post exit (p. 62):

> It is a difficult feeling to describe. The only ones who can describe it are probably those who have served, it is a feeling of being part of something, to contribute to something that is bigger than one's self; I support and contribute to something that I could not do by myself.

As in the other cases Oskar did not find, as long as this study was conducted, anything outside of the military context which could be compared to the sense of meaning and contribution to something larger than his self. This is suggestively also an example of lived religion of military service that includes an experience of profundity, meaning and community life with implicit religious dimensions.

Implicit religion and lived religion may allow for descriptions of the participants' communal life and military service which resonate with the profundity and depth of their storied experiences. Therefore, it is suggested that such perspectives and related ones, for example, invisible religion (Luckmann, 1967), spirituality and the sacred of everyday life (Pargament, 2008, 2011), and existential ultimate concerns (Tillich, 2014, 1957) may be useful among actively serving personnel to present deeper layers in military communal life and service. In fact, it is suggested that this is a promising and potential avenue for broadening research on military cultures (i.e., values, meanings, and practices) and military ways of life as lived implicit religion. This may also shape further nuances to existential and implicit religious elements in military identities which may be lost and/or difficult to reconstruct or restore during a transition from military to civilian life.

Additionally, it is well worth adding some words about the bodily dimension and embodied identities, a promising arena for future explorations of lived religion, implicit religion and spiritual reflections among service members and veterans. The results of the narrative analysis suggest that the body was highly involved in Peter's, as well as Emma's, self-identity work. In Peter's case his body was expected to act in specific ways according to his military identity (e.g., to take the lead in study situations, to behave militaristically). Similarly, Emma recounted that her body posture changed drastically when she positioned into her military Sergeant's position as a response to feeling nervous when talking in front of a crowd. Peter's body within the ski and rescue patrol became once again, rather as it had during military service, an integral part of a new team of comrades; additionally his body became even more interactive with

136

nature and outdoor activities as he moved to the mountains to work and live outdoors. Emma's physical body was also connected to her fulfillment of the dream to become a personal physical trainer. In the case of both Peter and Emma their evolutions of identities were not just related to narrative evolutions and formulations of new characters but also to a type of progressive bodily involvement of those new identities. This resonates very well with McGuire's (2008) understanding of lived religion as embodied practices. The emphasis of the narrative analysis throughout this chapter has focused upon how preexisting and new characters interact and evolve within the self over time throughout the study, yet these characters were at times expressed through a bodily dimension, as is well illustrated in the cases of Peter and Emma where their bodies were demonstrated to be important in the communal life for a member in a ski and rescue patrol as well as for a personal trainer who lived her dream within a community of athletes. This suggests that identities which correspond to implicit religious dimensions are likely lived through the bodies of their narrators.

CHAPTER 7

Existential and Religious Elements in the Process

Based upon the recently presented results of the analysis in chapters 5 and 6 it is suggested that military cultures develop military identities with corresponding I-positions which are more or less influential in the self, and thus among the participants, over time. Military narrative characters held counter features when compared to civilian characters, and these counter features were shaped in transition and particularly salient among those who transitioned via a linear civilian path. Influential yet divergent characters in the participants' selves implicated a potential for tension, or in some cases even conflict, within the self during the continued process of reorganization of positions which evolved throughout the transitions. Additionally, military I-positions had both agentic, unique, and individually applied attributes as well as being relatively exclusive as a result of the commonly perceived dichotomy between civilian and military which helped to bind military significant others even more tightly to one another, and this combination sculpted complex and varied military I-positions which were not just agentic or communal, but both. Throughout the transitions significant others served as promoters to the development of the participants, and meaningful preexisting or new occupations or life styles played major roles in the transitional movement to civilian lives and reintegration into civilian populations, or transition to a hybrid path, or return to full-time military service. However, for a richer understanding of the self-identity work in transition other empirical layers in the process also begged to be addressed. Those layers were the existential and religious elements in the process, which framed the third subquestion of the project. This chapter serves to present some of these themes or elements (two words which will be used interchangeably throughout this chapter) through the participants' own words so as to add another enriching layer to the understanding of identity reconstruction, identity maintenance, or identity renewal on the three paths of transition to civilian life or resumption to different types of military service.

This chapter has approached existential elements, or more precise: articulated questions of life, in the self-identity work during transition from a narrative point of view. It was assumed that questions of life in the process of identity reconstruction were significant for the lived life of a person and as such could be understood as existential elements. Thus this analysis has employed an open and inductive approach to questions of life/existential elements throughout the explorations of the self-identity work. Existential elements referred to storied experiences of the participants' questions of life in the transitional processes. *Existential concerns* was used as an open analytical code within Atlas.ti which had the potential to organize inductively storied experiences, or narratives about experiences, in regards to questions of life amongst the participants and their self-identity work. Individual inductive experiences from the participants were then developed into common existential themes or elements across the sample with a particular emphasis on the self-identity work and transitional paths. The method included asking explicit questions regarding experiences of significance for the lives of the participants throughout the process of transition, but also built upon personal stories within the interview narratives which have had major (past) or may have major (future) impacts on a participant's life. Examples of such question formulations include: *Could you reflect on a situation where you experienced significant life questions and maybe tell me that story? What is important in your life? What gives you direction in life?*

Six common existential themes or elements were developed based upon this analysis. These existential themes lacked explicit religious references (e.g., God, higher powers); therefore they are considered as non-religious existential elements. The six existential themes are listed below:

- Identities
- Meaningful work positions and/or life styles
- Significant others
- Beliefs and values
- Sacrifices imposed upon significant others and/or the self
- Temporary departure from society to instead envelope one's self in the natural world

The concept of religious elements in this dissertation referred to narrated experiences of relevance for the participants' questions of life which were connected to some type of belief in or experience of God and angels i.e. transcendent or higher powers (Astley, 2002; Hermans, 2015) and spiritual emotions such as uplift, awe, humility, mystery, gratitude, joy, peace, and serenity (Heelas, 2008; Pargament, 2008, 2011; Pargament et al., 2014). *Religious concerns* was used as an open analytical code with the potential to address storied experiences with relevance for the questions of life linked to self-identity work. The method included asking explicit questions in regards to the beliefs and experiences, but also personal stories which were revealed amid the open nature of the interviews which have had or may have religious/spiritual influences on a participant's life. Five participants described themselves as believing in God and in one instance angels, or experienced religious/spiritual feelings when immersed in nature or in church during musical events. The participants had quite disparate religious experiences, but one specific theme was the significance of nature for self-identity processes.

In this chapter, the most common and shared existential themes or elements among the participants will first be introduced, and then contrasted by a presentation of the differences demonstrated between the three paths in regards to the beliefs and values in self-identity work. A presentation of existential themes of sacrifices, which is suggested to be a part of the lived religion of many of the participants, and the significance of nature, which were both found across the paths, follows, and the chapter concludes with religious elements demonstrated in the process. Narrative accounts from the representative cases of Peter, Emma and Gustaf, will be complemented by voices from the wider sample.

7.1 Shared themes found within the process

Based upon the results of the analysis in chapters 5 and 6 some of the presented results can now be explicitly and properly introduced as existential themes or elements with a specific relevance for questions of life in the self-identity processes during transition among the participants across the sample. Throughout the third interview phase shared existential elements were discerned among the participants. These addressed identities, meaningful employment and/or life-styles, and significant others in life, all of which were crucial for the formulation of new, maintenance of, or renewal of preexisting personal narratives with characters. These three dimensions played a crucial role for life questions during transition. Preexisting and potential new narrative identities were understood as existential elements in the transitional process since those held relevance for the questions shared by the participants of *who I am*, what is my place in the world, and where am I going in this transition. Tailored to preexisting or potential new narrative identities were the storied experiences of meaning, for example where meaning was experienced in regards to a new job or education that supported the self-identity work in transition. However, experiences of a lack of meaning could work against the reconstruction of new identities, and this could in turn erode the participant's motivation to pursue a full transition from military to civilian life. Significant others had an influential impact upon the decision to exit full-time military service, endure a transition, and/or return to military service in one form or another. Significant others were found in both civilian and military contexts. The combination of significant military others and the experience of meaning attached to military service, concomitant with the experience of a lack of meaning in new identities, catalyzed a return to military service. Meanwhile civilian promoters and meaningful employment opportunities supported the process of transition to civilian life and reintegration into civilian population. The existential themes are given below:

- Identities: Questions such as who am I, who am I supposed to be, where do I fit in
- Meaning: Meaningful occupations and/or life styles which support the process
- Significant others: Who provides assistance and support in the process

Reflecting back on the narrative accounts in chapters 5 and 6, it seems that these existential themes or elements have already been implicitly introduced. Fragments from these larger narratives, and some articles, will follow to illustrate each existential element, including the path choice of the narrator.

7.1.1 Identities: Storied experiences and questions related to self-identity work

In the first interview Private First Class Mattias was referring to a self-identity experience when he stated: "I have a harder time to identify who I am today than when I served (p. 89)." [Full transition]

In the first interview Lieutenant Maria described her initial self-identity experience such as: "Really weird. Like being without an identity (p. 93)." [Full transition]

In the first interview Sergeant Emma described a storied experience: "I feel a bit confused in life, in regards to my occupation, so maybe I should stick to it right now since it provides me with meaning, but in the same time I believe that I should not be afraid of letting go of it either (p. 117)." [Hybrid outcome]

In the first interview presented elsewhere Lieutenant John recounted, in regards to his self-identity work, that the values and attitudes he encountered in the university setting: "With my military experience, the values that I have are not sufficient and it becomes a pretty big identity crisis, it prevents me from shaping a new identity... (Grimell, 2017b, p. 12)." [Full return]

In the first interview Sergeant Gustaf described his self-identity process: "So, yes, it feels like some kind of identity crisis... (p. 124)" [Full return]

141

7.1.2 Meaning: Employment and/or life styles

In the first interview presented elsewhere Captain Lennart had found meaning in life as a retiree with a new contemplative life style and declared satisfaction in regards to life when he proclaimed: "But there is one thing: to feel that life is actually rather amazing. It is enough if the sun is shining; you go and take a swim after a workout at the gym or in a small lake just a few kilometers from here, ride back with the bicycle, pass a café and have a cup of coffee and a small sandwich (Grimell, 2016b, p. 215)." [Full transition]

In the second interview Lieutenant Peter experienced new meaning in a civilian life as a member in a ski and rescue patrol who lived together with his girlfriend in the Swedish mountains where they shared an immediate possibility to enjoy outdoor activities and stated: "Perhaps I don't think so much about the meaning of life, but I feel the joy of living, and that has significantly changed since I left the Armed Forces (p. 113)." [Full transition]

In the first interview Sergeant Erik experienced the lack of meaning in regards to his university studies and the papers he produced in social science and stated: "As soon as it is examined by the teacher it is a dead mass, a dead piece of paper. Nothing more. And then it is hard, too, it is what makes it so difficult to find motivation (p. 90)." [Hybrid outcome]

In the first interview Private First Class Adam still found meaning in part-time military service and stated that in between study courses "then I can do what I think is fun in service: join the field exercises; I'm a signaler, and I signal which is damn fun (p. 91)." [Hybrid outcome]

In the second interview Sergeant Emma experienced new meaning in her recent employment as a governmental analyst: "I work with something I find extremely relevant... (p. 120)" [Hybrid outcome]

7.1.3 Significant others: Partners, family and friends who supported progression down the paths

In the first interview during the first phase of transition Lieutenant Peter narrated: "My girlfriend, she motivates me to everything I do here... (p. 111)" [Full transition]

In the second interview Lieutenant Peter explained that he had found new significant others in his recent civilian employment who aided his navigation of a civilian path as he experienced that "we have a community and belonging in what we do (p. 113)." [Full transition]

In the first interview Sergeant Gustaf expressed the power of social support during a transitional time of vacuum when he explained: "It was when I met my [current] girl-friend, so that was like a factor which led me to become more structured, and then I started to complete the exams in different subjects. I found my energy again (p. 99)." [Full return]

In the first interview Sergeant David similarly narrated the importance of social support during his initial transition as he stated that: "The most important thing for me is to feel that I still have my friends [civilian] remaining here, that they haven't disappeared, and they have not, so that was damn nice to feel when I returned. And with family, they have supported me... (p. 100)" [Full return]

In the second interview Lieutenant Gustaf, who had been promoted from Sergeant to Lieutenant as a condition of enlistment as a reserve officer, expressed the impact cama-raderie had upon his decision return to full-time service as "in this case it was a good friend who asked me if I wanted to assist him in the unit, so it was based on personal reasons (p. 125)." [Full return]

The turning point in the quest to answer the general questions of life regarding identities, meaning and significant others was found somewhere within the crucial period of two months to two years post exit, as described in chapters 5 and 6, when the participants traversed upon one of the three paths which either sustained a full civilian identity reconstruction, or led to the development of a hybrid military and civilian identity, or to a return and renewal of military identity. However, this was a process which implied that time, in correspondence to the presented existential elements, was essential in order to rebuilt new meaningful identities or return to preexisting meaningful identities which offered the answers to existential issues such as identity, meaning and significant others. In the case of the full transition from military to civilian life these existential elements were generally answered in new ways, whereas on a return to full-time service old solutions were typically re-employed. All of these existential elements were connected to preexisting or new characters and I-positions. These life questions were shared across the sample provided the analysis with an introductory insight in regards to existential elements in the transitional process, but they did not sufficiently describe deeper existential layers which commingled in the self-identity work in regards to the chosen paths during the transitional process. These deeper layers emerged, as introduced in the end of chapter 5, when looking at the different types of beliefs and values narrated by the participants as they traversed the three paths.

7.2 Divergent themes found between paths

One specific interest throughout the analysis was the attempt to find patterns across the narrative accounts which could further reveal the nuances within influential identities, meaningful occupations/life styles, and significant others in life with the goal of better understanding the identity work processes that in the end manifested as progression down one of three specific identity paths. Such nuances could indicate narrative distinctions or cues as for the potential development of self-identity work across time. One particular distinction which was found in the analysis regarded the beliefs and values inherent to the different paths. The majority of the participants who had either from the onset planned to serve part-time, or crossed over to reenlist in service part-time (hybrid path) or full-time (full return) voiced a shared set of beliefs and values in their narratives and/or their response to the question what they believed in. The shared set of beliefs and values revolved around an emphasis on and beliefs in national safety and, security, feminism, and democracy which absolutely and ultimately deserved to be safeguarded and protected. Such types of beliefs and values were, in contrast, not emphasized among the participants on the path of a full transition from military to civilian life. Upon the path of full transition the emphasis in general centered on the new individual lives that the participants were living, and those lives were filled with individually centered aspirations and ideas sustained by civilian culture (e.g., fulfill your personal desires and needs, pursuit of a career, live a good life). Therefore, based on the distinction and distribution it is suggested that the type of beliefs and values in national safety and security, feminism, and democracy which truly deserved to be safeguarded and protected, according to the participants, was a type of collective military voice which was heard within the personal narratives of the participants who continued with or returned to different types of military service. Such a collective military voice, in the eyes of these participants, ultimately was a motivating reason for the existence of the Armed Forces, and for the military interventions on a national and even a global level. Narrative accounts in this section help to highlight the differences between the paths; Sergeant Emma and Sergeant Gustaf expressed the collective voice among the two military tailored paths while Lieutenant Peter recounted a full transition with an individual emphasis on personal desires and needs.

Lieutenant Peter, who had followed a full transition from military to civilian life, responded to the question of what he believed in during the third interview:

> What I believe in is that everyone should follow their own path and do what they think is the most important to them, to live a life that you really live, whether it is to sit on a desk in a store or work only during summers throughout your life or not to work at all but buy a surf bus and go around the world. It is up to each and every one. And I more and more discover what I want to do and try and how to live, well, maybe not live because how to live life for me may shift quite often. But I try to live my life to the fullest and not postpone things but rather to do them.

Sergeant Emma, on the hybrid path, described another set of beliefs and values in the third interview:

> My time in the Armed Forces has shaped me very much in such a manner that in my world Sweden is something precious worth being protected, if you know what I mean. So even if it is not always explicitly stated in the context [military] this is what you are nurtured to value. That perspective is present in my job today, too [as a security analyst]. [...] That is what we do, to protect Sweden first and then democracy. That is the thing. For me I believe that becomes more concrete that way. So this is something that I value. And in Sweden it is seen by others as a little bit ugly to be a patriot, and I don't use that word since it can give wrong connotations. But if you look at the content of the word it matches with me very well. For me it is very concrete, it is Sweden, the Swedish government and society and my values and things like freedom and similar things.

Former Sergeant Gustaf, who was at the time a Lieutenant and serving full-time as a reserve officer, said in regards to what he believed in during the third interview:

> I don't know if I believe in anything. I believe in humans' equal value, freedom and rights, feminism and things like that. These are profound values to me. But if I believe in anything beyond that, no, that is not really my thing. Instead I think that everyone should have the same presuppositions to make it in life; that is what I believe in. [...] I am willing to go very far, and I believe that it is maybe one of the reasons for why I do

what I do today. It revolves around, even if it is only a support unit, the protection of freedom and rights. So it means a lot to participate in that.

In summary, within the narrative accounts of the participants travelling down military tailored paths a collective voice was discerned which profoundly emphasized and upheld the value and significance of human freedoms and rights via democracy, a process which needed to be defended. These are beliefs and values which western Armed Forces explicitly and implicitly are intended to ultimately protect and safeguard, and which in turn give reason for existence of the Armed Forces themselves. Such beliefs and values resonated well with the maintenance of military identities on both the hybrid path and the path of renewal via a full return to military service. The narrated beliefs and values of Emma and Gustaf could also be viewed as a significant part of the lived religion of military service for many of the participants in this study. They were serving a higher purpose, something larger than themselves, while they were protecting these beliefs and values of democracy and human rights. It is suggested that Sweden was the sacred entity which embodied those values, and the Armed Forces was the sacred structure which served as a means for the protection of this higher purpose of their military service. Yet these beliefs and values were equally powerful in the construction of meaning within the civilian sector for Emma, and thus in sustaining her on a hybrid path where the civilian identity also championed Sweden and democracy. In stark contrast, more recently developed civilian characters such as Peter's were fundamentally different in regards to beliefs and values in that they were individually tailored towards the individual's subjective aspirations in life and emphasized the call for individual exploration, development and pursuits within a civilian life. Although meaning was very important for Peter's new main character as a ski and rescue member, it was not about protecting beliefs and values embodied in the Swedish society. The stories told along the full transition from military to civilian life often emphasized living in and making use of individual freedom, while across the military paths stories were frequently told of a collective responsibility to unite to protect individual liberty and freedom. Beliefs and values were an existential element throughout self-identity work in that they held relevance for questions of life in such ways that beliefs and values influenced the processes in regards to identities, meaning and occupations or life styles. The different types of sets of beliefs and values found among those on a full transition from military to civilian life in comparison to those found among the participants travelling either of the two military tailored paths illuminated a sharp distinction between the participants who traversed purely civilian versus military routes. An interesting perspective presented by the sociologist van den Brink (2012a, 2012b) can widen this discussion. He identified three sets of existential values which could, at least by some, be seen as replacements for religious versions in a secular context. The three sets are the sacral, the social, and the vital. The sacral dimension involves religion, state, and abstracts, while the social dimension includes family, friends, and networks. The third vital set in turn involves nature, health, and the body. Taking van den Brink's suggestion into consideration would imply that those who travel upon military tailored paths demonstrated the sacral dimension, while those on a full transition from military to civilian life emphasized the vital dimension. All of the path-choices included the social existential values.

7.3 Themes of sacrifices

One theme which influenced questions of life among the participants, articulated most often retrospectively on the full transition from military to civilian life and on the hybrid path, revolved around different types of sacrifices which military service implicated upon the participants and their relationships with significant others. Many of the participants articulated such storied experiences of this condition which came with military service. This included, for example, how deployments to Afghanistan or elsewhere had impaired or even ended relationships with family, partners and friends; the pursuit of military life styles implicated that family was subordinated to the loyalty to battle buddies and military community in lived life. Additionally, military service could involve sacrifices of personal physical or mental health. Such personally articulated reflections and insights as those shared in the interview narratives in regards to what had been forsaken or even sacrificed in the line of duty were in some cases unavoidable, and in other cases were avoidable and thus became points of criticism which had significance during the decision to leave full-time service and sustain a full transition or a hybrid outcome. These types of reflections upon sacrifices actualized questions of life in regards to military and civilian identities, meaning, and employment/life styles in the aftermath of service. Within this section, several participants will expound upon such sacrifices.

7.3.1 Sacrifice imposed upon relationships with significant others

Captain Lennart, who had followed a full transition from military to civilian life, had divorced several years previously, had served for *36 years or more*, and during the third interview narrative approximately two years post exit described that military duty came first:

That bullshit that I heard during my career that the family comes first relative to the officer's duty, it did not! When I had my uniform on I was hundred percent loyal to the military career. Most of us were. […] I believe that the Army was built like that, otherwise it would not work. If I had some cough, I seldom called in sick; I didn't want to be home because then the colleague had to take the evening shift till 22:00, so there was nothing to debate. […] The task needs to be executed, execute the task! And I was totally focused on that. It was so from the onset of basic training, and continued throughout my conscription in commanding positions. I never laid down to be sick because then the buddy had to perform my duties.

Lennart's family grew more important to him as his retirement was proceeding, and his grandkids also held a prominent place in his life.

Major Stig had served *36 years or more* when the first interview was conducted shortly before his scheduled retirement. The interview was conducted in Stig's military office, and in regards to his family he revealed:

So I have forsaken the family really very much, and you can notice that amid colleagues too. Former colleagues that I had, those of us who were given recommendations to continue our careers as Lieutenant Colonels, those who did are divorced, another had to quit due to alcoholism, one died of stress, and much more. So I believe that we have forsaken our families a lot in the line of duty, but it also depends on who you are, if you can relax. However, I think that it is really difficult since we work so intimately together, you can't say "no, I can't work tonight"; I would become an outcast; I would not be a member of the team. So the family will come second, and it is the same nowadays with this position. […] Of course it is about loyalty, but it revolves more around that we are trained from day one to solve the task, and that lives implanted within all of us. Now we are supposed to solve this, and when I feel that I can't do this tonight, but all of my colleges are here, then the psychological cost to me is higher to go home to the family than to stay and know that the family is alone but I will meet my family the next day anyway. If something acute happens in the unit everybody volunteers. If we have an exercise and the instructor grows ill and I am free then I go there to work because we must solve the task. […] I still regret that, when the kids were growing up my wife had to make it by herself, and I notice that now on my children who have grown up, too. I worked, I had vacation, and I worked, and it was more when I had my medical condition that life caught up with me. Then I started to think "damn, what a boot full of shit I have been". They were gathered in my hospital room, "but why were they?" I was not there when they needed me, "but now they are here anyway!" I think I have forsaken all too much, and I have tried to communicate that to younger colleagues, too, who call and say "my kid is sick so I will be an hour late…", but I reply "stay home all day!" [Stig grew more emotional, with tears in his eyes] I have tried to make it work in such a way.

As Stig retired from full-time service he kept his position as a commander in the Home Guard which equated a hybrid outcome with part-time service. In the aftermath of everything that had happened throughout Stig's career his family grew more and more important to him throughout the second and third interview narratives, particularly his grandchildren and his wife. In regards to his grown up children Stig stated: "My own kids, it is the same relationship."

Colour Sergeant Andreas, who was at the time a university student, had served approximately eight years and eventually turned to a hybrid outcome. In regards to neglecting his co-habiting girlfriend throughout military service, amid his dedication to service, Andreas stated in the first interview, three months post exit:

Fortunately my co-habiting girlfriend, who has been with me for a long time, is accustomed to the condition that I am away much. We have always had such a relationship since day one, so she is used to it. But I felt some guilt on those days when I had said that I was going to call but did not. And when I called, my mind was set on the next exercise anyway. I was somewhat egoistic then, I held a position and felt so natural in the uniform, so when I got the comment "can't you just be you for a while?", I noticed that myself, too, that damn it took several hours after I had returned from a two week field exercise before I had readjusted. So I was torn apart, sadly I must confess, between two identities.

Sergeant First Class Lars was about to deploy for an international mission during the second interview as he followed a hybrid path about nineteen months post exit. He had postponed his civilian studies during the deployment and was about to leave his co-habiting girlfriend at home; they had recently met. His girlfriend was sad, as was Lars, but he had made the decision to deploy before they had met, and although he had the possibility to cancel the deployment he did not because he was highly motivated to deploy. In regards to this process Lars stated in the second interview narrative:

The most difficult thing is to know that my decision has such negative consequences for her, and I have some type of guilt over that. But I have chosen to be tactical about it and talk as much as possible about it, and really try to encourage her to express what she feels. I know that she knows that I want to deploy. I think back to when I first told her and asked "how do you feel about this?" she said "it is hard to see anything other than your eyes sparkle", but I have tried to be clear about it. Even if she knows how eager I am to deploy, she should be honest and say what she thinks and feels. Even though she knows how much I want this, she is free to think other things.

Lars deployed, and after completion of the deployment he returned to Sweden. When the third and final interview was conducted one year later he had resumed the university studies. Moreover, Lars said that his co-habiting girlfriend had supported him in the readjustment of the perception of life and he stated:

Lately I have realized that there are many other pieces which I wish could fall in place too. So, before I was willing to sacrifice anything for the career, but today it is not that black and white anymore. Previously, the meaning of life was that I had a dream and was willing to walk over bodies to get there. Today the plan for where I want to go is more nuanced, and maybe somewhat more based on several dimensions, both career and family. The goal and dream of a career in a certain area, or whatever it may be, means less today. I still see the dream but am not willing to sacrifice all things to get there. I suddenly realized that I may have to sacrifice family aspects and friends and so on in order to get there; I may not be prepared to do that. Although I may always be tempted by that dream, my perception today includes that even if I am very ambitious, I more and more realize somewhere that I need to moderate those ambitions in order to make it work well with the girlfriend, family, and friends and so on. That is likely a change, which I have discovered.

7.3.2 Sacrifice imposed upon the self

Lieutenant Maria had served for eleven years and was at the time working within a civilian company with leadership development while pursuing her full transition from military to civilian life. During the second interview narrative approximately twenty-five months post exit, in regards to the way she had served as a platoon commander, she stated:

I have reflected a lot upon my previous military service and the employment in the Armed Forces, and I have realized that I have invested extreme amounts of energy and time as the platoon was supposed to be the best, and it was at the expense of about everything else, yes, everything else. And I don't regret that I did it that way; I understand why I did that, and I thought it was right then and there, but I will probably never do that again in any kind of employment. Today it is more a feeling that a job is a job, it is supposed to be carried out in an efficient way, but I will never allow it to take over my life more than what is reasonable. It is just an employment, and it is maybe not such an existential question for other people, but for me it is because my prior military job was such an extremely large part of my life where I didn't just say that I worked as an officer, I was an officer. And that is a condition which I never will chose again, and it feels great to get some distance to it. Even though I am happy at my work today and have no ideas of quitting, I don't want to be so emotionally linked to my work.

Sergeant Helen had served for almost three years, including her last deployment which had introduced her course down a hybrid path from the perspective of this study. In regards to the physical costs which she had come to recognize after her last deployment she stated during the third interview narrative:

It has costed me knee damage and shoulder problems, and these I must always carry with me. I have had substantial problems with the shoulders since I returned from the previous deployment. So physically it has costed quite a lot.

Sergeant David, who had served for three and a half years prior to his full return to military service, stated in the first interview narrative that he had protected the others in his group as a squad commander and recounted a story which described who he was at the time:

We were on an exercise when someone accidently dropped a real hand grenade in all too short distance and did not recognize the danger, but I did, and then the hand grenade was activated, so I launched myself from behind to place myself in front of the battle buddy and then cast him behind me, deliberately using my own body as a shield between the grenade and the rest of the group. Everyone came away from the accident unharmed. So this describes me as a person; the battle buddies come before me.

In summary, participants across the three paths had made myriad types of sacrifices because of military service. The costs of these sacrifices revolved around the relationships with significant others and the self and deeply influenced narratives about experiences, emotions, decisions and reflections upon life among the participants during their transitions. Some sacrifices could not be undone, for example a lifelong military career which included consequences such as forsaking children and partners, or psychical injuries. Absence, even in the most subtle forms, from one's child(ren) during youth could potentially create voids in the relationship(s) which could not easily be bridged later in life. Meanwhile, some sacrifices which were recognized early within military careers taught some participants, in collaboration with significant others, to readjust their aims and attitudes to life so as to include more in this perception and focus of life than just military or civilian careers and advancements. Moreover, it is suggested that military identities among this sample included a type of loyalty and willingness to serve which in many instances presupposed sacrifices of the selves, wives, children, and/or co-habiting boyfriends/girlfriends in order to achieve what the military organization required. The collective military cultural voice of beliefs and values that must be protected (presented in section 7.2) tended to overrule other voices in the selves related to significant others. Sacrifices appear to be inbuilt in military cultures and service for the greater good, for the sake of collective values such as freedom and democracy. This also implies that participants who had returned to full-time service were therefore less inclined to talk about potential and/or ongoing sacrifices. Embedded within the military cultures, as described by many participants, were both the significance of executing the tasks when serving at any cost and the vital nature of loyalty to battle buddies. However, those sacrifices which also encumbered significant others implied storied experiences and emotions of guilt, another by-product which stemmed from the increasing dialogue between military culturally shaped characters and civilian culturally constructed characters, such as a father or a husband or a co-habitant boyfriend or girlfriend, throughout the transition. The widespread narratives of sacrifices across the generations of the participants can also be viewed through the proposition of military service as a type of lived religion which includes subordinating one's self to a higher purpose, which in turn equates sacrifices. The lived religion of military service among many of the participants has provided them, and still provides some of them, with profundity and meaning, camaraderie and community but also the potential for losses and sacrifices.

7.4 The theme of nature

Throughout the narrative analysis it became clear that nature held a profound effect and role in life for a significant number of participants across the three paths. Nature assisted self-identity work and life in transition and post-transition as harmony and strength were drawn from outdoor activities in nature. Nature was often described as an entity which was experienced as a specific power source in many participants' lives. Nature became a salient resource which instilled balance, deeper insights and energy in life, especially when experienced in solitude. Amid the self-identity processes nature offered quality, peace and serenity in life. In this section narrative accounts from Lieutenant Peter, Colour Sergeant Andreas, First Class Sergeant Oskar and Sergeant David are presented in order to demonstrate the significance of nature for the self-identity process.

Lieutenant Peter, who made a full transition from military to a civilian life in the Swedish mountains, had a particular relationship to nature which permeated all three interviews. Peter's relationship to nature facilitated the process of becoming a civilian, and that was also the reason why he and his girlfriend moved to the mountains; he stated in the first interview six months post exit in regards to the decision to move to the mountains:

> It has a lot to do with the outdoor interests. I love cycling, and walking during the summer season, and skiing during the winter season, and riding the snow mobile. Everything that I have here is that which I previously sought under my free time. All my money was spent to get up here when I served in the military. So, "why shouldn't I live here?"

In the third interview, approximately thirty-three months post exit, Peter stated in regards to the significance nature held in his life:

> Nature and outdoor adventures are my big passions. I like to be out on my own, and to be outdoors a lot. But I should not claim that I am always on my own, but I really like to do two to three days on my own in the mountains during both the winter and the summer seasons. To just be on my own, no need to check the wrist watch, instead when I am tired I am tired and then rest when I need it. That is quality of life to me! It is the same to be outdoors with friends or my girlfriend and to share this of course. It is fine to compromise or change route; that is an adventure too. But particularly nature and the adventure I experience when I am outdoors and explore. That is amazing; that fills me with peace and serenity, even if I do pretty demanding things, and it is still what creates an amazing life.

Colour Sergeant Andreas, who was then committed to a hybrid outcome which at the time included university studies, said that nature was significant to him in order to reach deeper thought processes, and in the third interview narrative approximately twenty-seven months post exit he stated:

> Nature, and fire, and water, are three amazing things to get access to, and then to create the bubble wherein I am allowed to think those rather deep thoughts, so nature is important, indeed. Without adding any aspects of why nature looks like it does or who has made it such, but to instead just accept it and be amazed at how it is. I can't make that happen in a city. [...] It is a very broad thinking process which includes past, present and future, and often an incredible gratitude for what I have. Thoughts of that type appear in such situations. A kind of peace, too, I would say, since I seldom can make time for this in the everyday life. The everyday life can be so stressful with a lot of factors to consider, but when I found myself in those situations then and there without having to think about what to have for dinner, then these broad thought processes begin as everyday life is barred out. [...] I feel very at peace afterwards, and I have processed within myself where I am supposed to go with these thoughts; and goals that I had, some may have been strengthened, and I really want to go there, and with other goals I may conclude that those I have reached, or some aspirations that I have had are no longer relevant as I may have a new one. Today it has become more time for family, for the home. In order to find out what is most important in different phases in life I really need this to feel strength in the decisions that I made, and to ignore previous decisions.

First Class Sergeant Oskar, who adjusted through a hybrid outcome, was approximately thirty-two months post exit during the third interview. He was at the time working as a security consultant, and in regards to what he experienced in his soul when he was in nature Oskar stated:

> Serenity! I am surrounded by digital things, stress and the city all the time. For me to get outdoors, to be by myself, listen to birds singing, and to be in nature; it does things to my senses! It is huge to just walk, not being occupied by my fingers on the dashboard, but just walk, and carry things like a backpack. It gives me so extraordinarily much. It is that serenity and some strange type of satisfaction. But is visual too! I think it is very beautiful to see the sun rise when I have spent my night in a tent or paddling the kayak or something else. Most of all it is about serenity.

Sergeant David decided to leave full-time service due to an injury in his back which caused him significant personal and professional stagnation. He endured two rough years of transition and reintegration into a civilian life prior to his return to full-time service two years post exit. David stated in the third interview narrative that the most burdensome aspect throughout transition to civilian life was the evenings which were very, very tough. He had great difficulties to fall asleep as his thoughts just kept going and going and going. His thoughts were exclusively centered on the Armed Forces; meanwhile he perceived himself to be worthless outside of the military context. He slept about one to two hours per night, and by the end of the week he normally just fell asleep due to exhaustion. It became difficult to be alert on the temporary civilian jobs that he held throughout this period of two years. However, nature was his reservoir where energy and strength were reinvigorated in order to go on with life, and David stated in the third interview narrative: "Therefrom I mostly got the energy to continue to try to get a hold on myself." In regards to his special relationship to nature David replied:

> I am raised in the northern part of Sweden where you are out in the forest, and I have always been in the forest with my grandpa, and my dad, tenting and making own shelters for the night to sleep without a sleeping bag and stuff like that. So I have always enjoyed the forest and particularly fishing, which is great fun. But most of all I believe it is the peace and to be in solitude, without having anyone to judge me. To do whatever I want to do without being corrected or told that I am a fool or anything. I am in solitude with my own thoughts and can do whatever I want. I have no better explanation.

In summary, nature in a broad sense (e.g., mountains, forests, waters, sea, or to walk, to tent and build fire outdoors) was discovered to hold a significant existential position during self-identity processes throughout and after transition among many of the participants within this sample. Solitude in nature was a common and shared storied theme among Peter, Andreas, Oskar, David and many others in the sample. The outdoor characters had the capacity to assist the selves on an existential level in regards to self-identity work and questions of life throughout transitions. Nature even functioned as a type of promoter position for Peter which guided his decision over where to go in life during the process of exit: to the mountains. The mountains continued to support his self-identity work on an existential level throughout transition and reintegration into civilian life and population. The quality and passion of life was found in the mountains, and the nature and arctic area supported Peter's path to civilian life. From another perspective nature facilitated Andreas's thought processes during transition, and he perceived that he needed that arena to assist and order decisions in regards to questions of life (e.g., goals aspirations, prioritizations, significant others). Andreas found a peace in nature which assisted him to conduct deeper reflections on significant questions of life. Oskar emphasized that nature affected his senses and instilled serenity. It appeared that nature held a particular type of quality in life which could not be sustained elsewhere. Oskar tapped into some type of force while he was in nature which became a sharp contrast to his new civilian life behind a computer and surrounded by a digital world. Finally nature assisted David to rekindle his energy to go on with life during his two years of transitional struggle to become a civilian which preceded his return to the Armed Forces. David found peace and solitude in the nature. This type of commitment to nature narrated by the participants, including its existential prominence for their inner lives, can also be understood as a type of lived religion wherein nature became the entity for worship and awe which in turn provided its practitioners with power, peace, and serenity in their selves and lives. The significance of nature upon the existential lives of the participants could also be described through van den Brink's (2012a, 2012b) methodology as a vital dimension.

7.5 Religious/spiritual themes

As already introduced, five participants narrated individual religious/spiritual beliefs and/or experiences. The storied experiences from four of them were related to the processes of self-identity work in transition, but there was diversity between these narratives in regards, for example, to what they believed in (e.g., God, angels, transcendence, nature, biblical ideas of God and creation, transcendent reunions with deceased parents). Yet there was one commonality discerned among three of these five, and that commonality was the experience of the power of nature, which corresponds to the experiences of nature given above in section 7.4. However, the participants in section 7.4 did not connote their experiences with any explicit religious/spiritual world views (or I-positions). This section, on the other hand, focuses on those who explicitly expressed religious world views (or I-positions). Interestingly, all four of the retiring/recently retired service members were explicit in their religious/spiritual experiences, in contrast to only one of the remaining fifteen younger participants expressing such. But these four more often experienced religious/spiritual feelings in nature rather than, for example, within congregational life and sermons. The participants did not reject or deny institutional and/or official religious beliefs, but they rather preferred activities and life styles within nature which then generated religious/spiritual experiences and feelings. Such a link between nature and spirituality was acknowledged more than a century ago by William James

(1902); he also defined religion in terms of experiences in solitude such as "the feelings, acts, and experiences, of individual men in their solitude, so far as they apprehend themselves to stand in relation to whatever they may consider the divine" (p. 21b).

Captain Lennart, who made a full transition from military to civilian life throughout the study, answered the question of *what do you believe in?* with: "There is a God somewhere." Yet it was not in church or through institutional religion that Lennart found consolation, inspiration and energy in life but rather, as he stated in the third interview narrative:

> When I am in nature and perceive what a wonderful creation it is. When I sit in the canoe with a fishing rod in my hand, all is quiet, and then suddenly I hear a bird call far in the distance. To sit in the sun, it is really warm, everything is alive. Well, it is a power source, an amazing power source. I can feel that when I am sleeping in the morning, I get up around four in the morning to take a leak, and in the same time read the weather. Last time when I was outdoors when I got up around three or four in the morning, it was somewhat light and a devilish fog, then I saw the roe deer drinking near the river, foxes, and it was all crowded in the river with ducks. A moose was powerfully approaching the river, too, with the great horns, to drink and eat. And it was breathless and a little bit warm and humid. Incredibly amazing!

Major Tore, who was throughout the study committed to a hybrid outcome, claimed that a life style in nature had always played a significant role in his life and still did, and he stated in the third interview narrative:

> I haven't missed a moose hunt so far! When the vacation list was scheduled that was always the first thing I planned, that is sacred, the first Monday in September and that whole week. I still hope to do that for many years into the future. Additionally, on and off during the whole autumn I hunt a lot, although maybe not as much as when I had the dogs. Back then I hunted birds in the forest rather often. When the kids were little I kept on hunting, and I carried them in a special backpack. When the dogs barked on point on a bird I checked if the kid was asleep, and if so I leaned the backpack against a tree and went on to attempt to shoot the bird, shot at it, or in the best scenarios shot it, but often just scared it away, and then returned to get the kid if I had remembered approximately where I had parked him [the tone was humorous]. And this was a quite significant aspect; this was where I could clear my mind and recalibrate my body, to disconnect from

everything, the ordinary everyday life concerns and so on, to hunt and fish and spend time outdoors, and later to drive snowmobile in the nature.

In response to a question about faith and religion Tore presented the same type of beliefs and values associated with military paths, which implicated that these were associated with Tore's choice of a hybrid path which included part-time service on a more flexible basis. But as for institutional and official religion, Tore had a more complex relationship, and he stated that:

> I don't know if I am… I am not religious in that kind of way. I do have some type of belief I guess. I believed in the military system, which also is a type of belief where I thought I contributed to something. Maybe you experience that no matter what job you have, but for me I thought I contributed to something, or I know I contributed to something. In my mind I know I did, but if it was true or not, that is another question, it is some kind of faith anyway. But religiously, spiritually, I don't know. I can experience such a feeling in church, for example on a concert, which I experience as peaceful. But the biblical explanation of how you are supposed to believe, God and the trinity and all that, it doesn't necessarily fully cover it; I believe it is a much longer process. I don't mean to exercise Darwinism, but on the other hand I don't think that they are contradictory, either, it is just that the Bible is so narrow in a way which I can't really imagine myself. However, on the other hand, those parts including peace and serenity, those I experience in nature.

All through the interview narratives with Lennart and Tore, a life style in nature and thirst to live really close to nature continued to be explicitly narrated as salient parts of their lives as retirees. Since even more time could be spent in nature after retirement, their lives to a large extent were organized around the seasons of nature. Although Major Stig was a churchgoer, nature still had a prominence in his life in much the same way as for Tore and Lennart. Stig stated that he really enjoyed getting out into nature to experience serenity:

> It is incredibly wonderful to just go out into the forest and sit on a downed tree and think of totally other things. That is a big difference in regards to my wife who comes from a large city. My wife frequently wants to go to the city to sit in a café or something. I want to go thirty kilometers in the opposite direction, out to a lake in the forest to just sit down and enjoy the serenity.

Major Stig, who maintained a commitment to a hybrid path throughout the study, had a belief in God which continued to develop throughout the three interview narratives. Institutional religion was more central to Stig than to any other participant, and in the first interview Stig stated:

> Well, I may not go to church every Sunday, but a couple of sermons per year, and sometimes on Sunday I watch the sermons on television, so sure, I feel that there is a God, a God or something above me who takes care of me. Then whether He has created the world or not, that is another aspect, but there is something which steers in certain ways and looks after me.

In the second interview Stig was riddled by questions of the meaning of his life in regards to the loss of a former colleague. His colleague was a very healthy individual who had recently died instantly in his tracks during a walk in the city. Stig, on the other hand, had survived a severe medical condition earlier in his career, as presented earlier. Stig recounted lying incapacitated in the hospital, all the while regretting that he had been an "a boot full of shit" in regards to his kids and family (p. 149). The loss of a good, appreciated and healthy colleague activated deeper questions for Stig as he kept searching for the purpose for his survival:

> "Why did I make it?" I sit here and wonder and wonder and wonder. "What is the purpose for my survival; why me? Is it something they, someone, wants me to perform, and what would that be?" I can lay myself down and think about that for hours. "What can it be? Did I survive to help my daughter to buy the house? Did I survive to sit by dad's side when he died? Why?"

In the third interview narrative Stig said that he went to church several times per year and that he sometimes felt a specific need to go to church, that he must go there and sit there. When he was asked to describe why he had intensified his attendance he responded:

> When I go there then suddenly my mother [who had already passed away] sits beside me that day, and the next time then it can be my dad [who had also passed away], or some relative. It is like someone talks to me. That which I experience in church provides me with a deeper faith that there is something, someone that tells me to go there, and I don't experience that connectivity at home.

Stig experienced that the religious aspects in his life were growing more and more salient, which also was the case for his parents as they aged. Through the religious growth which Stig experienced and articulated throughout the interview narratives, he felt consolation and trust in that he was being cared for by higher powers.

Captain Roger, who traversed a full transition from military to civilian life, left the military life behind him. Roger appreciated the life as a retiree since he could follow and continue to deepen his interests, such as taking care of his cabin in the countryside and living a social life with his family and civilian friends. In the third and final interview narrative Roger unexpectedly described how his belief in angels gave him assistance and power in life.

> I don't know if I said it last time [which he did not], but I believe that there are angels. Someone who keeps my course when I can´t make it on my own. Someone who can tell me "do it in that way". Somehow, I become fascinated about those occasions when I discover "I probably didn't think that by myself". Instead someone else told me so. Sometimes when life is really hard then someone may call who I haven't talked to in four years, and then I think "why did he call now, I haven't talked with him in ages?" So somehow, somewhere in the subconscious, we take care of each other. [...] Well, today it has progressed that extensively so that I am no longer worried about any difficult situations. Somehow there is an inner power or something which throughout life has shaped my life. Sometimes someone may arise and say "but don't say so!" Or someone may arise and see that something is wrong without me knowing really who that is. In some ways I believe that something in our subconscious makes us capable of communicating with each other if we only give it some time and not just rush through it. Even if I don't have any visible evidence, when considering events that are particularly trying, "from where do I get the power to accomplish them? Suddenly there it is, and I am stronger than ever." I never have to think about it. I was in a Nordic nation where there was a belief in elves and other things. I believe that in all cultures there are such things that people think about in regards to the subconscious, invisible elements which steer and assist.

In summary, for Lennart, Tore and Stig nature had always played a significant role in their lives, and as they retired nature continued to be a profound arena to which their lives were partly organized via, for example, different forms of hunting, particularly the sacred moose hunt, camping, skiing, fishing, and picking berries and so on. Preexisting outdoor characters were sustained and developed throughout transition and retirement in close relations to their life styles in nature. All of these characters narrated characteristics which were often found while in solitude: serenity, peace and power in nature, as did the participants in section 7.4. A difference was that Lennart, Tore, and Stig had religious/spiritual world views (or I-positions) which collaborated with the outdoor life styles, whereas the other participants in section 7.4 did not have such I-positions even amid the similarities of experiences and feelings that nature had upon their selves. For Lennart and Tore religious/spiritual experiences of serenity, peace, and power were channeled via their outdoor characters rather than through institutional and official religion. In fact, for all three of them, their lived religion was primarily exercised in nature through all of their outdoor activities which influenced their existential well-being, and this exhibits much resemblance to similar cases presented by McGuire (2008) and Ganzevoort & Roeland (2014). However, concerts and music events in church also had a self-described religious/spiritual effect on Tore. Meanwhile, for Stig church was a particularly significant arena for transcendent reunions with his deceased parents which deepened Stig's faith. In the second interview after a colleague to Stig had suddenly and unexpectedly died, deeper questions of survival and guilt haunted Stig; he pondered why he was still here when a physically well-trained colleague who had deliberately maintained such a healthy life had died. Was there a purpose? All of those questions were addressed to some transcendent power which had spared Stig for some reason.

An unexpected religious rumination was revealed in the third and final interview narrative when Roger shared his belief in angels, angels who had assisted him in life. The belief in angels appeared to have a processual character wherein Roger in the third narrative had reached a state wherein he no longer had any worries for difficult or demanding situations in life. These angels were not described as transcendent beings sent from God, but rather immanent beings without any explicit reference to God or transcendent powers.

CHAPTER 8

Investigating the Influence of the Interviews

8.1 Assisting the participants' self-reflection

As the interview cycles proceeded it was often emphasized by the participants, typically after we concluded the structured data collection, that the interviews provided them with opportunities for deeper reflection upon subject matters which were seldom discussed or elaborated otherwise. Several participants explained as we met that he or she had already begun reflecting over identities, self, meaning and direction in life in regards to the past, present and future some time prior to and in anticipation of the interview. Furthermore, in subsequent interviews it was frequently narrated that reflection had continued for a time after our previous interview(s) and departure(s). This was seldom recorded on tape as it rarely occurred during the official interview, but instead came during the introductions or after the structured recording phase had been completed, and was also recounted in some evaluation letters. The interview cycles included both a number of repeated semi-structured questions (se Appendix III) and more interview specific follow up questions which appeared to stimulate self-reflecting processes. Based upon such interview statements the researcher drew the tentative conclusion that the interviews activated some type of introspection which could be beneficial to at least some of the participants. However, the original design of this study did not include any evaluation of a potential self-reflecting effect of the interview cycles. In correspondence with the first supervisor (Prof. R. Ganzevoort) the decision was made to equip each participant with an evaluation letter (see Appendix IV) during the last interview cycle to, among a number of things, investigate what potential implications the interview design had upon the participants. All of the participants answered and returned the evaluation letters to the researcher. This section serves to present the answers from the evaluation letters which addressed the outcome. This is felt to be crucial in the interest of full transparency when considering potential interview influence upon the interviewees' self-identity work across the time of the interview-study. The interpretative conclusion of the content analysis will then be elaborated into the theological theory on transition from military to civilian life in chapter 9. Of specific interest are the narrative accounts in regards to question 1 [What experiences have you gathered by participating in a three year study, with repeated interviews focusing on your military narrative (identity), meaning and that which you experienced during the transition throughout the study period?] and question 3 [In what way have the interviews affected you in this process?]:

The content analysis of questions 1 and question 3 generated four conclusions wherein the first (A) was shared by a majority of the participants. It was concluded that the interview cycles in general assisted the participants to reflect upon their self-identity process, and that this reflection has subsequently provided some of them with:

(A) An increased self-understanding and awareness about military identities and other identities in regards to the temporal and spatial (within self) dimensions in transition to civilian lives or return to (different forms of) military service

(B) An opportunity to process emotions and memories, traumatic events, or to open up and share inner life and experiences from military service and transition

(C) An experience of peace, harmony or satisfaction in regards to decisions and directions in lives based upon repeated reflections

(D) An opportunity to share personal experiences with a person who has conducted a similar journey

The narrative accounts of the participants, as translated from Swedish, will be fully presented below and were organized and ordered through the displayed developmental paths of transition: a full transition, a hybrid outcome, a full return to military service. No specific trends could be found in the evaluation letters related to the discovered paths. In order to protect the anonymity of the participants the original handwritten responses were transferred (in content and style) by the researcher into a typed form and are presented as such:

8.2 A full transition to civilian life (six participants)

Second Lieutenant Karl

[Question 1] The interviews cycles (3) have been occasions to me for deeply reflect and look back upon my military service and the time after that. This has been a powerful experience as it has provided me with peace and a certain harmony to look back upon the time which has passed and emotionally consolidate decisions and thoughts by articulation.

[Question 3] As mentioned previously – The opportunity to reflect has provided peace and harmony. I believe that this has increased my comfort in the process of consolidating the decisions which led me to who I am today, which moreover have helped me to appreciate my life today even more.

Lieutenant Peter

[Question 1] I experience that I have given words to my thoughts and wonderings. I have perceived it as good and peaceful to talk with a person who has also has done this, and furthermore given it additional thoughts than I did during my years outside of the Armed Forces.

[Question 3] These are almost the only times that I discuss the Armed Forces and the discussion is pleasant but for me everything has come naturally such as to leave the Armed Forces and to start a different life.

Lieutenant Maria (her account has been presented elsewhere in Grimell, 2007e)

[Question 1] It has been very enriching to reflect upon the journey that I have made once per year under structured circumstances. I have felt myself that my answers have evolved throughout the time which has past, which also suggests that I have evolved.

[Question 3] I have scheduled time for reflection in a more structured manner than if I would not have participated in this study. Not just the time during the actual interviews but also prior to and afterward them. It also feels good to have been participating in something which will contribute to important research.

Private First Class Mattias

[Question 1] I have learned that I somehow go through phases during a transition as you every year look back upon the same episode. The first interview felt more spontaneous in the answers and closer to the feeling that I actually had in regards to the exit point from military service. The second interview felt more reflective, and the third interview, then I felt I had an even broader perspective and reflected upon the wholeness. It also felt good to reflect upon why I have made those decisions which I have.

[Question 3] The interviews have influenced me to reflect upon the decisions that I have made and continue to make in life. It has been shown that there is a common and recurrent theme in my life. I don't think I would have identified that if it wasn't for the interviews. It would at least have been difficult to do that.

Captain Roger

[Question 1] My experiences of the participation in the study were that what I said in the first interview changed. I would call it a type of self-understanding. What I said in the first interview was so obvious and natural. With time came the insight of how much of my self and identity was related to military service. That also included the loss of camaraderie and community in military service.

[Question 3] There are many things that I have taken for granted, and the longer the process continued the more the thoughtfulness grew. The process still continues.

Captain Lennart

[Question 1] It assisted me to remember events, contexts, and experiences in a good way. The interviews have touched upon my whole professional military life and reactivated things I would otherwise forget.

[Question 3] See my answer in regards to the first question. Additionally, that the interview was not a one-time occurrence, but instead repeated over time. My participation grew much larger because of that.

8.3 A hybrid outcome of transition (nine participants)
Sergeant Erik (his account has been presented elsewhere in Grimell, 2017a)

[Question 1] I experienced that my understanding of my own process of leaving the Armed Forces was increased. I understood more about why I sometimes become disappointed or upset with myself when I in my civilian "me" couldn't perform in the same way as in my military "me." I experienced that the interviews have helped me to organize my thoughts and get a better sense of understanding of how my military background affects my identity, and why it was so difficult to stop serving in the Armed Forces.

[Question 3] I experienced that the interviews have helped me to organize my thoughts and get a better sense of understanding of how my military background affects my identity, and why it was so difficult to stop serving in the Armed Forces.

Sergeant Emma

[Question 1] Wow, a challenging question! So many different thoughts have emerged throughout the process, particularly in relation to the interviews, but also in-between. Most of all I have on a conscious level reflected upon my military professional role and

165

realized that I had one, which I really didn't reflect upon before. I have thought a lot about why I enlisted in the Armed Forces in the first place, and what has kept me going for so many years. Additionally, what motivated me in the end to take the step and quit. What is even more interesting is that I nowadays mostly think about how to find a type of military service which fits and feels meaningful in order to take a step back.

[Question 3] I have talked more to my friends about different experiences in regards to the Armed Forces, most of all I have asked more questions and encouraged them to talk. I have also shared some things in confidence with my male friends and former colleagues, and unfortunately heard from others some sad stories which concern them. We have basically began to talk more to each other, not just about experiences but also how it was and felt then, how it feels now, and how we think it has affected us in different contexts.

Colour Sergeant Andreas

[Question 1] An increased understanding of what has shaped me as a person and in what ways the experiences have formed me. A feeling of contributing to something in relation to the Armed Forces, even though I long for the uniform. I have much more self-understanding because of the qualitative and demanding questions wherein both spontaneous answers and more thoughtfulness are weaved together. My answers above were and in question 3 was somewhat a surprise to me. But it is also gratefulness and a re-strengthening of the military self even though the everyday life looks different as a civilian.

[Question 3] It has been a good reconnection to the decision to leave full-time service. Good to talk to someone with a similar background that has done the journey himself. I have developed my self-perception with a focus on what I can make use of in the civilian life, that I learned in the military service. The last interview was kind of special as the feeling compared with before was different "how shall I answer?", "what happens afterward?", "is it over now?"

Private First Class Adam

[Question 1] Some studies take a long time to conduct. To know how the interviews are conducted. I hope that the study brings more understanding to why some decide to become civilians.

166

[Question 3] To return to military experiences and to remember many funny and hard situations. It has been nice.

Sergeant Helen

[Question 1] It has been a therapeutic process with a big outcome for me as a person. It has provided me with a reason to reflect upon my experiences and my military identity. I have been able to track my own thoughts and how they have changed throughout the years. On a personal level I have had an opportunity to process some traumatic episodes and emotions which had partly blocked my development.

[Question 3] The interviews have influenced my awareness of the process. They have also provided me with some distance from my negative experiences during the process and my previous experiences.

First Class Sergeant Oskar

[Question 1] An understanding of how my own ideas change over time.

[Question 3] I have reflected upon how my previous answers are divergent from my latest.

First Class Sergeant Lars

[Question 1] I have become more conscious about how my military career has affected my identity. I can observe that the past years of military service have developed me as a person in a direction which I am very satisfied with today.

[Question 3] The interviews have increased my propensity to reflect upon the past and how it has influenced the present.

Major Stig

[Question 1] I realize that I am in a process which will take a couple years, to transition from being a service member with a structured life, to a civilian life that I "own" myself, and that I have to shape. That was experienced, but assisted by the interviews, as a stressful process in the beginning: the search for an identity, who am I, what group do I belong to? However, now in the end it has becoming a more harmonious life with family and friends in the centre. Now as I enter my golden years the meaning of life and the belief in God has increased.

[Question 3] In the days following the interviews I have tried to analyze my answers in order to find some answers to who I am and where I am going. After the last interview it has become much clearer.

Major Tore

[Question 1] -I am not alone.

-There are many aspects when leaving military service.

-People leave due to different reasons.

-I see more clearly differences in the Armed Forces then and now (it was not always better before... but more fun).

-I am still proud of my military career and long military service.

-I cannot still conform to the fact that the conscription was put to an end and to watch the Armed Forces be disarmed so much and so quickly.

[Question 3] -Difficult question. Some answers you'll find in other answers.

-Perhaps I have become more observant over myself and my reactions and that the political "betrayal" lies somewhere behind, disturbing and nagging me.

-I still compare with then and now, conscription versus professional Army, wherein I think that I have not changed?

-I have seen that time changes, and so do I, and that I may not always be updated.

8.4 A full return to military service (four participants)

Sergeant David

[Question 1] The experiences that I have won are that I feel that I have had time to discuss my situation. I have experienced that I really didn't feel as good as I thought I did, and it was foolish to keep that inside of me.

[Question 3] The interviews have affected me in a positive way. It feels good to have someone to talk to about this specific subject matter, since those who did not serve cannot relate to such matters.

Lieutenant John

[Question 1] By participating in the study I had the opportunity to actively reflect upon my own identity and self-perception. By the repeated approach it has stimulated me to look upon how I have developed my perception of what constitutes identity in general and military identity in particular. The military identity is something which I have taken for granted for almost a decade in a uniform. During the time I was a civilian I distinctly experienced how strong the common identity in the Armed Forces is and how I missed it in a civilian world. The reasoning that I have deepened in the interviews has allowed me to identify those parts of the military identity which are the most important, and to see where in my civilian life I may find that. That experience has assisted me to avoided spending energy on processes which include an incompatible outcome in regards to my own point of view.

[Question 3] The interviews have without any doubt assisted me in the valuation of different aspects in life. As I during the three years that I participated in the study went through big changes both professionally and privately, the interviews assisted to keep focusing and developing as an individual.

Sergeant Jonas

[Question 1] As a person I realize that I have experienced quite a lot in the military service, and that I realize that I have experienced more than others who have served longer.

[Question 3] I have become more conscious and realized that I have a military identity which I go in and out of.

Lieutenant (former Sergeant) Gustaf

[Question 1] I experience that the study has made me reflect upon my selection of profession, and I realize that I have several times changed my point of view and attitude, which I had perceived as being cemented.

[Question 3] It has brought me to reflect a number of extra times upon how I perceive myself and which identity is the strongest in myself.

CHAPTER 9

A Theological Theory on Transition from Military to Civilian Life

9.1 Potential advantages of practical theology

The previous chapters have built upon a longitudinal empirical investigation of existential and religious dimensions in identity reconstruction, culminating in the evaluation letters which were initially anticipated as coming after the study but which instead became an interesting extension of the study's data collection, among nineteen Swedish service members during the process of becoming civilians. The transitional experiences, the self-identity work, and finally the existential and religious elements in the processes have been analyzed through a narrative and dialogical framework. The results of the analysis were anchored in such a framework. Moreover, the results of the analysis have been used in theory building in chapters 5 and 6 wherein the lenses of implicit religion (Bailey, 1990; Hamilton, 2001) and lived religion (Ganzevoort, 2009, 2011b; Ganzevoort & Roeland, 2014; McGuire, 2008) were used to understand implicit religious military values, meanings, and practices among the participants such as serving a higher purpose, subordination of one's will, sacrifices, and commitment to battle buddies and military community. Participants testified that this type of lived and implicit religion was difficult to find demonstrated in other contexts.

In this chapter we will interpret the empirical material, based upon the results, from a theological outlook, and add a unique perspective to studies on self-identity work in transition from military to civilian life by building an existentially and spiritually oriented theological theory. A significant motive for doing this rests upon the long history of interpreting existential human questions that theology has always had, even in a context as pluralized and secularized as Sweden. From a theological point of view there are existential questions of the participants to which such a theological answer may resonate. It is expected that there is a layer of implicit theology among the participants which is waiting to be more deeply explored and which will further meld this theological theory on transition from military to civilian life with the long existential history of theology.[15] One answer to the participants' existential rumination and

---

[15] Implicit theology in this chapter refers to a type of theology which addresses existential contemplation and questions without explicitly connecting them to God or transcendent dimensions or explicit religious beliefs in a more traditional sense since the participants were not narrating these. The goal here of using implicit theology under the prerequisite that the participants did not narrate explicit religious dimensions is to provide potential answers to transition from military to civilian life through correlation together with critical investigation of Christian and/or religious sources and self-identity work. This could be contrasted to ordinary theology (Astley, 2002) which explicitly addresses participants' God-talk, ideas of transcendence, and religious beliefs.

questions in regards to self-identity work in transition from one culture to another is to acknowledge that there are spiritual depths of lives which have profound impacts upon the self. Thus this theory aims to assist the participants, and a wider military audience, to discern potential spiritual depths of life and their "importance, meaning, or significance," to their spiritual lives by making a "spiritual judgement", or preferably a *spiritual recognition* of such sources or fruits of life (James, 1902, p. 8a). As humans we are not exclusively psychological, social and physical beings, but spiritual beings as well (Ellens, 2011; Pargament, 2011). Practical theology may serve such a purpose of recognizing and nurturing spiritual lives in unique ways through correlation which also welcomes earnest critical investigation of Christian and/or religious sources and self-identity work in transition from military to civilian life.

Furthermore, a theological approach may interpret and equip storied experiences with words, expressions and concepts which introduce a theological language interplay with the potential of resonance to the storied experiences of the participants, military audiences and wider audiences, and as such create a focus upon, for example, the link between military communal life, or nature, and spiritual life. When considering the younger generation of participants who likely experienced the same feelings in nature (e.g., peace, harmony, serenity, joy, energy, power, awe) as the older generation did, yet did not narrate a connection to the divine, lived religion, or spirituality, this could be seen as correlating with Swedish society at large where religion is less and less explicit among the younger generations who are thereby left without a spiritual vocabulary. However, this theory intends to present nature and other sources of life as potential spiritual depths of life and thereby help to enable the use of spiritual language within such storied experiences.

It is also suggested that the evolution of practical theology in a pluralized, secularized, and deinstitutionalized Swedish context could benefit from methodologies or paradigms such as lived religion (Ganzevoort, 2009; McGuire, 2008) implicit religion (Bailey, 1990, 1997), and existential theology which all share an emphasis of spiritual (depths of) life to discern layers of implicit theology among Swedes with their secular presence that includes a Lutheran public heritage.

Taken together with the fact that I have not found a preceding theological theory within a Swedish context on self-identity work amid transition from military to civilian life, these are the motives for the application of theology in this dissertation, as well as to develop a theological theory around this subject matter. Therefore, this chapter of the dissertation aims to present a theological theory built upon the empirical investigation which has been presented in the previous chapters, an enterprise which extends this dissertation into a theological domain by contributing a theologically voiced theory to the research on military transition to civilian life. A further explanation of the prerequisites for the theory building is also found in chapter 2. Since this theological theory on transition from military to civilian life is existentially and spiritually oriented and primarily built upon both the storied experiences of transition, self-identity work, and existential/religious elements and the evaluation letters from the participants it implicates that the theory is simultaneously a proposal "for a journey, representations of a journey, and the journey itself" (Tweed, 2006, p. 9). Moreover, that the theory is a tentative and contextual theological proposal of such a journey which includes correlational and critical dimensions located in time and space. The disposition of this chapter rests upon a theological interpretation of the results which moves step by step, from the beginning of the transitional process to the end (in a full transition, a hybrid outcome, or a full return to military service), wherein a conversation between the findings and theological and spiritual perspectives have cooperated in the formulation of a theological theory of military transition to civilian life which may invite the participants, and a larger military audience, into dialogues with their selves and others during the processes. Definitions of concepts and descriptions of perspectives will be described across the sections of the chapter as the theory unfolds and takes form throughout the chapter.

9.2 A theological perspective on military communal life and service

In the introductory chapter, sociological perspectives were presented which consider the structured process of collectivistic socialization concomitant with an individual's entry into the military world. Each individual's military identities and I-positions are shaped and constructed within an influential military community which generates context specific behaviors, mindsets, and uniforms. Even so, as presented in chapter 1, service members are not passive recipients who simply absorb the institutional messages which are fed to them in their socialization processes. Service members are active agents who may have more or less unique ways of appropriating and interpreting military cultures to fit or resonate with their own selves and preexisting I-positions, and thus individuals position themselves differently within military institutions. As active agents, military personnel uniquely interpret the institutional contexts and take on a variety or multiplicity of perspectives according to their personal aspirations. The military communal life and service, with its wide range of implications, has a certain social, cognitive, emotional, routine-oriented, and even ritualistic effect on the military personnel. Therefore, more than half a century ago the military sociologist Huntington (1957) proposed an analogy between the military communal life of service members and that of Christian monastic communities. From one perspective there is much resemblance, such as an organized communal life which to varying degrees is separated from life in the civilian world, an organized communal life which cultivates strong beliefs, specific ethics and codes of conduct, devotion to a cause, loyalty to the members, potential sacrifices, and even standardized clothing which downplays individual uniqueness. Additionally, following sociologists such as Bailey (1990, 1997) and Hamilton (2001), it may be suggested that the deeply ingrained military communal life and service of military personnel can be labeled as implicit religious in regards to the dedication to the local community and a commitment to the human. Bailey (1990) suggested that commitment to the human was a form of experience that could be comparable to the sense of the sacred in contemporary societies (cf. Pargament, 2011). The strength and significance of the military community and the loyalty and commitment to battle buddies, until death if necessary, equip the bond between battle buddies with a type of sacredness which cannot, nor should not, be violated. In another manner, Pargament (2008) suggested that communities and communal life can take on a sacred character for their members. Humans have a basic and irreducible yearning for a relationship with something that transcends the selves. Not only in individual terms can the sacred be understood, but also in terms of relationships and communities. Such a proposal goes beyond explicit religious communities and includes non-religious military communities as well (Grimell, 2016b; Lunde, 2009). In related ways practical theologians have suggested that existential and spiritual questions in life can be addressed and understood beyond organized, institutional and official religious communal life as the lived religion of ordinary people in secular contexts (Ganzevoort, 2011b; Ganzevoort & Roeland, 2014). All of these approaches touch upon a critical insight: communities, practices, meaning, experiences, and storied accounts of lived life must not be limited or narrowed to specific Christian or explicit religious fields. Instead implicit religion (Bailey, 1990), invisible religion (Luckmann, 1967), lived religion (McGuire, 2008), spirituality and the sacred of everyday life (Pargament, 2008, 2011) and theological approaches to lived religion in secular and deinstitutionalized contexts (Ganzevoort, 2009, 2011b), ordinary non-technical and non-scholarly theology (Astley, 2002) or existential ultimate concerns (Tillich, 2014, 1957) may all provide people who live their lives outside of religious communities, and who do not necessarily share explicit confessional world views, with descriptions that resonate with the profundity and depth of their experiences in lived life. This corresponds to the embodied practices and lived religion of military communities as eloquently formulated by a distinct perception of McGuire (2008, p. 118):

> The body disciplines that produce a dancer capable of aesthetically pleasing virtuoso performances are not altogether different from those that hone the skills of a military commando capable of efficiently destroying many lives. If they are at all effective, embodied practices are hardly neutral. In order to understand individuals' religion-as-lived, we must avoid romanticizing certain embodied practices, while ignoring others we may deplore.

Concepts such as implicit religion, lived religion, or the sacred character of communal life serve as relevant ways of describing and interpreting the effects of military communal life and service of the participants in this project during their transitions. As presented, the embodied ideology of military service among many of the participants in this study included subordination to a higher purpose, which equated sacrifices and a commitment to a community of battle buddies who likewise devoted to and lived by such standards. The values, beliefs, commitment to local community and battle buddies are not considered as explicit religious but rather as implicit religious, or even as a type of lived religion which provided the participants with an embodied life style which included a higher purpose of life, sacrifices, meaning, and satisfaction. It was a lived religion which they proclaimed was hard to find demonstrated in other contexts. This and other closely related methodologies have been utilized in the interpretation of the narrative accounts and have been published as case study articles built upon the storied experiences of participants in this project (see Grimell, 2016b, 2017c, 2017d). In regards to the sample of this project as a whole, which was more inclined to talk about questions of life than religious beliefs, in combination with the secular Swedish context and the complete analysis of the material, the avenue for the theory building in this chapter has narrowed in on creating an existentially and spiritually tailored theology. Such a theological approach may serve as an alternate way to understand the narrative analysis of military transition to civilian life within the previous empirical chapters.

Existential refers, throughout the construction of this theory, to the participants' attitudes to existence during the specific life situation of transition from full time military service, wherein the participants thought of and articulated questions of life such as who am I, who am I supposed to become, where is my place in this world, where do I find purpose and meaning in my life, and so on (Koole et al., 2006; Scherer-Rath, 2014; Tillich, 2014; Wikström, 1993).

The strength of using the existential attitudes of the participants as a foundation for the approach to this theory building is that it does justice to participants' perspective. From the outlook of this dissertation in practical theology, an existential and spiritual theory is viewed both as a timely theological challenge as well as a potential approach to make such a voice relevant to the field of transition from military to civilian life.

9.3 The concept of spiritual depth of life

The theologian Paul Tillich served as the source of inspiration within existential theology for the elaboration of the concept of *spiritual depth of life*, a concept which provided powerful motivation for this theory and further exploration of the vocabulary, even if with a somewhat different interpretation was taken relative to the one created by Tillich. One of his students, Harvey Cox, wrote in the introduction to the third edition of *The Courage To Be* (2014, p. xxiv)[16]:

> He knew, both from his keen observation of modern culture and through his own spiritual struggles, that the words "grace" and "faith" and even "God" had not only lost much of their original power but had also been so distorted that they had often been evacuated from meaning. So he boldly experienced with a new vocabulary. If the word "God" no longer speaks to you, he once wrote, say "depth." Instead on "sin," say "separation." Instead of "forgiveness," say "acceptance."

The profundity of lived life can be experienced within a wide range of contexts or situations such as in nature, music, relationships, art, religions, studies, communities and communal life, to name just a few, and is deemed *spiritual depths of life* in this theological theory on transition from military to civilian life. This concept of a spiritual depth of life implies that there is something valuable in each depth, that deeper meanings or extraordinary experiences interact with the mind, body, and soul of the individual and thereby transcend merely psychological, social or physical experiences. A spiritual depth entertains an experience of purpose and identity which transcends the self. A spiritual depth is not consumed by the individual, but rather some external, boundless entity that contains power, energy and meaning from which the individual can draw (Cavanaugh, 2007; Heelas, 2008). A spiritual depth of life invokes an experience of spiritual emotions such as uplift, awe, humility, mystery, gratitude, joy, peace, and serenity (Astley, 2002; Ganzevoort, 2009; Pargament, 2011; Pargament et al., 2014). A spiritual depth of life sustains life, but also has the potential to absorb life, and taken together

---

[16] *The Courage To Be* was originally published in 1952.

these imply that a spiritual depth is not just an entity which sustains life, it potentially sustains death too. An absence of spiritual depths of life may result in feelings of emptiness which question the very meaning with life, yet a spiritual depth itself may also consume a life and everything within it. A service member may gradually become so integrated into the meaning or purpose of military communal life and service that he or she ultimately sacrifices everything, including relationships and the self, in the line of duty. The concept of a spiritual depth serves as an entity which may host all of these experiences within its depth. Cultural contexts such as the Armed Forces, universities, congregations, political movements, and sports teams and families, to name several, may all be potential arenas wherein spiritual depths of life can be experienced and linked to a contextually constructed I-position. Spiritual depths of life are connected to certain I-position(s) of the self (e.g., I as an outdoor person, I as a music lover, I as a father, I as a painter, I as a believer in God, I as a service member) which serve as the mediation between the spiritual depth and the self. While sketching the contours of the concept it may also be said that one particular spiritual depth of life, related to one particular I-position, may stand out as a specific influential entity which is surrounded by other less pervasive, but still important, depths of life. Such an influential spiritual depth may have a corresponding impact upon the self via the mediating I-position.

9.3.1 A potential military spiritual depth of life

Although this study was not initiated with such a strong focus on military communal life but instead upon the departure from such, the profundity of the participants' storied experiences of military communal life and service, together with observed parallels to other research reports such as those presented in chapter 1, led to a reconsideration of the narratives of the study participants as a potential shared and collectivistic military depth of life. Military communities and service provided the participants with a military spiritual depth of life which transcended (and possibly still transcends) and resonated (and possibly still resonates) in their selves through specific military I-positions. Tillich's timeless invitation was helpful in the service of broadening the theological mind during this context specific theory building so as to better apply and expound the first part of this theory on military transition to civilian life while considering the depth of the overwhelming experiences of military communal life and service. This, however, does not imply that a military spiritual depth is another word for God, but rather that the concept of a military spiritual depth may have the potential to host and speak to a majority of the participants who have expressed profound storied experiences of belonging, togetherness, identities, meaning, significant others, beliefs and values, sacrifices, nature, life and death, derived from military communal life and service. Such profound narratives of experiences, according to the theological interpretation, are addressed as a military spiritual depth which transcends the self. This military spiritual depth is what was lost in transition and that which appeared difficult, for a majority of the participants, to find or discover, replace or reconstruct in a civilian life.

9.3.2 Characteristics of a military spiritual depth of life

A military spiritual depth of life is not a type of thing which can be strictly controlled or regulated by individual battle buddies, officers, military organizations, or mental health organizations, family members or the partners, or even the service member him- or herself. The components and aspects of the military cultures and organizations coalesce, in different degrees with complex interactions and reactions, in the evolution of a unifying collectivistic military spiritual depth, which is then hosted on a more personal level within each of the service members. This overarching military spiritual depth is an entity which enriches and sustains life through the experiences of military communal life and service, camaraderie, and meaning. So on the one hand, a military spiritual depth enhances, and then itself further strengthened by, military identities, extraordinary relationships, commitment, loyalty, meaning, careers, life styles and world views. However, a military spiritual depth also includes and embraces death and darker dimensions such as violence, killing, sacrifices and loss of battle buddies, psychiatric diagnoses, and moral injuries. So on the other hand, a military spiritual depth may have a consuming and darker character which resonates with what McGuire (2008, p. 117) acknowledge as darker "spiritual practices" or "darker elements" of lived religion. Such darker images serve to further elucidate the complexity of a military spiritual depth and furthermore help to avoid romanticizing its implications. A service member may become absorbed by the spiritual depth of military communal life, and as narrated by the participants this service amid absorption may entail extended sacrifices of both others and the self which the individual well recognizes and laments: "damn, what a boot full of shit I have been" (p. 149). Somewhere in the line of service, in some instances gradually accumulated as what were thought to be calculated costs while at other times appearing to be very random, sudden and unanticipated, a descent too deep into a military spiritual depth may break a service member and leave him or her him unfit to serve. Even worse, such costs may make it more difficult for an individual to assess life as worth living when dark dimensions of a military spiritual depth such as injuries, PTSD, TBI and moral injury may burden life in the aftermath of military service; an individual may very well need to process and formulate a new life story which includes trauma, guilt, scars and/or stigmata (Bragin, 2010; Ganzevoort, 2008; Janoff-Bulman, 1992). The cost of absorption by a military spiritual depth of life may be ultimate.

The experience of a military spiritual depth of life challenges questions of life, or promotes existential concerns, outside of the military context such as a loss of identity, status, meaning, job and money, which imply that many aspects which belong to a contextual spiritual depth of military communal life and service may be hard to find and sustain in a civilian life. But even if those aspects may be found in a civilian life, these may not have the same thrilling effect of the self as a military spiritual depth. When considering the identity reconstruction among the participants in this project it appeared as though some type of spiritual depth, old or new, needed to be connected to the reformulated (or retold) stories of who I am in order to advance the process of self-identity work in transition. If a military spiritual depth was present in military communal life and service, but lost and not substituted in transition, it impacted the well-being of that participant who continued to dream about, and long back to, the military life since military service continued to be the only avenue to a spiritual depth of life. Such military selves did eventually reenlist in some way, shape, or form to thereby reunite with the entity of a military spiritual depth so that they could collaboratively reinstate the existential well-being. This suggestively functions well from the perspective of the individual's health as long as it does not serve to avoid other unspoken, yet significant, questions of life such as an honest exploration of who I am to become as a civilian, or to mask potential psychiatric conditions, or lead to an all too costly absorption.

9.4 Transition from military to civilian life as a period of estrangement from civilian world

Transition from military to civilian life implicates a process wherein a service member leaves the military communal life and service for a life in other cultural contexts which includes different collections of values, meanings, and practices in the shaping of new identities. Such a decision was not taken lightly among the participants, and the process of mulling over this dilemma in some instances spanned more than a year. Many participants expressed stagnation and disappointment as reasons to leave full-time service. Some appreciated the initial feelings of freedom and self-determination felt shortly after departure, but in several instances this was a short-lived joy; the importance of the organized and collectivistic life style which included a military community, identity, meaning, significant others, and a uniform had now become obvious, as demonstrated in the interview narratives. Eventually the narrated contrast between the military culture and the civilian culture and the struggle of rooting one's self amid this upheaval resulted in existential experiences, life questions, and reflections. Such existential experiences marked the acceleration of the feeling of estrangement from a civilian world during the transitional process. Estrangement is a concept borrowed from Tillich (1957) but is here applied on a different level. In this theological theory on transition from military to civilian life estrangement is construed to mean that each service member belongs to the same civilian world to which he or she, from the military outlook, is estranged. Estrangement includes a self-perception of being the stranger, of being alienated or seen as the other, an outsider who has a vastly different sense of belonging, identity, experiences, beliefs and values, and to a degree even a different (professional) language (for alienation also see Adler, Britt, Castro, McGurk & Bliese, 2011). Such storied experiences were categorized and can be found in chapter 5 within the overarching themes of identity issues, a pro-militaristic position in self, emotional issues, and the importance of significant others. Feelings of estrangement are also shared to some extent in chapter 7 by existential elements such as identities, meaningful employment and/or life styles, significant others and beliefs and values. This estrangement was intensified by the distinct dichotomy between military and civilian worlds/relationships. In spite of such feelings of belonging to the military community, those who have left full-time service do, in fact, also belong to the civilian world from which they may have felt estranged.

In general, after a potential initial period of relief, the feeling of estrangement from a civilian world in transition accelerated sometime between two to eight months post exit and culminated about two years post exit when a transitional path had been chosen, albeit with some exceptions among the participants. The feeling of estrangement from a civilian world intensified both because of the encounters with new unfamiliar values, meanings, and practices, and because of an increasing sense of a loss of something significant in life which unfolded across time and which the self had to process. Many participants expressed in the early phases of transition that something with a deeper amplitude in life had been disconnected from their military selves. This theory suggests that this deeper amplitude was the spiritual depth of military communal life and service that surrounded their military identities, meaning, significant others, beliefs and values and so on, that the spiritual depth was the nebulous root system which fed the sense of estrangement from a civilian world and context. Across time, thirteen participants resolved such concerns by engaging in different forms of military communal life and service. Only six participants sustained a civilian linear path throughout the study period. According to this theory, the military depth which potentially engulfs military communal life, military identities, and other profound experiences of service had fueled tension, anxiety, alienation, and estrangement during a military transition to civilian life, and ultimately propelled the majority of the sample to entrench at least one foot within the military context in order to reunite with that military spiritual depth of life.

Many researchers have suggested that former service members who are undergoing transition may find it difficult to navigate new cultural perspectives, ideas, and attitudes within a civilian context (Beder, 2012; Brunger et al., 2013; Burkhart & Hogan, 2015; Coll et al., 2012; Higate, 2008; Jolly, 1996; Moore, 2012; Pellegrino & Hoggan, 2015; Wheeler, 2012; Yanos, 2004; Zinger & Cohen, 2010). This likely includes viewpoints which stand in stark opposition to the military outlook of former service members. The feelings of estrangement from a civilian world are often discovered when encountering such new cultural influences. In the eyes of a service member during transition the military identity and the military cultural lens (or a military I-position) may still be quite vivid and salient in his or her self (Grimell, 2015, 2017a, in press a). Meanwhile new civilian peers, for example in a university setting or in a civilian job context, may be naïve to such a military perspective and background. A former service member may be perceived as a civilian, yet inside the self he or she may harbor an influential military I-position which conducts much of the day to day interactions, internalization of data, and construction of meaning within that civilian world. A former service member may also be perceived in a stereotypical militaristic manner, and this simplification and generalization can likely have a counterproductive effect on the self-identity work in transition (Grimell, 2015, 2017b; Rumann & Hamrick, 2010). Such experiences deepened the sense of estrangement for Lieutenant Peter and Sergeant Gustaf, for example. The narrative struggle of the self already included identity questions such as who I am, who am I supposed to become, where am I supposed to go, and where is my place in the world, and thus whenever the dichotomy between the military and civilian worlds was further accentuated feelings of estrangement from a civilian world likewise grew more acute. The self-identity work in transition includes the invention and refinement of an I-position which can bridge such a dichotomy to thereby overcome these feelings of estrangement from a civilian world. It is important to add that for female service members there may potentially exist additional layers of estrangement and alienation as the military community and service, from the onset, has been dominated by service men (initial estrangement from a male military world), and former service women are an even more uncommon occurrence within the civilian world (estrangement and alienation from a civilian world as a military service woman in transition), something even more novel and *other* for the vast majority of their new peers (Grimell, 2017e).

A perspective from the psychology of religion is added as a potential layer of understanding to the feeling of estrangement from a civilian world during transition; "the healthy-minded" (James, 1902, p. 45b) in contrast to "the sick soul" (p. 72b). This concept also reflects two fundamental personality types which were originally described by William James (1902) but which are given an alternate understanding through the lens of a dialogical self. James (1902) described the healthy-minded and the sick soul as two ideal typological distinctions; here they are employed as temporal I-positions, with a risk of the sick soul growing more permanent depending upon the evolution of the transition.[17] The healthy-minded, according to James (1902), tend to see everything in life as good, and this suggests happiness and satisfaction as potential outcomes throughout life. The sick soul, however, serves as the counter-position to the healthy-minded; the sick soul is sensitive to life's discords and thus eternally wrestling with existence, meaning, suffering, darkness, destruction, and evilness of the world and self. But, on the other hand, a sick soul also allows itself to open up, perhaps to the deepest levels of truth (Wulff, 1997). Additionally, from a dialogical perspective, the voice of a sick soul has the potential of seeing things as they really are without the risk or intent of glorifying war or combat; a sick soul is keen to acknowledge meaninglessness, destruction, and darkness. The escape from the burden of the voice of an overwhelmingly dominant sick soul is possible through a gradual transformation or dialogue, which could be understood as an identity reconstruction, wherein life can be perceived through and lived in new ways by other positions (e.g., the voice of a healthy-minded position). Such a dialogical transformation would eventually include feelings of peace and harmony.

In this theory of transition from military to civilian life, feelings of estrangement from a civilian world may imply a temporary I-position of a milder form of a sick soul who grapples with meaning, the search for identities, direction if life, and likewise mulls over sacrifices, suffering, and potential evilness and destructiveness experienced in the line of duty. Among several of those who traversed upon a full transition to civilian life milder forms of temporarily nar-

---

[17] The evolution of self-identity work in transition is also dependent upon the nature of the military experiences in war zones which make, for example, moral injury to a promising concept which could be widened and linked to the concept of a sick soul in the interest of better serving veterans' health. This could also be even more nuanced and employed through a dialogical self framework wherein the voice of the sick soul is not the only voice which populates and therefore defines the self but rather one of a chorus which must include somewhere in the shadowlands a relic healthy-minded voice which, among others within the chorus, offers the potential for growth and resolution amid deliberately focused self-identity work and dialogue.

rating voices of sick souls were demonstrated by the participants' existential ruminations upon the process which eventually led into a gradual evolution, or dialogical transformation, of
the selves to embrace reconstructed identities and new ways of perceiving life which included
narratives of peace, happiness, and satisfaction (i.e., more influential from healthy-minded
positions). It is thereby suggested that a process of transition may create a temporary I-
position of a sick soul which is burdened with different types of agony and concerns. However, a temporary I-position of a sick soul may also prepare the self to see new potential spiritual
depths of life amid transition which may then be gradually cultivated into the self. If a temporary I-position of a sick soul becomes overly dominant in the self over time, there is a risk that
it could become a permanent and influential character in the position repertoire of the self
which can be plagued by a dark, cynical, pessimistic, and negative view upon of the world,
the life, and the self.

Through this theory on military transition to civilian life it is moreover suggested that the pervasive nature of a military spiritual depth can sustain its hold on a former service member for
an extended period of time into a transition to civilian life, and thus the military spiritual
depth can absorb or consume other potentialities of depths which exist within the civilian context. Such influences of a military spiritual depth can operate through battle buddies who continue to serve, local or world events, new prospects of military missions, relationship changes,
or simply grow more tempting when contrasted with perceived shortcomings of alternate spiritual depths within the civilian realm which can generate motivation, dreams and desires, civilian employment opportunities, identities, and/or significant relationships. This absorption
of potential civilian spiritual depths can also be accelerated by a constant perception of the
civilian world, life and experiences thereof through a military lens of the self which is extra
sensitive to and perceptive of estrangement in transition to civilian life. This equates the dom-
ination of a military I-position which undermines the dialogical capacity of the self. The prob-
able eventual outcome of such a situation is a return in some form to the military community
and service. In order to soften the influence of a military spiritual depth, feelings of estrangement must gradually be dissolved by exploration and discovery of other potential spiritual
depths through old or new I-positions which are brought into action and conversation by the
self. Such a process would enable a gradual narrative identity reconstruction wherein the narrative military claims continually decrease, as on the linear civilian path. In contrast, when the
military spiritual depth remains influential, it works in the interest of narrative maintenance or

even narrative renewal of military identities, as on the hybrid path and path of return to full-time service.

9.5 Potential avenues to alternate spiritual depths of life

There are other potential spiritual depths of life which may assist a service member in the transition from military communal life and service into a civilian population and life. Such spiritual depths have similar characteristics as a military spiritual depth such as deeper meanings, extraordinary experiences, devotion and emotions like awe, humility, gratitude, joy, peace, and serenity. Such spiritual depths may transcend the self. Additionally, these spiritual depths sustain life but potentially also include darker dimensions such as a consuming or absorbing character. For example, if an individual descends too deep into a spiritual depth of a career profession or a destructive relationship, this absorption may also include sacrifices of others, such as a partner and/or children, and/or the health and well-being of the self. Alternate spiritual depths are likewise mediated and experienced through different I-positions. Built upon the narrative analysis, mainly from chapter 7 and the evaluation letters (in chapter 8), four empirical avenues have been displayed among the participants which may support the exploration of alternate sources of spiritual depths: self-reflection, significant others, identity reconstruction through meaningful employment and/or life-styles, and nature.

9.5.1 Cultivation of new spiritual depths during transition utilizing self-reflection

A transition may be viewed as a movement from a potentially essentialist idea of the self by a service member, an idea which is narratively manifested as "I am a soldier in the broader sense of my person", in the very being of who I am (Grimell, 2015, p. 143), to a situation of existence where a former service member now has the freedom, and potentially acknowledges that freedom, to extensively rewrite his or her story (i.e., narrative identity), desires, dreams, and goals in life. A service member in transition is challenged by the specific life-situation to address and reflect upon the self, identities, meaning, and significant life questions in order to understand the responses and reactions within the self in the light of encounters with other cultural ideas and attitudes amid a new life situation. A transition requires answers from the individual instead of an escape from the situation, and although a form of escape may be to simply reenlist, hard won and profound answers may also lead to reenlistment. Such processes of reflection may eventually serve as an invitation for new insights and influences of the self and in life. As a service member reflects upon influential I-positions in the self he or she may begin to recognize, acknowledge, and cultivate other potential sources of spiritual depths in lived life. Self-reflection may, in other words, serve as one avenue to the perception and reali-zation of a new spiritual depth of life. One major impact of such a meta-cognitive activity, and a potential awareness of alternate spiritual depths, is to stimulate a dialogue between old and new I-positions of the self. Such a process may at some time(s) include the capacity to assume a meta-position which enables the self to leave the confines of specific I-positions to instead rise to a bird's-eye perspective from which different positions can be considered sim-ultaneously (Hermans & Hermans-Konopka, 2010). From a meta-position one can "take a broader array of specific I-positions into account and have an important executive function in the process of decision making" (Hermans, 2013, p. 86). The ability to take a meta-position facilitates the continuity, coherence, and organization of the self from a spatial point of view.

Such a process of self-reflection does not appear to necessitate a large number of sessions, but instead seems to center more on the quality, openness and sincerity of the self-reflection pro-cess. As presented in chapter 8, it was demonstrated that the three interview cycles assisted the participants' selves in at least four ways across time.

(A) An increased self-understanding and awareness about military identities and other identities in regards to the temporal and spatial (within self) dimensions in transition to civilian lives or return to (different forms of) military service

(B) An opportunity to process traumatic events, emotions and memories, or to open up and share inner life and experiences from military service and transition

(C) An experience of peace, harmony or satisfaction in regards to decisions and directions in lives based upon repeated reflections

(D) An opportunity to share personal experiences with a person who has conducted a simi-lar journey

Open systematic questions in regards to the stories of who I am, emotions and experiences, relationships, directions and aspirations in life and existential questions of life were often enough to begin a process of self-reflection, a process which cultivated a more reflective self which now enjoyed a deepened awareness of its identities (or I-positions) during the transition in regards to the impact of a military communal life and service and experiences of transition. This process had the potential to begin to dissolve feelings of estrangement. The reflective process was in a way initiated and guided by the researcher during the interviews, but in some instances narrated as preceding the interviews temporally as participants anticipated what would be shared, and was often recounted as continuing after the official interviews by the participants who, in solitude and/or together with friends or partners, continued to ruminate. The responses within the self in a civilian context and new situations were gradually better understood as a result of the processes of self-reflection and interviewing. Many participants eventually returned to different forms of military service and were satisfied with that path choice. Their satisfaction may also have been nurtured by the deeper reflections which accompanied the systematic elaborations to the interview questions.

9.5.2 Significant others as potential avenues to spiritual depths

Significant others serve as promoter positions which may assist a service member in his/her decision, whether it is to leave full-time service and sustain a civilian path or to return to military service (Hermans & Hermans-Konopka, 2010). Significant others in the civilian context may have the potential to cultivate or open up new spiritual depths of lives, such as a commitment and devotion to a partner and/or children (Kusner, Mahoney, Pargament & DeMari, 2014), to God, a congregation or a community (Kristeva, 1987; Pargament, 2008; Tillich, 1960, 1963), or to a meaningful career and aspirations in a civilian life (Pargament, 2011). Any of these can reduce or even erase the sense of estrangement from a civilian world via the revitalization or creation of I-positions. The observed importance of significant others in this study resonates with much of the recent research on military transition to civilian life (Beder, 2012; Blackburn, 2017; Moore, 2012; Sautter, Armelie, Glynn & Wielt, 2011; Tatum, 2015; Yanos, 2004). However, battle buddies or significant others in the military context may work in the service of a military spiritual depth to increase the sense of belonging in a military community and conversely accelerate the sense of estrangement from a civilian world. Significant others in a military context may, if significant others and new spiritual depth are lacking in a civilian life, motivate backtracking during transition and influence a former service member in favor of a return to military service. While some significant others may serve the spiritual depth of military worlds, other significant others nurture the discovery and realization of spiritual depths within the civilian realm, and thus it can be said that significant others work contextually in the interest of spiritual depths of life.

9.5.3 Meaningful employment and/or life styles as potential sources of spiritual depth

Meaningful jobs and/or life styles serve as another potential source of spiritual depth which may support a service member in the navigation out of military communal life and service and into a civilian population and life. This source of spiritual depth has two interesting alternatives in regards to the narrative analysis of beliefs and values in chapter 7. In a full civilian identity reconstruction, beliefs and values were manifested in civilian narrative characters which had salient counter features relative to the military characters, and these civilian narrative characters gradually steered these service members towards new meaningful jobs or life styles as retirees. The feelings of estrangement were thereby gradually resolved.

Meanwhile, when applying the other alternative, a hybrid path to civilian life, military beliefs and values steered service members in transition towards civilian employment which corresponded more or less with the previous set of military beliefs and values, such as those that esteemed the need of security and the protection of democracy and freedom. Thereby they appeared to in many ways continue their work in somewhat related domains to those with which they were familiar and found meaningful in the previous military employment. The new narrative characters had features which had more resemblance to old military characters. Suggestively, the closer a service member stayed to military beliefs and values, the more likely they found meaning in related contexts or in military service (or in a combination thereof). To stay connected to a military spiritual depth, or close to a related spiritual depth of a civilian career, can also be perceived in this theory as a way of decreasing estrangement.

9.5.4 Nature as a potential source of spiritual depth

Nature stands out as another particularly important source of spiritual depth, with or without explicit religious/spiritual connotations, which provided participants with peace, harmony, power, energy, well-being, and even identity and deeper reflections or insights about the self and life. This finding may have a context-specific relationship to Sweden in general, and the context of military service in particular. As already introduced, the status and role of Christianity in Scandinavia, and particularly in Sweden, has declined over a long period as Sweden has moved towards an individualistic and secular society (af Burén, 2015; Ahmadi & Ahmadi, 2015; Thurfjell, 2015). Meanwhile humans have continued to experience deeper meaning in aspects of life, for example when communing with nature, that go beyond the ordinary (Ahmadi, 2006, 2015; Bregman, 2006; Wikström, 1993). Simultaneously, several researchers have observed and suggested the development of a particular spiritual relationship between Swedes and nature. For example Herlitz (1995) noted that, "Swedes, generally speaking, have an almost sacred relationship to nature" (p. 36). Corresponding to such an understanding Ahmadi (2006, 2015) suggested in her research that for Swedes nature becomes laden with sacred connotations and holds a particular spiritual dimension in their modern lives. Adding to this contextual relationship between Swedes and nature in general is the exposure of service members to nature throughout their career (e.g., field exercises, physical training, patrolling, bivouacking). Service members are trained to survive and excel in the natural environment; therefore, the development of military identities through basic training, camaraderie, and missions are all closely associated with nature and potentially linked to the military spiritual depth of communal life and service. Service members in transition, and Swedish ones in particular, can easily be anticipated to experience a spiritual depth of nature which may resonate in their selves (in civilian as well as military I-positions) by providing energy, harmony, peace, or serenity. No storied experiences with a reference to estrangement from nature were displayed in the material. Every narrative account that mentioned nature clearly decreed that it works in the service of well-being and health. Once again, this dimension of nature, well-being, and health could also be illuminated as a vital dimension (van den Brink, 2012a, 2012b).

This theory, in consideration of the narratives, suggests that the spiritual depth of nature implies that deeper meanings or extraordinary experiences within nature interact with the mind, body, and soul of the individual to thereby transcend merely psychological, social, or physical experiences (Ellens, 2008). Moreover, this implies that the spiritual depth of nature is not consumed by the individual, but rather is some other, external entity that contains power, energy or meaning from which the individual can draw (Heelas, 2008). Thus the effect of the spiritual depth of nature is to provide peace, balance, focus, and power or strength to go on with the individuals' lives. These revitalized states of mind, body and soul may evoke what some researchers entitle spiritual emotions such as "uplift, awe, humility, mystery, gratitude, joy, peace, or serenity" (Pargament et al. 2014, p. 49). Experiences of a spiritual depth of nature connote some kind of openness to life that supersedes a strict secular atheistic position of a total disenchantment of the world; however, it does not necessitate a religious relationship (Heelas, 2008). Moreover, the storied differences of the experiences among the sample group regarding the more explicit religious/spiritual narratives given by the older service members compared with non-religious/spiritual narratives shared by many of the younger service members parallels the general religious decline in Sweden over the most recent decades. Additionally, taking William James (1902, p. 21b) definition of religion (i.e., "the feelings, acts, and experiences of individual men in solitude, so far as they apprehend themselves to stand in relation to whatever they may consider the divine") into consideration the experience may be the same, but the younger generations of service members do not connect it with the divine as did their elders. The interpretation of the findings in this project implies that older retired officers may benefit more from explicitly religious/spiritual ideas (or I-positions) of nature than younger service members, who can instead be better served with relatively less explicit ideas and I-positions which likewise tap this shared depth of nature. It may be beneficial for the younger generation to learn some spiritual language in order to open up for both a helpful dialogue like that which has served for a long time to describe such experiences, as well as to introduce alternate spiritual sources of understanding such as the link between nature, well-being, and life. Nature was experienced as a powerful source by many of the older and younger participants alike, independent of a religious/spiritual or non-religious framework of understanding, and thus can also serve as a promising bridge to deeper reflections about life.

9.6 The old being and the new being of the self

As new potential sources of spiritual depths are recognized, the routes to new potential identities open up to allow meaningful narrative identity reconstruction during the self-identity work in transition. But even as that happens, a military I-position will not simply disappear in the vacuum of a self; on the contrary, the old being of the service member will always exist somewhere in the space of the self. During the journey over a linear civilian path of identity reconstruction the military I-position will most likely move further into the shadows and grow more passive as new civilian identities, I-positions, and related depths take over the roles and duties of the old military being. Nonetheless, this evolution throughout transition from a dominant military I-position into a less salient position of the self does not necessitate that the story or the spiritual depth of military experiences and service is omitted or reduced into a single personal narrative story of ego-identity development wherein the military experiences and spiritual depth belong to the past and therefore are disconnected from any current influence upon the self. The self is a dialogical narrator with multiple I-positions which are constantly adapting to an ever-changing world, and depending upon events and circumstances in life, unexpected situations, significant others, desires, motives, and spiritual depths, different I-positions are continually called to the front while others take time on the bench (from which they can still be heard) amid the ever-changing lineup of players on the field (Hermans et al., 1992). Even as participants who followed a linear civilian path narrated strong reconstructed identities as civilians two to three years post exit, they also recounted that their military I-positions continued to interact upon the selves.

Additional lessons about the old and the new beings of the selves gleaned from the narratives in this longitudinal study included that the new civilian characters which were shaped by the participants were equipped with counter features (e.g., the perception of life, beliefs and values) in regards to the old military characters, especially on the full transition to civilian life. Meanwhile, those following military paths typically sustained much more dialogue with their old military I-positions and thus kept military values, meanings, and practices active in their lived lives. The difference between participants increased as the participants on a full transition to civilian life developed new characters with other beliefs, values, and life questions or existential focus. Additionally, other I-positions (and this was also true of those on a hybrid outcome within this study), such as a co-habiting girlfriend or boyfriend, husband, son or daughter demonstrated cooperation with the new identities which were constructed in the self in order to avoid repeating imposing sacrifices upon the relationships with significant others and the self, a mistake learned the hard way by the old military being who was being gradually displaced to the shadowlands of the self.

Sacrifices made by service members in military service may, from a theological perspective, resonate to some Christian perspectives which accept sacrifices in the line of service for a higher purpose such as democracy, freedom, a just war in order to sustain or restore peace, or a military crusade (or individual action) in order to protect beliefs and values (Bonhoeffer, 1959; Elshtain, 1995; Fowl & Jones, 1998; Hauerwas, 2001; Holmes, 2005; Winright, 2007). To be a service member and forsake or even sacrifice relationships with significant others and/or the health of the self or potentially life itself may be understood as a cost of wearing the cross which has been presented to a service member by the military service as sanctioned by the larger nation, federation or alliance, and/or even by theologians within an religious institution. This serves as a type of vocational perspective of military servants who wear a cross of military service that implicates a ready willingness to endure personal suffering, as well as the sufferings of significant others who long for a better relationship with the service man or woman, father or mother, son or daughter (Bonhoeffer, 1959; Elshtain, 1995; Fowl & Jones, 1998).

Forsaking loved ones and imposing sacrifices upon them as conditions of military communal life and service may, from a sociological perspective, be described as a competition between the family and the military organization for the serving individual's time, energy, and loyalty. Both the family and the military can be portrayed as greedy entities which are characterized by the pressures they place on the service member to weaken his or her ties with other persons or institutions, or to not form any such ties in the first place (Segal, 1986). There is often an underlying tension between the needs of the family and the military which a service member must navigate and negotiate, a struggle which ultimately leaves someone feeling forsaken, and this in turn can make redeployment seem like a better option (Beder, 2012). This serves as a sociological way of describing that which this theological theory suggests to be two different spiritual depths: the military depth and the family depth. In terms of van den Brink's (2012a, 2012b) existential sets it may also be suggested that the first is a sacral spiritual depth and the second is a social spiritual depth. However, the pervasive character or dimension of a military spiritual depth has a particular influence on the service member which may direct him or her back to military service and life. This does not only revolve around the difficulties to navigate different institutional demands, or a feeling of estrangement from a civilian world and alienation within a civilian life, but also draws from the experiences of profundity in life which may be sustained by a military spiritual depth, even amid recognition of its darker consuming character. This darker side of a military spiritual depth can narrow and absorb life at the expense of significant others outside of the military context, and the self in regards to physical and mental health and the connection with other sources of spiritual depths of life which are vital in order to sustain those linked identities.

It is important to mention that sacrifice is not necessarily a bad thing; this evaluation depends on what or who is sacrificed, to what extent and why. But as suggested earlier, a military spiritual depth of life cannot be controlled by the individual, and this equates that the questions of what or who, to which extent, and why are likewise beyond individual control. Even as dialogue between the spiritual depths of life exists (e.g., the family and the military) in the beginning of a military service, including good intentions and healthy relationships, both military service and family life will evolve and at some point an individual may become gradually lost in a military spiritual depth and sacrifices may be made which were never expected, or even imagined, upon enlistment. Even if a service member is single and has all the time in the world to commit him or herself to military communal life and service, and therein constructs a powerful military identity and I-position, it may nonetheless, or perhaps therefore, become quite a challenge to explore and invite new spiritual depths of life. This may eventually cripple a military transition to civilian life by accentuating the loss of a military spiritual depth and the sense of estrangement from a civilian world and alienation within a civilian life. This serves as an imperative for deeper reflection for each and every service member in military service or in the midst of transition. The complexity of a military spiritual depth, which sustains overwhelming experiences of togetherness, meaning, identity, and life, may also consume life and potentials within life though its pervasive and powerful impact upon a military I-position of the self.

9.7 The calling to friendship

As stated in the introduction of this dissertation, military cultures prepare their members in effective, organized, and systematic ways to break (civilian) cultural taboos and engage in the otherwise legally punishable act of killing other humans, and this implies that military cultures and professions stand in stark contrast to civilian entities within the Western world (Bragin, 2010; French, 2005; Goldstein, 2001; Kümmel, 2011; Strachan, 2006; Wilson, 2008). The ultimate purpose may be altruistic, such as to preserve democracy and freedom, but the underlying duty, and the ontological character of military professions, within military communities is to train, condition, and prepare service members in a variety of ways to kill, and face death, during military service. It is hard to avoid this fact as so much of the military organization and its personnel function in order to execute the ultimate act of the organization: to conduct combat and war. This implicates that as long as military personnel serve, they harbor an inbuilt dichotomy in their perception of the world: us versus the potential or factual enemies (Baumann & Gingrich, 2006; Verrips, 2006). This dichotomy of us and them is a necessary prerequisite to be able to execute combat and kill other humans and sustains some type of moral justification, and thus mental health, while doing so. However, there is also a potential risk and cost that accompanies the breaking of a cultural taboo to kill an enemy (for dehumanization processes see, for example, Zimbardo, 2008), even in the line of duty. The ontological problem with military cultures, professions, and therefore identities is that a service member must limit the cultivation and development of friendship outside of the military context in order to maintain suitable leeway to perform what the service may require. Such a dichotomy of *us and them* in military cultures and world views is transferred onto the military identity and I-position of each self, and this dichotomy may create tension and conflict between other civilian I-positions in the self which do not share this ontological military character of soldiery or military professions.

This theological theory on transition from military to civilian life suggests that reflection upon the dimensions of dichotomy in the perception of the self, others and the world may advance the progress of self-identity work during transition. The lens which imbues a dichotomy belongs to the military I-position, or the old being of the self, and enhances the feelings of estrangement from a civilian world and alienation within a civilian world. Such an outlook of the world may be further amplified by a military spiritual depth in life which potentially provides the military I-position with the energy to uphold this perception throughout encounters with others in life, and which can also consume alternate potential spiritual depths of life. Therefore, inspired by feminist theologians such as McFague (1982), Hunt (2009) and Thompson (2004) it is suggested that the new being of the self, the new I-position(s), may benefit by being partly constructed around a vocation of relationship with others in the world. Such a development of a new I-position(s) could benefit from cooperation with other I-positions in the self which may share such an approach to others and the world, I-positions which likely have previously been subordinated throughout military service.

The concept and nature of friendship offers an ability to create unexpected partnerships among people, as well as within the self in regards to resolving estrangement, so that a bridge can be built between the estranged parties. Friendship can nurture both external and internal collaborations. Hunt (2009) suggested that friendship has the potential to connect humans who, literally or figuratively speaking, are antagonists or enemies. Friendship has the capacity to transcend dichotomies of the self and others in the world, which in turn gradually may contribute to a new era within the self in which internal dichotomies are bridged. A vocation of relationships functions on at least two levels: it serves as an invitation to talk, learn, share, and broaden the experiences of life, even when the chasm between people, including cultures and identities, appears to be vast. In the same manner, a vocation of relationships serves as an invitation for self-exploration of the cultures and I-positions which populate the self.

McFague also suggested (1982) that it is not common identities which bring friends together but rather shared ideas, dreams, and visions which nurture and sustain dialogue, and this postulation is applicable both towards the world and to the self. When applied to the world at large the reciprocal character of friendship mitigates the temptation to maintain, construct, or even reconstruct dichotomies, barriers and walls that distance others in life and the world. When this postulation that the sharing of ideas, dreams and, visions is the unifier of friends is applied to the self, then a calling to a vocation of friendship suggestively may have a positive impact on the dialogical capacity of the self as a whole. The spirit of friendship and relationships may support an inclusive and cooperative evolution within the self which can overcome the temptations of certain I-positions (identities of the self) to maintain distance, distinction, and/or us and them perspectives.

192

Thompson (2004) connects her feminist interpretation of friendship with the shift within the Johannine narratives from servant to a caring friend and thus Jesus's own reformulation, as recorded in the Gospel of John (chapter 15), of the disciples from servants to friends. She suggested that friendship has a special subversive character which can serve as an image for a vocation to friendship in a contemporary society; however, friendship has often been viewed as being too ordinary to include the divine. Thompson, on the other hand, proposed otherwise, that friendship may very well bear transcendence and depth which are potentially God's hidden presence within comparatively mundane and ordinary relationships. Such a theological proposal may be particularly interesting for an I-position as a believer, which may have a disposition for cooperation with such an evolving I-position and character of a friend in the self-identity work during transition. Viewing this theological concept of friendship from another angle (Tracy, 1975), any calling to friendship suggests that two principal sources are brought into friendly yet critical correlation, and in the instance of this dissertation and this theory which flows from it, Christian texts and the participants' experiences and narratives have collaborated throughout the results of the investigation.

This theological theory on military transition to civilian life suggests that the calling to friendship decreases the impact of a military spiritual depth, invites new potential sources of spiritual depths linked to old and/or new identities, dissolves feelings of estrangement, and supports the cooperative spirit within the self, which taken altogether advance the self-identity work during a transition. The calling to friendship implies dialogue and openness to the other, someone or something which was previously perceived as more unlike the self, as well as a collaborative and curious approach towards the self. One important contribution of friendship is that it advocates trust in other people and thus calms suspicious minds, which are a potential result of a military mindset which can function as a hindrance in regards to the establishment of trustful and honest relationships in a civilian life (Schok, Kleber, Lensvelt-Mulders, Elands & Weerts, 2011). The emerging perspective on soul repair when recovering from moral injury after war goes so far as to suggest that the strong bonds which are made between service members during military service and deployments can actually impede the development of emotional ties to family and civilian friends upon the return from deployment and may serve as a problem in the transition back to society and civilian life (Brock & Lettini, 2012).

9.7.1 Some challenges along the road

Other studies may suggest that there may be challenges to this aspect of this theory that vocation to friendship is a possible way to advance self-identity work in transition, especially during the early phase of a transition. This may be partly true, but over time this longitudinal study suggests otherwise, even for those participants who followed a hybrid path. There are both themes which are narrated in the military identities, as well as in the disposition of military I-positions, which can render such a vocation plausible in the long run. Service members, if anyone, know the value and significance of friendship, loyalty and commitment to others. However, this experience is often exclusive throughout military service to include only battle buddies, and it may persist in this exclusivity in early transition. However, over time such a perception may change and be widened as new relationships are brought into conversation with the self, and the military spirit of friendship may be transferred into new civilian identities. This was particularly evident on the linear civilian path whereupon the participants during the final interviews recounted their worlds and relationships quite differently than during their early phases of transitions, as narrated in the first interviews.

The calling to friendship is seen as a normative element in this theory on military transition to civilian life since it is suggested that it may advance the self-identity work. However, this vocation to friendship goes in mutual or reciprocal directions. Civilians, as well as service members, must invite each other to explore friendship opportunities, share life, talk, discuss, exchange experiences, and learn from each other. Then these outreaches of friendship have the potential to evolve into honest and sincere relationships and new spiritual depth(s) of life may be discovered and/or further developed. But not just that, there are signs in the empirical material of the need to accept a certain loss of the profundity of military camaraderie in order to open up to more inclusive friendship, which has a theological connotation. The act of acceptance, or rather to accept that one is accepted (by God), has been suggested by Tillich (2014) as an important but sometimes difficult existential theological dimension for an individual to acknowledge. Here, in this theory, acceptance is employed on another level as a part of the process of transition from military to civilian life in regards to acknowledgement of the loss of profound relationships, a difficult yet important consequence to process and fully accept. For example, Peter was haunted by a sense of emptiness and loss in regards to the military community and camaraderie during his transition, and he had no aspirations to fill that hole by cultivating relationships with student peers. However, over time Peter accepted the loss and testified in the second interview that he had found a new community wherein "you may not be as tight, but the camaraderie is the same." Accepting the loss of profound military relationships was necessary in order to established new ones. Another example is taken from Sergeant David; he could not accept the loss of military life and camaraderie and testified to the profundity that he still experienced during the second year of transition from military to civilian life (Grimell, 2016b, p. 213):

> Yes, well, it is tremendously, eh, it is so extremely difficult to explain how you can have such a connection to the Armed Forces, but it is, eh, because it is not always fun as you have these heavy field weeks and you just want go get back home and go to bed, it is difficult for people to understand why you want to get back all the time, but there is something that, it is something there which just make you want to get back to all the time… it is everything, camaraderie, the surroundings, basically everything that you miss.

Since David could not accept the loss of community, camaraderie, and the Armed Forces which, using van den Brink's (2012a, 2012b) paradigm had a sacral dimension for him, he returned to full-time service.

A further consideration is the mutual motivation to the calling to friendship; if it becomes overly one-sided, or even worse if neither party is interested in exploring the calling to friend-ship, then the result may instead be the consolidation of dichotomies and differences which then become even more difficult to bridge, increase feelings of estrangement, and eventually promote return to the military spiritual depth of communal life and service. Such an unfortu-nate development in transition from military to civilian life was narrated by Lieutenant John who described frustration, identity crisis, and the consolidation of dichotomies in the universi-ty setting between him (who represented *the military*) and the student peers (who represented *the others*) which made it all too difficult for either party to establish any deeper friendship (Grimell, 2017b, p. 12):

> Yes, I became crazy. During one seminar the other day we discussed something, and one of the students said ''nowadays soldiers don't really fight against each other.'' And I started to think, 'but you haven't actually been out there serving and I have colleagues of mine that have lost their legs...' So this has rather strengthened my military identity... It has been very frustrating, and I experience a lack of attachment to reality at the insti-tution I belong to, there are really great researchers in many areas but they are scholars and only deliver criticisms. With my military experience, the values that I have are not

195

sufficient and it becomes a pretty big identity crisis, it prevents me from shaping a new identity... It consumes so much energy because sometime I focus more on how detached the others are than I should, instead of focusing on my studies. It is related to the institution and everything that you are supposed to do. It is like criticizing everything that you are, that I believe in. Somehow I believe in these things, otherwise I wouldn't have ended up serving in the Armed Forces. But now I am supposed to sit and constantly criticize the system I am a part of, that consumes much energy, definitely.

CHAPTER 10

Conclusions

10.1 Lessons learned

This study showed that transition from military to civilian life among this qualitative sample was frequently a dynamic process of temporal narrative identity reconstruction and spatial self-identity work. A transition from military to civilian life required some type of reorganization of I-positions which in turn created decentering movements within the self as a preexisting organization of I-positions was prompted to change by reorganization and movement within the self (Hermans & Hermans-Konopka, 2010). From a narrative perspective the stories of who I am still exist but need to be reorganized and retold. Thus a reorganization of I-positions corresponds to a reorganization of stories. This study furthermore showed that the self-identity work during transition from military to civilian life, among this particular sample, was a complex process which led the participants onto three diverging paths of storied evolution in order to center and reintegrate their selves. One way of understanding the decision to traverse upon these different paths was through the dynamics of localization and globalization (Hermans & Dimaggio, 2007). It was suggested that military communal life consisted of a rather closed and local community with familiar and known values, meanings, and practices which were shared and denoted by the service members thereof. A transition from a local and military community exposed the participants to a variety of new and alternate values, meanings, and practices of a civilian world. The dynamics of localization and globalization could result in the invitation and elaboration of new values, meanings, and practices during the self-identity work as in a full transition from military to civilian life, but for some participants the outcome was a counter-positioning to the local, familiar and known military service. The transition had a malleable nature as it was dependent upon a number of variables such as preexisting military identities, significant others, the experience of meaningful employment and/or life styles, beliefs and values, and a potential reflection and awareness of sacrifices imposed upon significant others and/or the self. The majority of the sample kept at least one foot in the military context, at least upon completion of the study, and thus developed a hybrid civilian/military identity or returned to full-time military service. Although the majority intended to become civilians, only a limited number of participants sustained a full transition from military to civilian life. This suggests three types of narrative evolutionary and centering models for the self-identity work during transition in regards to this Swedish context and sample:

(1) A full transition from military to civilian life which equated a civilian storied evolution and included an identity reconstruction wherein a new story of who I am was richly developed and led by a main character which had counter features in comparison with the old military character, whilst the military story of who I am was, from a narrative point of view, left behind.

(2) A hybrid outcome of a bicultural civilian/military identity which equated a hybrid storied evolution and characteristically included a more gradual process of identity construction of a civilian character which was typically much more similar to the preexisting military character, while the military character was maintained as an active narrative I-position through part-time service.

(3) A full return to military service which equated a military storied evolution and included the renewal of military identity and in some cases construction of a new military character, whilst the development of a civilian character related to a new civilian profession was aborted. However, other civilian characters were also constructed over time to promote continued evolution of a storied self (also see Grimell, 2017a, 2017b).

For the participants in this study, the self-identity work in transition often implied existential reflections upon questions of life such as who am I, who will I become, where is my place in the world, and where am I going. The importance then of such existential elements has been demonstrated throughout the processes. It is suggested that beliefs and values were one distinct divergence point in regards to the selection of civilian or military tailored paths, and thus the storied evolution of the selves, in response to these existential issues. Additionally, such beliefs and values may amplify certain elements of military service such as the subordination of one's will to a higher purpose which included sacrifices, the commitment to a community, loyalty to the battle buddies, which could also be perceived through the lens of lived and implicit religion (Bailey, 1990, 1997; McGuire, 2008). This lived and implicit religion transcended the self and was hard to find demonstrated in other contexts. For a limited number of participants, explicitly religious reflections were also saliently narrated throughout the process. Nature played a crucial role for some of them and could be perceived as the way they lived their religion and gained existential power in their lives. Other participants also narrated such storied experiences as having an existential magnitude of the nature without connecting them explicitly to the divine or traditional religion.

198

Within the broader realm of research, it is less common to hear theological consideration and theory building around self-identity work during military transition to civilian life; this observation deserved more consideration from a theological outlook. The theological theory presented in chapter 9 on transition from military to civilian life, built upon the previous empirical chapters, serves as an alternate and contextual voice on the subject matter which expands this study beyond a merely psychological and narrative investigation. The emphasis given on the existential and spiritual approach of the theory is intended to resonate with the existential attitude of the participants, as well as to describe the profundity of the storied experiences of military communal life and service which had shaped, and continued to shape, the military identities and the storied and centering evolutions for many participants. This theory potentially offers a theological understanding of the nuances of military communal life, service, and identities which echo in the self during a transition. This theory may also serve as an assistant which may be invited by service members for further self-reflection prior to, during, and/or after the transitional processes.

A transition from military to civilian life is, for these participants, understood through the three evolutionary and centering models for narrative self-identity work throughout the process. From an existential perspective it could be suggested that a transitional evolution, no matter where it may lead a participant, has entered a more stable phase when the evolution of stories and characters has been shaped in dialogue with meaningful answers to the existential questions of life such as who I am, where am I going, and where is my place in the world. From a theological outlook it is suggested that a firmer footing is given to such a phase if it rests upon the existence of spiritual depth(s) of life, which is/are linked to identities of the self and brought into dialogue by the self. This theological point of view suggests that spiritual depth(s) appear(s) to provide stability in the self-identity work, a proposal which also works in the service of a military spiritual depth and military identities.

10.2 Possible routes for future development

The narrative results of this study, such as the transitional experiences presented in chapter 5 and the self-identity work in chapter 6, resonate to other psychological and sociological research projects on military transition to civilian life (Adler et al., 2011; Bélanger & Moore, 2013; Bragin, 2010; Brunger et al., 2013; Burkhart & Hogan, 2015; Coll et al., 2012; Drops, 1979; Haynie & Shepherd, 2011; Jolly, 1996; Rosenberg, 1993; Rumann & Hamrick, 2010; Savion, 2009; Wheeler, 2012; Yanos, 2004; Yarvis & Beder, 2012). Yet the strong empirical attraction of a hybrid outcome or a full return to a military path was not expected. Based upon the narrations of many participants within this sample, the possibility to reenlist in some way to military service to sustain or renew the military story of who I am and the spiritual depth therein was of major importance for the individual's quality of life and existential and spiritual well-being. A potential avenue to understand this desire was and is through the theological theory on military transition to civilian life which introduces the concept of military service as a potential spiritual depth of life. This theoretical viewpoint thereby acknowledges implicit religious dimension of military service which include a higher purpose, beliefs, values, camaraderie, and communal life which provided the participants with profundity and meaning but also potential losses and sacrifices. These findings serve as an invitation for other researchers, across disciplines, on the subject matters to investigate (a) how the contextual results of this study may resonate with other contextual research on transition from military to civilian life, or (b) how these qualitative sample results may resonate with other qualitative sample results within a Swedish context. The results of this study may also be used for (c) a quantitative exploration which could, for example, investigate both whether stressful experiences peak somewhere between the first months and second year of transition and how such experiences are related to existential questions of life such as who I am, my place in the world, meaningful employment and/ or life styles linked to identities, and/or the role of significant others. A quantitative approach could also be taken when considering (d) the broader applicability of the three paths present with this sample within a much larger body of service members transitioning from military to civilian life and how beliefs and values relate to the travels on such paths.

Another potential departure point for future exploration is an articulated possibility to do (e) a follow-up study on the participants to widen the longitudinal perspective even more in regards to the storied evolution of the paths in self-identity work, and with that data to then widen and fine-tune the theological theory. The majority of the participants have stated that they are willing to contribute further with their experiences.

10.3 The evolution of the PhD project
The theological theory presented in this dissertation, in combination with the unexpected extensiveness of the impact of the interviews, and even the participants' anticipations of and reflections over the interviews, upon the participants' self-identity work have relevance for the arena of spiritual care and reflection in order to foster spiritual fitness among service

members as a preparation for a forthcoming transition. Pargament & Sweeney (2011) presented the development of the spiritual fitness component of the US Army's Comprehensive Soldier Fitness (CSF) program. Spirituality was then defined "in the human sense as the journey people take to discover and realize their essential selves and higher order aspirations" (Pargament & Sweeney, 2011, p. 58). Utilizing a number of theoretically and empirically grounded arguments, they promoted the role of spirituality in the CSF program as a significant motivating force, a vital resource for human development, and a source of struggle that can lead to growth or decline. A conceptual model was presented (constructed by Sweeney, Hannah & Snider, 2007) that facilitated the progression of the human spirit, and an educational computer-based program was developed around that model with the goal of promoting spiritual resilience. The program of spiritual fitness consisted of three tiers (Pargament & Sweeney, 2011):

- Building awareness of the self and the human spirit
- Building awareness of resources to cultivate the human spirit
- Building awareness of the human spirit of others

The findings and insights throughout this study resonate with the ideas from Pargament & Sweeney (2011), and taken together these suggest an important applicability in a Swedish context for the implications of this longitudinal research project in order to psychologically, existentially, and spiritually assist service members to prepare for transition from military to civilian life. This attempt to better serve the spirituality of service members should also be connected to the intensifying focus on veterans' spiritual struggles which was recently highlighted by the journal *Spirituality in Clinical Practice* (Bryan, 2015; Bryan, Graham & Roberge, 2015; Currier, Kuhlman & Smith, 2015; Grimell, 2016b; Kopacz & Connery, 2015) as well as in other journals such as *Psychological Services* (Bobrow, Cook, Knowles & Vieten, 2013) and the *Journal of Health Care Chaplaincy* (Nieuwsma & Rhodes et al., 2013). In resonance with voices and perspectives which emphasize the spiritual components in service members' self-identity work, this dissertation proposes a method which can be used for further elaboration within a Swedish context by building spiritual fitness through a number of sessions during a one year period:

- The first session utilizes the theological theory on transition from military to civilian life and other related spiritual perspectives upon military service, self, and life as an introduction to widen the awareness of spiritual depths and thus foster explicit knowledge of spiritual fitness. Each participant is also given a manual including mate-

201

rial derived from this dissertation, other spiritual perspectives, exercises, and reflections to which he or she can return to during and after the sessions.

- The second session utilizes an interview method, similar to the one which was employed in this study, and thus invites the service members to reflect upon narrative identities, values, meanings, practices, and life questions in conversation with an interviewer who articulates open systematic questions.
- The third session, about six months after the second, repeats the same interview process and follows the same interview-guide.
- The fourth session has a concluding character and focuses upon evaluation and lessons learned during the process.

The interviews can, depending on the number of participants, be conducted by the service members themselves as they alternate between interviewer and interviewee to follow the interview-guide and are provided with instructions prior to the actual interviews. This process can be further elaborated by providing each participant with an existential diary to use after the session cycle has concluded. The purpose with such a diary would be to continue the reflection upon spiritual depths of life and/or help recognize alternate depths over time, including how such spiritual depths evolve and influence the participant. This diary could also serve to shape dialogue between such depth related I-positions.

This method focuses on three potential groups and/or phases which are best served with slightly different angles of approach which could, for any given individual, be cumulative and evolve over time.

- [Prior to transition] Building spiritual fitness through narrative self-reflection, *with a focus on preparation prior to the process*, among service members during full-time service: An exploration of the narrative self, military spiritual depths, and their implications. A focus on self-reflection to cultivate awareness and potentially open the self to other sources of spiritual depth(s) in life.
- [During transition] Building (or continuing to grow) spiritual fitness through narrative self-reflection, *with a focus on guidance during the process*, among service members in the midst of a transition to civilian life: An exploration of the narrative self, military spiritual depths and their implications. A focus on self-reflection to assist the exploration and potential discovery of spiritual depth(s) in a civilian life amid transition.

- [Post-transition] Building (or continuing to grow) spiritual fitness through narrative self-reflection, *with a focus on the enrichment of life*, among already transitioned former service members: An exploration of the narrative self, non-military spiritual depths and their implications. A focus on self-reflection to assist the exploration and potential discovery of spiritual depth(s) within a civilian life in the aftermath of a transition.

This method would, as implied, utilize a narrative approach to and a dialogical outlook of the self; it would combine these elements to serve as a framework for the understanding of the self, while the theological theory of transition from military to civilian life would enrich such self-reflections with existential and spiritual perspectives.

This method was included in a project proposal which was accepted by the Swedish Soldiers Homes Association during May 2017. The project is planned to result in the published manual, referred to in the first bullet above, during 2018 which can then be used by service members, as well as the local directors and/or counselors of the association and potentially military chaplains. The Swedish working title of the project is *Övergången till ett liv efter tjänstens slut, jaget och militära identiteter* [The transition to a life after service, the self and military identities]. The working title opens up two ways of understanding transition to a life after service. The first understanding focuses upon active serving members who need to transition back to a civilian life (i.e., with other values, meanings, and practices) when the working day ends and to recognize, appreciate, and cultivate different spiritual depths during such day-to-day transitions. The second understanding focuses upon a transition from military to civilian life of a more final character once the military service is concluded. In summary, this project has established a promising dialogue between empirical practical theological research and an organization with the potential to make use of such research to cultivate even better conditions to nurture self-identity work among military personnel in the midst of service and a forthcoming transition, in addition to transitioned service members who still reach out for contact and support from the association.

10.4 Limitations and contributions of the study

This study has been conducted as a qualitative and narrative investigation, and it encourages further research to test the findings quantitatively. Meanwhile, the depth and detail of a qualitative study are its real strengths, and taken together these implicate that it is counterproductive to judge a qualitative study by the criteria and assessment of quantitative research: random sampling of a large representative group of a highlighted population in order to sustain the potential for generalizations and predictions (Merriam, 2002, 1998; Polkinghorne, 2005). This postulation serves as the starting point for the discussion of limitations in this qualitative study on storied experiences during transition from military to civilian life amongst a limited number of snowball sampled participants.

The original design intended to begin to follow the participants with the first interview (Time 1) conducted at the onset of exit from full-time service. However, difficulties to assemble a sufficient sample in enough time to conduct a longitudinal study rendered this aspiration impossible, as has been described in greater detail in chapters 4. This is recognized as a limitation in regards to the original design but not a limitation in the light of the revised design. Nonetheless, the participants typically chose one of the three types of narrative evolutionary and centering models for the self-identity work during transition during the crucial period of two months to two years post exit. Additionally, as a consequence of the longer than first hoped time frame between exit and the first interview for some individuals, the study itself came to capture a longer and broader time and with this an image which displayed even more plasticity amid military transition to civilian life.

Especially considering the relatively unique qualitative and narrative focus of this study, it is acknowledged that other researchers may discover, apply, and/or construct other categories and themes through an analysis of this rich amount of longitudinal material, and how to sift through such massive data compilations could be perceived as a limitation in any qualitative study and in qualitative research in general. However, this quality can also be seen as a strength of qualitative research and this particular study; they are never finalized and fixed but instead allow for ever more meaningful analysis, nuance and enrichment, for new and/or deeper qualitative insights which flow from different analysis approaches. Through the lens of Polkinghorne's (1988) understanding of a meaningful analysis as a measure of validity, it is suggested that the results of analysis in chapter 5 (transitional experiences), chapter 6 (identity construction and reconstruction) and chapter 7 (existential and religious elements) were examples of meaningful analysis, among other potentially meaningful analyses, upon which theory was built.

It is a challenge to present longitudinal narrative accounts in a balanced yet relevant and succinct way in order to demonstrate thoroughly the results of the analysis while still promoting an interest to read the entire dissertation. As for transparency, it is hoped that the presentation of the research project and the inclusion of a balanced amount of narrative accounts (along with the possibility to read both the full narrative accounts and/or related articles derived from the research), have equipped the project, as well as the dissertation, with the degree of integrity and honesty which can only be upheld through transparency (Kvale & Brinkmann, 2009; Lincoln & Cuba, 1985; Mishler, 2004; Polkinghorne, 1988; Riessman, 1993). The trustworthiness of the data should not be a matter of theoretical argumentation due to analytical protocols, but rather presented via narrative analysis and the narrative accounts made by participants (Clandinin & Connelly, 2000; Crossley, 2000; Webster & Mertova, 2007). The heart of the dissertation, as was stated in the disposition within chapter 1, was embedded in the empirical chapters of storied lived experiences and laid bare through the narrative accounts. This transparency was additionally vital in order to render the dissertation potentially relevant for a wider military audience; the transparency serves as an invitation to such an audience to compare the participants' detail-rich storied accounts to their own experiences and processes during and after transition.

Another group of experiences which should be shared revolve around the character of the longitudinal design in regards to the nineteen participants. Unique insights were taken from the process of following military transition to civilian life via three annual interviews per participant, which ultimately stretched across Sweden and grew undeniably personal to at least some degree as one interacted repeatedly with similar individuals during a potentially vulnerable phase of life. It was time consuming and expensive to travel approximately 30 days around Sweden per year, and then a vast number of interviews needed to be transcribed. This is not perceived as a limitation but rather as an invitation for consideration and preparation for researchers interested in conducting longitudinal research.

As a conclusion, in the end of this PhD project, it is suggested that the following contributions have been attained throughout the project and by this dissertation:

- It helps to fill a specific void in the research on military transition to civilian life as it presents portraits of long term self-identity work with a specific emphasis on existential and religious dimensions.
- It presents a unique contextual longitudinal study of self-identity work among service members in transition.
- It provides the field of military research, which is primarily populated by voices from psychology, sociology, health care and medicine, with a practical theological voice.

- It offers existential and spiritual perspectives derived from service members in a pluralized and secularized context to those working with health care and spiritual care.
- It assisted the participants' self-identity work during transition.

Summary

Reconsidering the Uniform

Existential and religious identity reconstruction among Swedes after military service

Military cultures shape the narrative identities of service members which may resonate deeply within the individuals' selves. This implies that the transition from military to civilian life begins in an existing narrative definition of a person, from which the journey to new civilian presuppositions calls for a narrative re-definition or reconstruction of the story of who I am, a process which may be experienced as a challenge, perhaps even as a threat, by the self. A shift from military service to a civilian life equates to a transitional journey from one culture to another, from one identity to another, wherein the different cultural content likely shapes rather different narrative identities of the self. Relatively little research has been conducted on narrative identity reconstruction among voluntarily released service members, and a significant missing aspect is to sustain through a longer period of time this exploration of identity processes; there was a paucity of such temporally long investigations. Moreover, existential, spiritual or religious dimensions in the longitudinal identity reconstruction among service members in transition are rarely discussed in preceding research. Taken all together, these observations were the impetus for the design of an empirical, longitudinal and contextual research project on self-identity work. The focus and approach of the project were included within the body of practical theology which equated that the interpretation of the analysis was formulated in conversation with theological traditions and related areas of existential, spiritual, and religious research.

The overarching purpose of this study was to describe the role of existential and/or religious dimensions in identity reconstruction among Swedish military personnel during the process of becoming civilians. The formulated purpose called for a contextual, qualitative, empirical, and longitudinal focus with a narrative approach to lived life experiences among service members in transition. The research project adopted an annual interview design to cover the transitional processes among the participants, and the interviews were conducted from 2013 to 2016. The sample was derived by a snowball sampling method and consisted of nineteen Swedish service members in transition to a civilian life. They had numerous variations due to age, rank, branches, mission experiences and total years of service. The majority of the sample included service members aged between twenty-three to thirty-five years old. Four service members were around sixty years old, and thus their transition was actually the process of retirement.

There were no confessional requirements to participate in the study. The participants were initially organized into three groups, roughly equal in size, depending upon the amount of time which had elapsed between the exit and the first interview.

The central research question derived from the purpose of the project was: What is the role of existential and religious dimensions in identity reconstruction among Swedish military personnel in the process of becoming civilians?

The following subquestions outlined the analysis of the project:

- What are the experiences of Swedish military personnel in the process of becoming civilians?
- How is the identity constructed and reconstructed in the transition from a service member's to a civilian's narrative?
- What are the existential and/or religious elements in this process?

The analysis was conducted by utilizing a narrative approach within a Dialogical Self Theory framework, a pairing which demonstrated to be particularly useful in the enterprise of understanding experiences and identity processes in lived life. A transition implied a disruption of a story that created voids in a personal narrative into which new characters may progressively emerge and grow. Meanwhile preexisting characters continue to act. One of the basic premises of Dialogical Self Theory was that different I-positions produced different narratives. The narrative analysis was tailored to be an inductive inquiry, and the research design was built around the interview. This was approached as a qualitative inquiry process which addressed self-identity work in transitional movement wherein stories were compared across time. This meant that the longitudinal focus must be significant in order to describe the narrative identity reconstruction as an ongoing process. Such an analysis included content as well as process analysis of narrative accounts. The combination of a narrative and longitudinal approach was vital to capture the content and the evolution of each individual's identity reconstruction process throughout the transition from military to civilian life. The longitudinal approach, together with existential and religious dimensions in self-identity work, rendered this project a novel contribution to the field of research that addresses transition from military to civilian life.

The first subquestion on transitional experiences was considered as an inductive and individual content analysis which thereafter was developed into five overarching organizing themes as a result of the analysis. Within the five common themes, a number of transitional experiences were titled as issues or subthemes so as to organize the experiences within the overarching themes. The hermeneutical principle for the development of these themes was that the issues or subthemes could be understood in reference to the overarching theme and vice versa.

The five overarching transitional themes which organized the experiences were:

- Identity issues
- A pro-militaristic position in the self
- Emotional issues
- Satisfaction
- The importance of significant others

It unfolded throughout the study that the transitional experiences led the participants onto three narrative evolutionary paths: a full transition from military to civilian life (which eliminates a relationship with the Armed Forces), a hybrid outcome of a civilian/military path (which alongside the civilian life at some point sustains a more formal or informal relationship with the Armed Forces), or a full return to military service (which at some point aborts the civilian transition). In fact, thirteen participants eventually entered onto a military tailored path and followed that path as long as the study continued, while six followed a full transition from military to civilian life. The timeline in the sample suggests that the crucial time to select a path, in regards to transitional experiences, spanned between roughly two months to two years post exit. Participants who traversed upon the same path often varied strongly in terms of post exit time. Thereby it became more meaningful to organize the sample based upon the evolutionary paths of transition.

The second subquestion of how identity was constructed and reconstructed referred to how preexisting and new I-positions shaped the identity claims in the interview narratives during transition, and how these narrative claims changed their stories of who I am across time. It was assumed during the analysis that storied characters of the self (e.g., military, student, employee, and other civilian identities) held corresponding I-positions in the self, which was driven to reorganization amid transition. The results of the analysis were presented as representative processual cases belonging to one of the three paths: a full transition from military to civilian life, a hybrid outcome, or a full return to military service. The three paths gave a specific type of storied evolution among the participants, and below are three tables which summarize the content of the self-identity work within the three paths as expressed throughout the interviews and finalized during the third and final interview cycle (Time 3) by the participants.

A full transition from military to civilian life

Overarching themes	The content of identity reconstruction (Time 3)
Identities	• A reversed asymmetry between military/veteran identities and new civilian identities wherein the new civilian identities become more influential; a salient tendency is that new civilian characters tend to be constructed with counter features in relation to the military characters • A clear sense of a military "me" persists, but without particular adjustment problems • A richly developed reconstruction of a new meaningful story of who I am as a civilian wherein several civilian I-positions/characters appear to cooperate in pursuit of shared desires • A withdrawal from military community and camaraderie in favor of a salient relational positioning to civilian friends and life
A pro-militaristic position	• Pride of having served and positive emotions attach to it
Emotional issues	• Wholly ameliorated or at least not demonstrated
Satisfaction	• Embracement of a new way of life and identities
Significant others	• Preexisting and new civilian promoters are significant for the processes of reconstructing identities and lives

A hybrid outcome

Overarching themes	The content of identity maintenance and reconstruction (Time 3)
Identities	• Co-existence of military/veteran identities and new civilian identities, where military/veteran identities may maintain an influential position in the self, and where the perception from time to time may be filtered through a military/veteran lens; the new civilian characters tend to be tailored with different features than the military ones but not be as salient as in a linear path to civilian life; from time to time tension may exist between military and civilian I-positions • A clear sense of a military "me" but without particular adjustment problems • A growing reconstruction of a new meaningful story of who I am as a civilian wherein several civilian I-positions appear to cooperate in shared desires • A decline in regards to military community and camaraderie in favor for relational positioning to civilian friends and life
A pro-militaristic position	• Pride of having served and positive emotions attach to it • Reenlistment to part-time service
Emotional issues	• Grew less painful, even wholly ameliorated or at least were not demonstrated
Satisfaction	• Embracing both military and civilian life to varying degrees
Significant others	• Civilian promoter positions assist the transition to a civilian life while military others and battle buddies have significance for the maintenance of service and military identities

Overarching themes	The content of military identity renewal (Time 3)
Identities	• A distinct asymmetry between military/veteran identities and new civilian identities, where military/veteran identities maintain a dominant position in the self, and where the perception is filtered through a military/veteran lens • A clear sense of a military "me", and in some cases relatively minor adjustment problems in civilian life • Distinct difficulties to find meaning and/or motivation in a new civilian life, which implies difficulties of reconstructing the story of who I am within a civilian realm • Reunion with the extraordinary community and camaraderie • Dichotomy between military and civilian worlds/relationships
A pro-militaristic position	• Pride of having served and positive emotions attach to it • Reenlistment to full-time service
Emotional issues	• Grew less painful, even wholly ameliorated or in the least undemonstrated
Satisfaction	• Embracement of the return to a military way of life and identity
Significant others	• Military others and battle buddies have been significant for the return, while the lack of civilian promoter positions hindered the transition to a civilian life

It was also suggested in the interpretation of this analysis that the embodied ideology of military service among many of the participants included subordination to a higher purpose, which demonstrated to equate potential sacrifices and a commitment to a community of battle buddies who shared and lived by such standards. The values, beliefs, commitment to local community and battle buddies were considered as implicit religious. It was also proposed that for some participants this served as a type of lived and implicit religion which provided them with a higher purpose of life, sacrifices, meaning, and satisfaction, and participants described this meaning as difficult to find demonstrated in other contexts.

The exploration of the third a final subquestion on existential and religious elements or themes in the process opted for an inductive approach to articulated questions of life in the self-identity work. Existential elements referred to storied experiences with relevance for the questions of life in the transitional process. The method was to ask explicit life questions which explored the lived life of the participants in the present process of transition, but also reflections upon personal stories within the interview narratives which had major (past) or may have significant (future) impact on the participant's life. *Existential elements* was used as an open code with the potential to address and inductively organize such storied experiences in the self-identity work. The result of the analysis included six common existential elements or themes across the sample with relevance for the self-identity processes, as presented below:

- Identities
- Meaningful employment and/or life styles
- Significant others

211

- Beliefs and values

- Sacrifices imposed upon significant others and/or the self

- Temporary departure from society to instead envelope one's self in the natural world

The concept of religious elements or themes was chosen within this dissertation to refer to narrated experiences of relevance for the participants' questions of life which were connected to some type of belief in or experience of God and angels, i.e. transcendent or higher powers, and/or spiritual emotions such as uplift, awe, humility, mystery, gratitude, joy, peace, and serenity. The method was to ask questions in regards to the beliefs and experiences, but also considered personal stories within the interview narratives which have had or may have religious/spiritual influence on a participant's life. *Religious elements* was used as an open code with the potential to address and inductively organize storied experiences with relevance for the questions of life which narrated explicit religious elements. Again, there were no confessional requirements to participate in the study, yet with time five participants described themselves, under their own ambitions, as believing in God or angels or having experienced a religious/spiritual dimension in the Swedish nature or in church during musical events.

In addition to the empirical inquiry of the process an evaluation letter was given to each participant when the third interview was concluded. This was not part of the original research project proposal but was considered as an interesting addition to the design since several participants had articulated positive effects throughout the interviewing. It was concluded from these evaluation letters that the interview cycles in general assisted the participants to reflect upon their self-identity process, and that this reflection has subsequently provided some of them with an increased self-understanding and awareness about military identities and other identities in regards to the temporal and spatial (within self) dimensions in transition to civilian lives or return to (different forms of) military service.

In the final part of this dissertation, a theological theory on transition from military to civilian life is constructed using the empirical results of the analysis in the previous chapters as a foundation. This theological theory is existentially and spiritually oriented and integrated with a narrative and dialogical framework. This theory provides the research field on transition from military to civilian life with an alternate voice which presents a tentative and contextual, existential and spiritual theological proposal of such a journey, a journey of transition that can benefit from correlational and critical dimensions located in time and space. This theological theory on transition from military to civilian life suggests that the calling to friendship decreases the impact of a potential shared and collectivistic military spiritual depth, invites new potential sources of spiritual depths linked to old and/or new identities, dissolves feelings of estrangement, and supports the cooperative spirit within the self, which taken altogether may advance the self-identity work during a transition. The calling to friendship implies dialogue and openness to the other, someone or something which was previously perceived as more unlike the self, as well as a collaborative and curious approach towards the self.

The conclusion of this dissertation suggests that three types of narrative evolutionary and centering models for the self-identity work during transition have been displayed in regards to this Swedish context and sample. For the majority of the participants in this study, the self-identity work in transition implied existential reflections upon questions of life such as who am I, who will I become, where is my place in the world, and where am I going. It is also suggested that beliefs and values were one distinct divergence point in regards to the selection of civilian or military tailored paths, and thus the storied evolution of the selves, in response to these existential issues. From an existential perspective it could be suggested that a transitional evolution, no matter where it may lead a participant, has entered a more stable phase when the evolution of stories and characters has been shaped in dialogue with meaningful answers to the existential questions of life such as who I am, where am I going, and where is my place in the world. From a theological outlook it is suggested that a firmer footing is given to such a phase if it rests upon the existence of spiritual depth(s) of life, which is/are linked to identities of the self and brought into dialogue by the self. This theological point of view suggests that spiritual depth(s) appear(s) to provide stability in the self-identity work, a proposal which also works in the service of a military spiritual depth and military identities.

The theological theory presented in this dissertation, in combination with the unexpected extensiveness of the impact of the interviews, and even the participants' anticipations of and reflections over the interviews, upon the participants' self-identity work have relevance for the arena of spiritual care and reflection in order to help build spiritual fitness among service members as a preparation for a forthcoming transition. In resonance with voices and perspectives which emphasize the spiritual components in service members' self-identity work, this dissertation proposes a method for further elaboration within a Swedish context: building spiritual fitness through narrative self-reflection.

APPENDIX I

I am searching for officers and private soldiers who are on the verge of leaving (or who have recently left) their professional careers in the Armed Forces in order to initiate civilian lives or careers and who are interested in sharing their experiences with me in my research project. Research regarding veteran military personnel in Sweden is in need of expansion and amplification and your experiences are vastly important in order to increase the understanding of the situations of soldiers and officers upon demobilization.

By interviewing 30 officers and soldiers, I intend to explore *meaning and military identity* and how these are affected upon conclusion of a military career in the Armed Forces.

What a person perceives as meaningful is something highly subjective and might be anything that you think gives (or has given) your life meaning and direction. It might, for example, be colleagues, battle buddies, your group, unity, camaraderie, freedom, challenges, excitement, values, routines, structure, contributions for the benefit of others, testing of abilities in real-life situations, religion, faith, family, interests and so on. There might, on the other hand, also be a perceived lack or loss of meaning in life or an experience of cogitating, loneliness, guilt, consequences of ones decisions, grief, or anxiety.

In order to examine experiences of *meaning*, or the lack thereof, and *military identity* before, during and after demobilization, I would like to conduct three interviews over a period of three years. The first of these interviews will take place upon demobilization/when you leave your employment in the Armed Forces, the next interview one year later and the final interview one year after the second. Such long-term follow-up with military personnel has never before been conducted in Sweden or Europe.

The interviews will each last approximately between 45 minutes and one hour. As a participant, you are guaranteed complete anonymity, and all interviews will be anonymized and stored safely. No details that may reveal your identity will be published. When and where the first interview will take place is for you to decide. Travel expenses will not be covered.

The project is classified as ongoing veteran research at the Veterans Affairs, Swedish Armed Force's Headquarters (reference Monica Larsson). *By sharing your experiences*, you will make a valuable contribution to Swedish and international veteran research.

The project is located at the Faculty of Theology at Vrije Universiteit (VU) in Amsterdam. The subject area in which I conduct this study is practical theology, and the project will result in a doctoral thesis.

If you wish to participate in this project, please fill in the enclosed application form (or contact me by e-mail) and send it through the enclosed envelope as soon as possible. I will then contact you.

If you have any questions, please do not hesitate to ask!

Best regards,

Jan Grimell

PhD-Candidate in Practical Theology, Vrije Universiteit (VU)

Former tactical officer Norbottens Regemente, I19

070-5934866

jan_grimell@hotmail.com

References

First supervisor

Professor R. Ruard Ganzevoort

Professor of Practical Theology

Vrije Universiteit Amsterdam

T+31-30-2758503

F+31-30-2758501

M+31-6-23080850

r.r.ganzevoort@vu.nl

Second supervisor

Associate Professor Thomas Girmalm

Religious Studies and Theology

Umeå University

T+46(0)90-7867821

thomas.girmalm@umu.se

Headquarters

Monica Larsson, Research coordinator

Veterans Affairs

monica.s.larsson@mil.se

Fill in, cut off and send in the envelope!

Enclosed application form

Name	
Age	
Regiment / Battalion	
Company / Platoon	
Rank	
Position(s)	
Years of service	
What made you decide to	

leave full-time service (you don't have to answer if you don't want to)	
Your suggestion for a time/place to conduct the first interview	
Phone	
Email	

APPENDIX II

Informed Consent Agreement (translated from Swedish)

I confirm that I am informed about the research project *Existential and religious dimensions in identity reconstruction among Swedish military personnel during the process of becoming civilians*. I confirm that I have knowledge of my rights as an informant and of the research ethics applicable to the project (anonymity, storage of data, publishing, etc.). I participate freely and with informed consent in this research project.

Name _____

APPENDIX III

(A) Questions to grasp the central military story line

- If you think for a while, in what way would you describe your life as a soldier or an officer?
- Are there any memories that are especially important and vivid for you which you would like to share?
- Are there any events that are especially important and vivid for you which you would like to share?
- Are there any experiences that are especially important and vivid for you which you would like to share?
- What made you decide to leave the life as a soldier or an officer?
- What emotions do you carry with you now as you are leaving the life as a soldier or an officer?

(B) Questions to grasp relationships

- If you reflect a while over your relationships, what persons are important for you?
- If you think a while, are there any events that are important for you and your friends?

(C) Question to outline narrative identity

- If you reflect a while, do you find a situation or a pattern in a variety of situations which may describe you as a person or bring clarity of who you are?
- In what way does this situation or pattern over a variety of situations describe you?

(D) Questions to grasp existential concerns

- Can you reflect on a situation where you experienced significant life questions and maybe tell me that story?
- What is important for you in life?
- What gives you direction in life?

- What do you believe in? (Added in the third interview cycle)

APPENDIX IV

Evaluation Letter (translated from Swedish)

To begin with, I would like to thank you for participating in the study *Existential and religious dimensions in identity reconstruction among Swedish military personnel during the process of becoming civilians.* Your participation is highly valuable and will help fill a gap in the research, especially in a Swedish context, regarding military identities, new identities and different types of meaning in the transition to a civilian life. Hopefully, this thesis will contribute to an increased understanding of (Swedish) military personnel conducting this transition, and thereby your experiences from such a process will support and facilitate similar processes for future military personnel as they leave their employment.

In order to complete this study in such a way so as your experiences of participation might strengthen the project, I hope that you have the possibility to answer the four questions below and return this data in the enclosed envelope.

(1) What experiences have you gathered by participating in a three year study, with repeated interviews focusing on your military narrative (identity), meaning and that which you experienced during the transition throughout the study period?

(2) How have you experienced the interview questions (some of them have been recurrent and others spontaneously asked, depending on what has been said during the interviews)?

(3) In what way have the interviews affected you in this process?

(4) Is there anything you would like to point out in order for me to develop my skills, way of communicating, or other aspects of the ways in which I have interacted with you?

When the thesis is completed, I will send you a copy. Please, fill in your address below (if you would like a copy). If you have any questions, don't hesitate to contact me.

Once again, thank you for participating in this study!
Jan Grimell
PhD-Candidate
Phone 070-5934866
Email: j.m.grimell@vu.nl or jan_grimell@hotmail.com

221

BIBLIOGRAPHY

Abrahamson, B. (2011). *Kärnvärden och den militära framgångsformeln: Huset som Clausewitz byggde* [Core values and the military recipe for success: The house that Clausewitz built] (Report from the Swedish Defense University). Försvarshögskolan, Stockholm, Sweden.

Adler, A. B., Britt, T. W., Castro, C. A., McGurk, D., & Bliese, P. D. (2011). Effect of transition home from combat on risk-taking and health-related behaviors. *Journal of Traumatic Stress*, 24(4), 381–389.

Adler, A. B., Zamorski, M., & Britt, T. W. (2011). The psychology of transition: Adapting to home after deployment. In A. B. Adler, P. B. Bliese, & C. A. Castro (Eds.), *Deployment psychology: Evidence-based strategies to promote mental health in the military* (pp. 153–174). Washington, DC: American Psychological Association.

Adler, A. B., Bliese, P. D., & Castro, C. A. (Eds.). (2011). *Deployment psychology: Evidence-based strategies to promote mental health in the military.* Washington, DC: American Psychology Association.

af Burén, A. (2015). *Living simultaneity: On religion among semi-secular Swedes* (Doctoral dissertation, Södertörn University, Stockholm, Sweden). Retrieved from https://www.diva-portal.org/smash/get/diva2:800530/FULLTEXT01.pdf

Ahmadi, F. (2006). *Culture, religion, and spirituality in coping: The example of cancer patients in Sweden.* Uppsala, Sweden: Uppsala University.

Ahmadi, F. (2015). *Coping with cancer in Sweden: A search for meaning.* Uppsala, Sweden: Acta Universitatis Upsaliensis.

Ahmadi, F., & Ahmadi, N. (2015). Nature as the most important coping strategy among cancer patients: A Swedish survey. *Journal of Religion and Health*, 54, 1177–1190.

Agrell, W. (2013). *Ett krig här och nu: Sveriges väg till väpnad konflikt i Afghanistan* [A war here and now: Sweden's path to armed conflict in Afghanistan]. Stockholm: Bokförlaget Atlantis AB.

Alcorn, M. (2008). Psychoanalysis and narrative. In D. Herman, M. Jahn, & M-L. Ryan (Eds.), *Routledge encyclopedia of narrative theory* (pp. 469-470). New York: Routledge.

Alvesson, M., & Billing, Y. D. (1997). *Understanding gender and organizations.* London: Sage Publications.

222

American Psychiatric Association. (2013). *Diagnostic and statistical manual of mental disorders* (5th ed.). Retrieved from https://psicovalero.files.wordpress.com/2014/06/dsm-v-manual-diagnc3b3stico-y-estadc3adstico-de-los-trastornos-mentales.pdf

Andreassen, B., & Ingalls, C. E. (2009). Genderperspektivet og norsk militær profesjonsidentitet [The gender perspective and the Norwegian military professional identity]. In E. Edström, N. T. Lunde, & J. Haaland Matlary (Eds.), *Krigerkultur i en fredsnasjon* [Warrior culture in a peace nation] (pp. 239-276). Oslo, Norge: Abstrakt Förlag.

Arnett, J. (2002). The psychology of globalization. *American Psychologist, 57*, 774-783.

Astley, J. (2002). *Ordinary theology: Looking, listening and learning in theology.* Farnham, England: Ashgate Publishing Limited.

Badaró, M. (2015). "One of the Guys": Military women, paradoxical individuality, and the transformations of the Argentine Army. *American Anthropologist, 117*(1), 86-99.

Bailey, E. (1990). The implicit religion of contemporary society: Some studies and reflections. *Social Compass, 37*(4), 483-497.

Bailey, E. (1997). *Implicit religion in contemporary society.* Kampen: Kok Pharos.

Bakhtin, M. (1973). *Problems of Dostoevsky's poetics.* Ann Arbor, MI: Ardis.

Baumann, G., & Gingrich, A. (Eds.). (2006). *Grammars of identity/alterity: A structural approach.* New York: Berghahn Books.

Beder, J. (Ed.). (2012). Those who have served in Afghanistan/Iraq. In J. Beder (Ed.), *Advances in social work practice with the military* (pp. 137-147). New York: Routledge, Taylor & Francis Group.

Bélanger, S. A. H., & Moore, M. (2013). Public opinion and soldier identity: Tensions and resolutions. In A. B. Aiken, & S. A. H. Bélanger (Eds.), *Beyond the line: Military and veteran health research* (pp. 103-120). Montreal and Kingston: McGill-Queen's University Press.

Bell, S. E. (1988). Becoming a political women: The reconstruction and interpretation of experience through stories. In A. D. Todd, & S. Fisher (Eds.), *Gender and discourse: The power of talk* (pp. 97-123). Norwood; NJ: Ablex.

Bell, M. E., & Reardon, A. (2012). Working with survivors of sexual harassment and sexual assault in the military. In J. Beder (Ed.), *Advances in social work practice with the military* (pp. 72-91). New York: Routledge.

Ben-Ari, E. (1998). *Mastering soldiers: Conflict, emotions, and the enemy in an Israeli military unit.* New York: Berghahn Books.

Birren, J. E., & Cochran, K. N. (2001). *Telling the stories of life through guided autobiography groups*. New York: John Hopkins University Press.

Blackburn, D. (2016a). Transitioning from military to civilian life: Examining the final step in a military career. *Canadian Military Journal*, 16(4), 53-61.

Blackburn, D. (2016b). Affectations obligatoires: s'inspirer de nos alliés pour innover et prévenir des problèmes psychosociaux [Mandatory posting within Canadian Armed Forces: Be inspired by our allies to innovate and to prevent psychosocial problems]. *Journal d'actualités militaires 45eNord.ca*. Retrieved from http://www.45enord.ca/2016/10/affectations-obligatoires-sinspirer-de-nos-allies-pour-innover-et-prevenir-des-problemes-psychosociaux/

Blackburn, D. (2017). Out of uniform: psychosocial issues experienced and coping mechanisms used by Veterans during the military–civilian transition. *Journal of Military, Veteran and Family Health*, 00(00), 1-8. Retrieved from http://jmvfh.utpjournals.press/doi/pdf/10.3138/jmvfh.4160

Bobrow, J., Cook, E., Knowles, C., & Vieten, C. (2013). Coming all the way home: Integrative community care for those who serve. *Psychological Services*, 10(2), 137–144.

Bonhoeffer, D. (1959). *The cost of discipleship*. New York: MacMillan.

Boose, L. E. (1993). Techno-muscularity and the "boy eternal": From the Quagmire to the Gulf. In M. G. Cooke, & A. Woollacott (Eds.), *Gendering war talk* (pp. 67-106). New Jersey: Princeton University Press.

Bragin, M. (2010). Can anyone here know who I am? Co-constructing meaningful narratives with combat veterans. *Clinical Social Work Journal*, 38(3), 316-326.

Bregman, L. (2006). Spirituality: A glowing and useful term in search of meaning. *Omega: Journal of Death and Dying*, 53(1-2), 5-26.

Bruner, J. (1986). *Actual minds, possible worlds*. Cambridge, MA: Harvard University Press.

Brunger, H., Serrato, J., & Ogden, J. (2013). "No man's land": the transition to civilian life. *Journal of Aggression, Conflict and Peace Research*, 5(2), 86-100.

Bryan, C. J. (2015). Adjusting our aim: Next steps in military and veteran suicide prevention. *Spirituality in Clinical Practice*, 2(1), 84–85.

Bryan, C. J., & Morrow, C. E. (2011). Circumventing mental health stigma by embracing the warrior culture: Lessons learned from the defender's edge program. *Professional Psychology, Research and Practice*, 42(1), 16-23.

Bryan, C. J., Graham, E., & Roberge, E. (2015). Living a life worth living: Spirituality and suicide risk in military personnel. *Spirituality in Clinical Practice*, 2(1), 74–78.

Buber, M. (1970). *I and thou: A new translation with a prologue "I and You" and notes by Walter Kaufmann*. Edinburgh: T. & T. Clark.

Buell, S. D. (2010). *Life is a cruise: What does it mean to be a retired naval officer transitioning into civilian world?* (Doctoral dissertation, University of St. Thomas, Minnesota, United States of America).

Buitelaar, M. (2014). Dialogical constructions of a Muslim self through life story telling. In R. R. Ganzevoort, M. de Haardt, & M. Scherer-Rath (Eds.), *Religious stories we live by: Narrative approaches in theology and religious studies* (pp. 143-167). Leiden, Netherlands: Brill.

Burkhart, L., & Hogan, N. (2015). Being a female veteran: A grounded theory of coping with transitions. *Social Work in Mental Health*, 13(2), 108-127.

Brock, R. N., & Lettini, G. (2012). *Soul repair: Recovering from moral injury after war*. Boston, MA: Beacon Press.

Brotz, H., & Wilson, E. (1946). Characteristics of military society. *The American Journal of Sociology*, 51(5), 371-375.

Bruner, J. (1990). *Acts of meaning*. Cambridge, MA: Harvard University Press.

Castro, C. A., & Kintzle, S. (2014). Suicides in the military: The post-modern combat veteran and the Hemingway effect. *Current Psychiatry Reports*, 16(460), 1-9.

Cavanaugh, W. T. (2007). Consumer culture. In D. M. McCarthy, & M. T. Lysaught (Eds.), *Gathered for the journey: Moral theology in Catholic perspective* (pp. 241-259). Grand Rapids, MI: William B. Eerdmans Publishing Company.

Clandinin, J. D. (2013). *Engaging in narrative inquiry*. Walnut Creek, CA: Left Coast Press, Inc.

Clandinin, J. D., & Connelly, M. F. (2000). *Narrative inquiry: Experience and story in qualitative research*. San Francisco: A Wiley Imprint.

Clandinin, J. D., & Rosiek, J. (2007). Mapping a landscape of narrative inquiry: Borderland spaces and tensions. In J. D. Clandinin (Ed.), *Handbook of narrative inquiry: Mapping a methodology* (pp. 35-76). Thousand Oaks, CA: Sage Publications.

Coll, J. E., Weiss, E. L., & Yarvis, J. S. (2012). No one leaves unchanged - Insights for civilian mental health care: Professionals into the military experience and culture. In J. Beder (Ed.), *Advances in social work practice with the military* (pp. 18-33). New York: Routledge, Taylor & Francis Group.

Connelly, F. M., & Clandinin, J. D. (2006). Narrative inquiry. In J. Green, G. Camilli, & P. Elmore (Eds.), *Handbook of complementary methods in education research* (3rd ed., pp. 477-487). Mahwah, NJ: Lawrence Erlbaum.

Crites, S. (1986). Storytime: Recollecting the past and projecting the future. In T. R. Sarbin (Ed.), *Narrative psychology: The storied nature of human conduct* (pp. 152-173). Westport, CT: Praeger.

Crossley, M. L. (2000). *Introducing narrative psychology: Self, trauma and the construction of meaning*. Philadelphia: Open University Press.

Crotty, M. (1998). *The foundations of social research: Meaning and perspective in the research process*. Thousand Oaks, CA: Sage.

Currier, J. M., Kuhlman, S., & Smith, P. N. (2015). Empirical and ethical considerations for addressing spirituality among veterans and other military populations at risk for suicide. *Spirituality in Clinical Practice*, 2(1), 68–73.

Day, J. M., & Jesus, P. (2013). Epistemic subjects, discursive selves, and dialogical self theory in the psychology of moral and religious development: Mapping gaps and bridges. *Journal of Constructivist Psychology*, 26(2), 137-148.

Devries, M. R., Hughes, K. H., Watson, H., & Moore, B. A. (2012). Understanding the military culture. In B. A. Moore (Ed.), *Handbook of counseling military couples* (pp. 7-18). New York: Routledge, Taylor and Francis Group.

Dickstein, B.D., Vogt, D.S., Handa, S., & Litz, B.T. (2010). Targeting self-stigma in returning military personnel and veterans: A review of intervention strategies. *Military Psychology*, 22, 224-236.

Dimaggio, G., Salvatore, G., Azzara, C., & Catania, D. (2003). Rewriting self-narratives: The therapeutic process. *Journal of Constructivist Psychology*, 16(2), 155-181.

Drescher, K. D., Nieuwsma, J. A., & Swales, P. J. (2013). Morality and moral injury: Insights from theology and health science. *Reflective Practice: Formation and Supervision in Ministry*, 33, 50-61.

Drops, G. J. (1979). *Change in self-concept and identity during a time of mid-life transition* (Doctoral dissertation, the Union for Experimenting Colleges and Universities, Union Graduate School West, San Diego, United States of America).

Edström, E., Lunde, N. T., & Haaland Matlary, J. (Eds.). (2009). På jakt etter den militære profesjon [In the search of the military profession]. In E. Edström, N. T. Lunde, & J. Haaland Matlary (Eds.), *Krigerkultur i en fredsnasjon* [Warrior culture in a peace nation] (pp. 17-47). Oslo, Norge: Abstrakt Förlag.

Elliott, M., Gonzalez, C., & Larsen, B. (2011). U.S. military veterans transition to college: Combat, PTSD, and alienation on campus. *Journal of Student Affairs Research and Practice*, 48, 279–296.

Ellens, J. H. (2008). *Understanding religious experiences: What the bible says about spirituality*. Westport, Connecticut, London: Praeger.

Ellens, J. H. (2011). *Light from the other side: The paranormal as friend and familiar (real life experiences of a spiritual pilgrim)*. Eugene, Oregon: Resource publications.

Elshtain, J. B. (1995). *Women and war*. Chicago: The University of Chicago Press

English, A., & Dale-McGrath, S. (2013). Overcoming systematic obstacles to veteran transition to civilian life. In A. B. Aiken, & S. A. H. Bélanger (Eds.), *Beyond the line: Military and veteran health research* (pp. 249-264). Montreal and Kingston: McGill-Queen's University Press.

Estrada, A. X., & Berggren, A. W. (2009). Sexual harassment and its impact for women officers and cadets in the Swedish Armed Forces. *Military Psychology*, 21(2), 162-185.

Flick, U. (2002). *An Introduction to Qualitative Research* (2nd ed.). London: Sage Publications.

Fowl, S. E., & Jones, L. G. (1998). *Reading in communion*. Eugene, OR: Wipf and Stock Publishers.

Frankl. V. (2006). *Man's search for meaning*. Boston, MA: Beacon Press.

Franks, T. (2004). *American soldier: General Tommy Franks*. New York: ReganBooks.

French, S. E. (2005). *The code of the warrior: Exploring warrior values past and present*. Maryland: Rowman & Littlefield Publishers.

Fromm, E. (1947). *Escape from freedom*. New York: Rinehart.

Försvarsmakten. (2014). Personalredovisning för Försvarsmakten efter genomförd planering [Personnel accounting of the Armed Force post conducted planning]. FM2013-546:13. Retrieved from http://www.forsvarsmakten.se/sv/aktuellt/2014/05/forsvarsmaktens-forslag-pa-ny-organisation/

Försvarsmakten. (2017). Vem är veteran? [Who is a veteran?]. Retrieved from http://www.forsvarsmakten.se/sv/anhoriga-och-veteraner/for-veteraner/

Ganzevoort, R. R. (1993). Investigating life-stories: Personal narrative in pastoral psychology. *Journal of Psychology and Theology*, 21(4), 277-287.

Ganzevoort, R. R. (1994). Crisis experiences and the development of belief and unbelief. In D. Hutsebaut, & J. Corveleyn (Eds.), *Belief and unbelief: Psychological perspectives* (pp. 21-36). Amsterdam: Rodopi.

Ganzevoort, R. R. (1998). Reading by the lines: Proposal for a narrative analytical technique in empirical theology. *Journal of Empirical Theology*, 11(2), 23-40.

Ganzevoort, R. R. (2008). Scars and stigmata: Trauma, identity and theology. *Practical Theology*, 1(1), 19-31.

Ganzevoort, R. R. (2009, August 3). *Forks in the road when tracing the sacred: Practical theology as hermeneutics of lived religion.* Paper presented at the International Academy of Practical Theology, Chicago. Retrieved from https://www.researchgate.net/publication/238070309_Forks_in_the_Road_when_Tracing_the_Sacred_Practical_Theology_as_Hermeneutics_of_Lived_Religion

Ganzevoort, R. R. (2011a). Narrative approaches. In B. Miller-McLemore (Ed.), *The Wiley-Blackwell companion to practical theology* (pp. 214-223). Chichester: Wiley-Blackwell.

Ganzevoort, R. R. (2011b). Framing the gods: The public significance of religion from a cultural point of view. In L. J. Francis, & H.-G. Ziebertz (Eds.), *The public significance of religion* (pp.95-120). Leiden: Brill.

Ganzevoort, R. R. (2014). Introduction: Religious stories we live by. In R. R. Ganzevoort, M. de Haardt, & M. Scherer-Rath (Eds.), *Religious stories we live by: Narrative approaches in theology and religious studies* (pp. 169-180). Leiden, Netherlands: Brill.

Ganzevoort, R. R., & Bouwer, J. (2007). Life story methods and care for elderly. An empirical research project in practical theology. In H-G. Ziebertz, & F. Schweitzer (Eds.), *Dreaming the land: Theologies of resistance and hope* (pp. 140-151). Münster: LIT.

Ganzevoort, R. R., & Roeland, J. H. (2014). Lived religion. The praxis of practical theology. *International Journal of Practical Theology*, 18(1), 91-101.

Gergen, K. J., & Gergen, M. M. (1986). Narrative form and the construction of psychological science. In T. R. Sarbin (Ed.), *Narrative psychology: The storied nature of human conduct* (pp. 22-44). Westport, CT: Praeger.

Goldstein, J. S. (2001). *War and gender: How gender shapes the war system and vice versa.* Cambridge, UK: Cambridge University Press.

Gonçalves, M. M., & Ribeiro, A. P. (2012). Narrative processes of innovation and stability within the dialogical self. In H. J. M. Hermans, & T. Gieser (Eds), *Handbook of dialogical self theory* (pp. 301-318). New York: Cambridge University Press.

Gorman, G. E., & Clayton, P. (2005). *Qualitative research for the information professional: A practical handbook* (2nd ed.). London: Facet Publishing.

Gregg, G. S. (2005). *The Middle East: A cultural psychology (series in culture, cognition, and behavior).* New York: Oxford University Press.

Grimell, J. (2015). A transitional narrative of military identity: Eric's story. *International Journal for Dialogical Science*, 9(1), 135-157.

Grimell, J. (2016a). The story of the self in the aftermath of crisis: A case study. *Journal of Constructivist Psychology*, 29(1), 66-79.

Grimell, J. (2016b). Existential spiritual life among Swedish service members in transition: Marking out trends. *Spirituality in Clinical Practice*, 3(3), 208-219.

Grimell, J. (2017a). A service member's self in transition: A longitudinal case study analysis. *Journal of Constructivist Psychology*, 30(3), 255-269.

Grimell, J. (2017b). Advancing an understanding of selves in transition: I-positions as an analytical tool. *Culture & Psychology*, 0(0), 1-22.

Grimell, J. (2017c). Reflections on spiritual themes in a narrative psychological investigation of a secular Swede: Practical theology's potential contributions. *Practical Theology*, 10(1), 88-100.

Grimell, J. (2017d). Embodiment of the spirit: A case study. *Spiritual Psychology and Counseling*, 2(1), 57-72.

Grimell, J. (2017e). Self-reorganization in transition from military to civilian life: Maria's way. *Mental Health in Family Medicine, 13, 544-553.*

Grimell, J. (2017f). Making dialogue with an existential voice in transition from military to civilian life. *Theory & Psychology*, 00(0), 1-19.

Haaland, T. L. (2009). Den norske militaere profesionsidentiteten; Kriger, hjemlandsforsvarer og statsansatt tjenstemann [The Norwegian military professional identity: Warriors, homeland defenders and governmental employees]. In E. Edström, N. T. Lunde, & J. Haaland Matlary (Eds.), *Krigerkultur i en fredsnasjon* [Warrior culture in a peace nation] (pp. 48-71). Olso, Norge: Abstrakt Förlag.

Haaland, T. L. (2011). A Norwegian expeditionary mindset? In H. Fürst, & G. Kümmel (Eds.), *Core values and the expeditionary mindset: Armed forces in metamorphosis* (pp. 165-177). Baden-Baden, Germany: Nomos Verlagsgesellschaft.

Hall, L. K. (2012a). The importance of understanding military culture. In J. Beder (Ed.), *Advances in social work practice with the military* (pp. 3-17). New York: Routledge, Taylor & Francis Group.

Hall, L. K. (2012b). The military lifestyle and the relationship. In B. A. Moore (Ed.), *Handbook of counseling military couples* (pp. 137-156). New York: Routledge, Taylor and Francis Group.

Hamilton, M. (2001). Implicit religion and related concepts: Seeking precision. *Implicit Religion*, 4(1), 1-7.

Hauerwas, S. (2001 [1984]). Should war be eliminated? A thought experiment (1984). In J. Berkman, & M. Cartwright (Eds.), *The Hauerwas reader* (pp. 392-425). Durham, NC: Duke University Press.

Haynie, J. M., & Shepherd, D. (2011). Toward a theory of discontinuous career transition; Investigating career transitions necessitated by traumatic life events. *Journal of Applied Psychology*, 96(3), 501-524.

Heelas, P. (2008). *Spiritualties of life: New age romanticism and consumptive capitalism.* Malden, MA: Blackwell Publishing.

Herlitz, G. (1995). *Swedes: What we are like and why we are as we are.* Uppsala, Sweden: Uppsala Publishing House AB.

Hermans, H. J. M. (1996a). Opposites in a dialogical self: Constructs as characters. *Journal of Constructivist Psychology*, 9, 1-16.

Hermans, H. J. M. (1996b). Voicing the self: From information processing to dialogical interchange. *Psychological Bulletin*, 119(1), 31-50.

Hermans, H. J. M. (1997). Dissociation as disorganized self-narrative: Tension between splitting and integration. *Journal of Psychotherapy Integration*, 7(3), 213-223.

Hermans, H. J. M. (1999). Dialogical thinking and self-innovation. *Culture and Psychology*, 5(1), 67-87.

Hermans, H. J. M. (2001a). The dialogical self: Toward a theory of personal and cultural positioning. *Culture & Psychology*, 7(3), 243-281.

Hermans, H. J. M. (2001b). The construction of a personal position repertoire: Method and practice. *Culture and Psychology*, 7(3), 323-365.

Hermans, H. J. M. (2002). The dialogical self as a society of mind: Introduction. *Theory & Psychology*, 12(2), 147-160.

Hermans, H. J. M. (2003). The construction and reconstruction of a dialogical self. *Journal of Constructivist Psychology*, 16, 89-130.

Hermans, H. J. M. (2004). Introduction: The dialogical self in a global and digital age. *Identity: An international Journal of Theory and Research*, 4, 297-320.

Hermans, H. J. M. (2008). How to perform research on the basis of dialogical self theory? Introduction to the special issue. *Journal of Constructivist Psychology*, 21, 185-199.

Hermans, H. J. M. (2012a). *Applications of dialogical self theory: New directions for child and adolescent development.* Jossey-Bass, San Francisco: Wiley Periodicals, Inc.

Hermans, H. J. M. (2012b). *Between dreaming and recognition seeking: The emergence of dialogical self theory*. Lanham, Maryland: University Press of America, Inc.

Hermans, H. J. M. (2013). The dialogical self in education: Introduction. *Journal of Constructivist Psychology*, 26(2), 81-89.

Hermans, H. J. M., Kempen, H. J. G., & van Loon, R. J. P. (1992). The dialogical self: beyond individualism and rationalism. *American Psychologist*, 47, 23-33.

Hermans, H. J. M., & Hermans-Jansen, E. (1995). *Self-narratives: The construction of meaning in psychotherapy*. New York: The Guilford Press.

Hermans, H. J. M., & Dimaggio, G. (2007). Self, identity, and globalization in times of uncertainty: A dialogical analysis. *Review of General Psychology*, 11(1), 31-61.

Hermans, H. J. M., & Hermans-Konopka, A. (2010). *Dialogical self theory: Positioning and counter-positioning in a globalizing society*. New York: Cambridge University Press.

Hermans, H. J. M., & Gieser, T. (Eds.). (2012). Introductory chapter: History, main tenets and core concepts of a dialogical self theory. In H. J. M. Hermans, & T. Gieser (Eds.), *Handbook of dialogical self theory* (pp. 1-28). New York: Cambridge University Press.

Hermans-Konopka, A. (2012). The depositioning of the I: Emotional coaching in the context of transcendental awareness. In H. J. M. Hermans, & T. Gieser (Eds.), *Handbook of dialogical self theory* (pp. 423-438). New York: Cambridge University Press.

Hermans, C. A. M. (2015). Towards a theory of spiritual and religious experiences: A building block approach of the unexpected possible. *Archive for the Psychology of Religion*, 37, 141-167.

Higate, P. R. (2008). Ex-servicemen on the road: Travel and homelessness. *Sociological Review*, 48(3), 331-347.

Higgins, L. A. (1993). Sexual fantasies and war memories: Claude Simon's narratology. In M. G. Cooke, & A. Woollacott (Eds.), *Gendering war talk* (pp. 249-259). New Jersey: Princeton University Press.

Holmes, A. F. (Ed.). (2005). *War and Christian ethics: Classic and contemporary readings on the morality of war*. Grand Rapids, MI: Baker Academic.

Hunt, M. (2009). *Fierce tenderness: A feminist theology of friendship*. Minneapolis, MN: Fortress Press.

Huntington, S. P. (1957). *The soldier and the state: The theory and politics of civil-military relations*. Cambridge, MA: The Belknap Press of Harvard University Press.

Jackson, C., & Branson, Y. (2012). Assessing and responding to suicidal risk among OIF/OEF veterans. In J. Beder (Ed.), *Advances in social work practice with the military* (pp. 164-179). New York: Routledge, Taylor & Francis Group.

James, W. (1890). *The principles of psychology volume 1.* New York: Henry Holt and Company.

James, W. (1902). *The varieties of religious experience: A Study in human nature.* Retrieved from http://www.templeofearth.com/books/varietyofreligiousexperience.pdf

Janoff-Bulman, R. (1992). *Shattered assumptions: Towards a new psychology of trauma.* New York: The Free Press.

Janowitz, M. (1960). *The professional soldier: A social and political portrait.* Glencoe, IL: Free Press of Glencoe.

Jolly, R. (1996). *Changing step.* London, UK: Brassey's Ltd.

Knowles, C. H. (2013). Notes toward a neuropsychology of moral injury. *Reflective Practice: Formation and Supervision in Ministry, 33,* 76-78.

Kohler, N., & Wigfield, R. (2013). Group for children and families having a parent with an operational stress injury. In A. B. Aiken, & S. A. H. Bélanger (Eds.), *Beyond the line: Military and veteran health research* (pp. 139-149). Montreal and Kingston: McGill-Queen's University Press.

Koole, S. L., Greenberg, J., & Pyszczynski, T. (2006). Introducing science to the psychology of the soul: Experimental existential psychology. *Current Directions in Psychological Science, 15*(5), 212-216.

Kopacz, M. S., & Connery, A., L. (2015). The veteran spiritual struggle. *Spirituality in Clinical Practice, 2*(1), 61–67.

Kristeva, J. (1987). *Tales of love* (trans. Roudiez, L.). New York: Columbia University Press.

Kusner, K. G., Mahoney, A., Pargament, K. I., & DeMari, A. (2014). Sanctification of marriage and spiritual intimacy predicting observed marital interactions across the transition to parenthood. *Journal of Family Psychology, 28* (5), 604–614.

Kvale, S. (2007). *Doing interviews.* London: Sage.

Kvale, S., & Brinkmann, S. (2009). *Den kvalitativa forskningen* [The qualitative research] (2nd ed.). Lund, Sverige: Studentlitteratur AB.

Kümmel, G. (2011). Identity, identity shifts and identity politics: The German soldier facing a pre/post-Westphalian world risk society, ambitious national politics, an ambivalent home society and a military under stress. In H. Fürst, & G. Kümmel (Eds.), *Core values and the expeditionary mindset: Armed forces in metamorphosis* (pp. 51-67). Baden-Baden, Germany: Nomos Verlagsgesellschaft.

Laforce, J. C., Whitney, D. L., & Klassen, K. N. (2013). Service use in an outpatient clinic for current and veteran military and RCMP members. In A. B. Aiken, & S. A. H. Bélanger (Eds.), *Beyond the line: Military and veteran health research* (pp. 210-230). Montreal and Kingston: McGill-Queen's University Press.

Larner, B., & Blow, A. (2011). A model of meaning-making coping and growth in combat veterans. *Review of General Psychology*, 15(3), 187–197.

Liamputtong, P., & Ezzy, D. (2005). *Qualitative research methods* (2nd ed.). Oxford: Oxford University Press.

Lifton, R. J. (1992). *Home from the war: Learning from Vietnam veterans (with a new preface and epilogue on the Gulf War)*. Boston: Beacon Press.

Lincoln, Y. S., & Cuba, E. (1985). *Naturalistic inquiry*. Thousand Oaks, CA: Sage.

Litz, B. T., Stein, N., Delaney, E., Lebowitz, L., Nash, W. P., Silva, C., & Maguen, S. (2009). Moral injury and moral repair in war veterans: A preliminary model and intervention strategy. *Clinical Psychology Review*, 29(8), 695-706.

Luckmann, T. (1967). *The invisible religion: The problem of religion in modern society*. New York: Macmillan.

Lunde, N. T. (2009). Profesjonsetiske strategier: Nasjonal konsensus, liberal tilpasning og konservativ avskjerming [Professional ethical strategies: National consensus, liberal adjustment and conservative shielding]. In E. Edström, N. T. Lunde, & J. Haaland Matlary (Eds.), *Krigerkultur i en fredsnasjon* [Warrior culture in a peace nation] (pp. 156-197). Oslo, Norge: Abstrakt Förlag.

MacIntyre, A. (2007). *After virtue* (3rd ed.). Notre Dame, IN: University of Notre Dame Press.

Mancuso, J. C. (1986). The acquisition and use of narrative grammar structure. In T. R. Sarbin (Ed.), *Narrative psychology: The storied nature of human conduct* (pp. 91-110). Westport, CT: Praeger.

Malmin, M. (2013). Warrior culture, spirituality, and prayer. *Journal of Religion & Health*, 52, 740-758.

Mark. C. I., & Pike, G. B. (2013). Novel functional magnetic resonance imagining to quantify neuronal hemodynamic and metabolic underpinnings of cognitive impairment in mild traumatic brain injury and amyotrophic lateral sclerosis. In A. B. Aiken, & S. A. H. Bélanger (Eds.), *Beyond the line: Military and veteran health research* (pp. 20-34). Montreal and Kingston: McGill-Queen's University Press.

McAdams, D. P. (1988). *Power, intimacy and the life story: Personological inquiries into identity.* New York: The Guilford Press.

McAdams, D. P. (1997). *The stories we live by: Personal myths and the making of the self.* New York: The Guilford Press.

McAdams, D. P. (2001). The psychology of life stories. *Review of General Psychology,* 5(2), 100-122.

McAdams, D. P. (2013). *The redemptive self: Stories Americans live by.* New York: Oxford University Press.

McAdams, D. P., Josselson, R., & Lieblich, A. (Eds.). (2002). *Turns in the road: Narrative studies of lives in transition.* Washington, DC: American Psychological Association.

McAdams, D. P., Josselson, R., & Lieblich, A. (Eds.). (2006). *Identity and story: Creating self in narrative.* Washington, DC: APA Books.

McCracken G. (1988). *The long interview: Qualitative research methods series 13.* London: Sage Publications.

McFague, S. (1982). *Metaphorical theology: Models of God in religious language.* Philadelphia: Fortress Press.

McGuire, M. (2008). *Lived religion: Faith and practice in everyday life.* New York: Oxford University Press.

McMackin, R. A., Newman, E., Fogler, J. M., & Keane, T. M. (Eds.). (2012). *Trauma therapy in context: The science and craft of evidence-based practice.* Washington, DC: American Psychological Association.

Mead, G. H. (1934). *Mind, self, and society.* Chicago: University of Chicago Press.

Merriam, S. B. (1998). *Qualitative research and case study: Applications in education* (2nd ed.). San Francisco: Jossey-Bass.

Merriam, S. B. (Ed.). (2002). *Qualitative research in practice: Examples for discussion and analysis.* San Francisco: Jossey-Bass.

Mishler, E. G. (1986). The analysis of interview-narratives. In T. R. Sarbin (Ed.), *Narrative psychology: The storied nature of human conduct* (pp. 233-255). Westport, CT: Praeger.

Mishler, E. G. (1991). *Research interviewing: Context and narrative.* Cambridge: Harvard University Press.

Mishler. E. G. (2004). *Storylines: Craftartistis' narratives of identity.* Cambridge, MA: Harvard University Press.

Moore, B. A. (Ed.) (2012). *Handbook of counseling military couples.* New York: Routledge, Taylor and Francis Group.

Moskos, C. C., Williams, J. A., & Segal, D. R. (Eds.). (2000). *The postmodern military: Armed forces after the cold war*. New York: Oxford University Press.

Neimeyer, R. A. (2012). Reconstructing the self in the wake of loss: A dialogical contribution. In H. J. M. Hermans, & T. Gieser (Eds), *Handbook of dialogical self theory* (pp. 374-389). New York: Cambridge University Press.

Nieuwsma, J. A., Rhodes, J. E., Jackson, G. L., Cantrell, W. C., Lane, M. E., Bates, M. J., ...Meador, K. G. (2013). Chaplaincy and mental health in the Department of Veterans Affairs and Department of Defense. *Journal of Health Care Chaplaincy*, 19, 3–21.

Nir, D. (2012). Voicing inner conflict: From a dialogical to a negotiational self. In H. J. M. Hermans, & T. Gieser (Eds), *Handbook of dialogical self theory* (pp. 284-300). New York: Cambridge University Press.

Noy, C. (2008). Sample knowledge: The hermeneutics of snowball sampling in qualitative research. *International Journal of Social Research Methodology, 11*(4), 327-344.

Pargament, K. I. (1999). The psychology of religion and spirituality?: Yes and no. *The International Journal for the Psychology of Religion*, 9, 3-16.

Pargament, K. I. (2008). The sacred character of community life. *American Journal of Community Psychology*, 41, 22–34.

Pargament, K. I. (2011). *Spiritually integrated psychotherapy: Understanding and addressing the sacred*. New York: The Guilford Press.

Pargament, K. I., & Mahoney, A. (2002). Spirituality: The discovery and conservation of the sacred. In C. R. Snyder, & S. J. Lopez (Eds.), *Handbook of positive psychology* (pp.646-659). New York: Oxford University Press.

Pargament, K. I., & Sweeney, P. J. (2011). Building spiritual fitness in the Army: An innovative approach to a vital aspect of human development. *American Psychologist*, 66(1), 58–64.

Pargament, K. I., Lomax, J. W., Shealy McGee, J., & Fang, Q. (2014). Sacred moments in psychotherapy from the perspectives of mental health providers and clients: prevalence, predictors, and consequences. *Spirituality in Clinical Practice*, 1(4), 248-262.

Park, J. (2008). A profile of Canadian forces. *Perspectives, Statistics Canada*, 75-001-X, 17-30.

Parkinson, G. W., French, L. M., & Massetti, S. (2012). Care coordination in military Traumatic Brain Injury. In J. Beder (Ed.), *Advances in social work practice with the military* (pp. 55-71). New York: Routledge, Taylor & Francis Group.

Patton, M. Q. (1990). *Qualitative evaluation and research methods* (2nd ed.). Newbury Park, CA: Sage.

Pellegrino, L., & Hoggan, C. (2015). A tale of two transitions: Female military veterans during their first year at community college. *Adult Learning*, 26(3), 124-131.

Polkinghorne, D. E. (1988). *Narrative knowing and the human sciences*. Albany: State University of New York Press.

Polkinghorne, D. E. (2005). Language and meaning: Data collection in qualitative research. *Journal of Counseling Psychology*, 52(2), 137-145.

Porter, M., & Gutierrez, V. (2012). Enhancing resilience with culturally competent treatment of same-sex military couples. In B. A. Moore (Ed.), Handbook of counseling military couples (pp. 295-319). New York: Routledge, Taylor and Francis Group.

Raggatt, P. T. F. (1998). *The personality web protocol*. Townsville, Queensland, Australia: James Cook University.

Raggatt, P. T. F. (2002). The landscape of narrative and the plural self: Exploring identity using the personality web protocol. *Narrative Inquiry*, 12, 290-318.

Raggatt, P. T. F. (2006). Multiplicity and conflict in the dialogical self: A life-narrative approach. In D. P. McAdams, R. Josselson, & A. Lieblich (Eds.), *Identity and story: Creating self in narrative* (pp. 15-35). Washington, DC: APA Books.

Raggatt, P. T. F. (2012). Positioning in the dialogical self: Recent advances in theory construction. In H. J. M. Hermans, & T. Gieser (Eds), *Handbook of dialogical self theory* (pp. 29-45). New York: Cambridge University Press.

Rambo, S. (2010). *Spirit and trauma; A theology of remaining*. Louisville, KY: Westminister John Knox Press.

Ricoeur, P. (1991). Narrative identity. In D. Wood (Ed.), *On Paul Ricoeur: Narrative and interpretation* (pp. 188-200). New York: Routledge.

Ricoeur, P. (1992). *Oneself as another* (trans. By Blamen, K.). Chicago: The University of Chicago Press.

Ricoeur, P. (1998a). The narrative function. In J. B. Thompson (Ed.), *Paul Ricoeur: Hermeneutics & the human sciences* (pp. 274-296). New York: Cambridge University Press.

Ricoeur, P. (1998b). Appropriation. In J. B. Thompson (Ed.), *Paul Ricoeur: Hermeneutics & the human sciences* (pp. 182-193). New York: Cambridge University Press.

Ricoeur, P. (1998c). Metaphor and the central problem of hermeneutics. In J. B. Thompson (Ed.), *Paul Ricoeur: Hermeneutics & the human sciences* (pp. 164-181). New York: Cambridge University Press.

Riessman, K. C. (1993). *Narrative analysis*. London: Sage.

Rosenberg, S. D. (1993). The threshold of thrill: Life stories in the skies over Southeast Asia. In M. G. Cooke, & A. Woollacott (Eds.), *Gendering war talk* (pp. 43-66). New Jersey: Princeton University Press.

Rossman, G. B., & Rallis, S. F. (2003). *Learning in the field: An introduction to qualitative research* (2nd ed.). London: Sage Publications.

Roth, M., St Cyr, K., & McIntyre-Smith, A. (2013). Evidence-based treatments for military-related PTSD: A review of advances in psychotherapy. In A. B. Aiken, & S. A. H. Bélanger (Eds.), *Beyond the line: Military and veteran health research* (pp. 198-209). Montreal and Kingston: McGill-Queen's University Press.

Rowan, J. (2012). The use of I-positions in psychotherapy. In H. J. M. Hermans, & T. Gieser (Eds), *Handbook of dialogical self theory* (pp. 341-355). New York: Cambridge University Press.

Ruddick, S. (1993). Notes toward a feminist peace politics. In M. G. Cooke, & A. Woollacott (Eds.), *Gendering war talk* (pp. 109-127). New Jersey: Princeton University Press.

Rumann, C. B. (2010). *Student veterans return to community college: Understanding their transitions* (Doctoral dissertation, Iowa State University, Iowa, United States of America). Retrieved from http://lib.dr.iastate.edu/etd/

Rumann, C. B., & Hamrick, F. A. (2010). Student veterans in transition: Re-enrolling after war zone deployments. *Journal of Higher Education*, 81(4), 431–458.

Sarbin, T. R. (Ed.). (1986). The narrative as a root metaphor for psychology. In T. R. Sarbin, (Ed.), *Narrative psychology: The storied nature of human conduct (pp.* 3-21). Westport, CT: Praeger.

Sautter, F. J., Armelie, A. P., Glynn, S. M., & Wielt, D. B.(2011). The development of a couple-based treatment for PTSD in returning veterans. *Professional Psychology: Research and Practice*, 42(1), 63–69

Savion, S. M. (2009). *How do retired officers start anew in civilian society? A phenomenological study of life transition* (Doctoral dissertation, The George Washington University, Washington, United States of America). Retrieved from http://sunzi.lib.hku.hk/ER/detail/hkul/4354853

Scheibe, K. E. (1986). Self-narratives and adventure. In T. R. Sarbin (Ed.), *Narrative psychology: The storied nature of human conduct* (pp. 129-151). Westport, CT: Praeger.

Scherer-Rath, M. (2014). Narrative reconstruction as creative contingency. In R. R. Ganzevoort, M. de Haardt, & M. Scherer-Rath (Eds.), *Religious stories we live by: Narrative
approaches in theology and religious studies* (pp. 131-142). Leiden, Netherlands: Brill.

Schok, M. (2009). *Meaning as a mission: Making sense of war and peacekeeping* (Doctoral
dissertation, Utrecht University, Utrecht, The Netherlands). Retrieved from
https://dspace.library.uu.nl/handle/1874/35944

Schok, M., Kleber, R. J., Lensvelt-Mulders, G. J. L. M., Elands, M., & Weerts, J. (2011).
Suspicious minds at risk? The role of meaning in processing war and peacekeeping experiences. *Journal of Applied Social Psychology*, 41(1), 61–81.

Segal, M. (1986). The military and the family as greedy institutions. *Armed Forces and Society*, 13(1), 9-38.

Seidman, I. (2006). *Interviewing as qualitative research: A guide for researchers in education
and the social sciences* (3rd ed.). New York: Teachers College Press.

Skomorovsky, A., Thompson, A., & Emeno, K. (2013). Life satisfaction among Canadian
forces members. In A. B. Aiken, & S. A. H. Bélanger (Eds.), *Beyond the line: Military and
veteran health research* (pp. 84-102). Montreal and Kingston: McGill-Queen's University
Press.

Slocum-Bradley, N. (2009). The positioning diamond: A trans-disciplinary framework for
discourse analysis. *Journal for the Theory of Social Behaviour*, 40(1), 79-107.

Spence, D. P. (1986). Narrative smoothing and clinical wisdom. In T. R. Sarbin (Ed.), *Narrative psychology: The storied nature of human conduct* (pp. 211-232). Westport, CT: Praeger.

Stallinga, B. A. (2013). What spills blood wounds spirit: Chaplains, spiritual care, and operational stress injury. *Reflective Practice: Formation and Supervision in Ministry*, 33, 13-31.

Strachan, H. (2006). Morale and modern war. *Journal of Contemporary History*, 41(2), 211-
227.

Strong, C-A. H., & Donders, J. (2012). Traumatic brain injury. In B. A. Moore (Ed.), Handbook of counseling military couples (pp. 279-294). New York: Routledge, Taylor and
Francis Group.

Sweeney, P. J., Hannah, S. T., & Snider, D. M. (2007). The domain of the human spirit. In L.
J. Matthews (Ed.), *Forging the warrior's character: Moral precepts from the cadet prayer*
(pp. 23–50). Sisters, OR: Jericho.

Sørensen, H. (2011). Core values of Danish expeditionary soldiers. In H. Fürst, & G. Kümmel (Eds.), *Core values and the expeditionary mindset: Armed forces in metamorphosis* (pp. 179-189). Baden-Baden, Germany: Nomos Verlagsgesellschaft.

Tatum, D. (2015). *Towards a deeper understanding of the posttraumatic growth factors leading to an improved quality of life for military combat veterans* (Doctoral dissertation, Governors State University, University Park, United States of America). Retrieved from http://opus.govst.edu/capstones/138/

Thornborrow, T., & Brown, A. D. (2009). Being regimented: Aspiration, discipline and identity work in the British parachute regiment. *Organization Studies, 30*(4), 355-376.

Thompson, D. A. (2004). *Crossing the divide: Luther, feminism, and the cross*. Minneapolis, MN: Fortress Press.

Thompson, J. M., & Lockhart, W. (2015). *Backgrounder for the road to civilian life (R2CL) program of research into the mental health and well-being of Canadian armed forces members/veterans during military-civilian transition*. Charlottetown, PE: Veterans Affairs Canada. Research Directorate Technical Report.

Thurfjell, D. (2015). *Det gudlösa folket: De postkristna svenskarna och religionen* [The godless people: The post Christian Swedes and the religion]. Stockholm: Molin Sorgenfrei Förlag.

Tick, E. (2005). *War and the soul: Healing our nation's veterans from post-traumatic stress disorder*. Wheaton, Illinois: Theosophical Publishing House.

Tillich, P. (1957). *Systematic theology volume two*. Chicago: The University of Chicago Press.

Tillich, P. (1963). *Systematic theology volume three*. Chicago: The University of Chicago Press.

Tillich, P. (1960). *Love, power, and justice: Ontological analyses and ethical applications*. Oxford: Oxford University Press.

Tillich, P. (2014). *The courage to be* (3rd ed.). New Haven, CT: Yale University Press.

Tracy, D. (1975). *Blessed rage for order: The new pluralism in theology*. New York: Seabury.

Tweed, T. A. (2006). *Crossing and dwelling. A theory of religion*. Cambridge, Massachusetts, and London, England: Harvard University Press.

Valsiner, J. (2004, July 11-15). *The promoter sign: Development transformation within the structure of the dialogical self*. Paper presented at the Biennial Meeting of the International Society for the Study of Behavioral Development, Ghent.

Valsiner, J. (2005). Scaffolding within the structure of dialogical self: Hierarchical dynamics of semiotic mediation. *New Ideas in Psychology*, 23, 197-206.

van den Brand, J., Hermans, C., Scherer-Rath, M., & Verschuren, P. (2014). An instrument for reconstructing interpretation in life stories. In R. R. Ganzevoort, M. de Haardt, & M. Scherer-Rath (Eds.), *Religious stories we live by: Narrative approaches in theology and religious studies* (pp. 169-180). Leiden, Netherlands: Brill.

van den Brink, G. (2012a). *Eigentijds idealism. Een afrekening met cynisme in Nederland* [Contemporary idealism: A reckoning with cynicism in the Netherlands]. Amsterdam: Amsterdam University Press.

van den Brink, G. (2012b). *De lage landen en het hogere. De betekenis van geestelijke be-nigselen in het moderne bestaan* [The Lowlands and the Higher: The meaning of the spiritual principles in modern existence]. Amsterdam: Amsterdam University Press.

Verey, A., & Smith, P. K. (2012). Post-combat adjustment: Understanding transition. *Journal of Aggression, Conflict and Peace Research*, 4(4), 226-236.

Verrips, J. (2006). Dehumanization as a double-edged sword. In G. Baumann, & A. Gingrich (Eds.), *Grammars of identity/alterity: A structural approach* (pp. 142-154). New York: Berghahn Books.

Verschuren, P., & Doorewaard, H. (2010). *Designing a research project* (2nd ed.). Hague, Netherlands: Eleven International Publishing, the Hague.

Wall, R. B. (2008). Healing from war and trauma: Southeast Asians in the U.S. human architecture: *Journal of the Sociology of Self-Knowledge*, 6(3), 105-111.

Webster, L., & Mertova, P. (2007). *Using narrative inquiry as a research method: An intro-duction to using critical event narrative analysis in research on learning and teaching.* London: Routledge Taylor & Francis.

Wertsch, M. E. (1991). *Military brats: Legacies of childhood inside the fortress.* New York: Harmony Books.

Wheeler, H. A. (2012). Veterans' transition to community college: A case study. *Community College Journal of Research and Practice*, 36(11), 775-792.

White, H. (1990). *The content and the form: Narrative discourse and historical representa-tion.* Baltimore, Maryland: The John Hopkins University Press.

Whiteman, S. D., Barry, A. E., Mroczek, D. K., & MacDermid Wadsworth, S. (2013). The development and implications of peer emotional support for student service members/ veterans and civilian college students. *Journal of Counseling Psychology*, 60(2), 265–278.

Winright, T. (2007). Gather us in and make us channels of your peace: Evaluating war with an entirely new attitude. In D. M. McCarthy, & M. T. Lysaught (Eds.), *Gathered for the journey: Moral theology in Catholic perspective* (pp. 281-306). Grand Rapids, MI: William B. Eerdmans Publishing Company.

Wikström, O. (1993). *Om heligheten: Religionspsykologiska perspektiv [About the sacredness: Perspectives of the psychology of religion]*. Stockholm: Natur och Kultur.

Wilson, P. H. (2008). Defining military culture. *The Journal of Military History*, 72(1), 11-41.

Woodward, R. (2008). "Not for queen and country or any of that shit". In D. Cowen, & E. Gilbert (Eds.), *War, citizenship, territory* (pp. 363-384). New York: Routledge.

Woodward, R., & Jenkings, N. K. (2011). Military identities in the situated accounts of British military personnel. *Sociology*, 45(2), 252-268.

Wulff, D. M. (1997). *Psychology of religion: Contemporary and classic* (2nd ed.). New York: John Wiley & Sons, Inc.

Yalom, I (1980) *Existential psychotherapy*. New York: Basic Books, Inc.

Yanos, R. C. (2004). *Perceptions of transition to civilian life among recently retired Air Force officers* (Doctoral dissertation, University of Maryland, College Park, United States of America). Retrieved from http://drum.lib.umd.edu/handle/1903/2321

Yarvis, J. S., & Beder, J. (2012). Civilian social worker's guide to the treatment of war-induced post-traumatic stress disorder. In J. Beder (Ed.), *Advances in social work practice with the military* (pp. 37-54). New York: Routledge, Taylor & Francis Group.

Zimbardo, P. (2008). *The Lucifer effect: Understanding how good people turn evil*. New York: Random House Trade Paperbacks.

Zinger, L., & Cohen, A. (2010). Veterans returning from war into the classroom: How can colleges be better prepared to meet their needs. *Contemporary Issues in Education Research*, 3(1), 39–51.

BIOGRAPHY

Jan Grimell is an ordained minister in the Church of Sweden who has been combining working as a minister in the northern part of Sweden with his PhD research. He is also a former military officer in the Swedish Armed Forces; he served actively for ten years on several locations inside and outside of Sweden and is currently a reserve officer. Jan is an alumnus of Umeå University, Sweden and holds a MA in religion and theology with a main field of specialization in social sciences of religion. He also holds a BA in social science with psychology as his main field of specialization. He has published several articles in international journals.

Religion und Biographie/Religion and Biography
hrsg. von Prof. Dr. Detlev Dormeyer (Dortmund), Prof. Dr. Ruard Ganzevoort
(Amsterdam), Prof. Dr. Linus Hauser (Gießen) und Prof. Dr. Friedhelm Munzel
(Dortmund)

Dorothea Mecking
Die Toten sitzen mit am Tisch
Verlusterfahrungen von verwaisten Eltern und ihr Umgang mit dieser Lebenskrise
Ein Kind zu verlieren ist für Mütter und Väter eine existenzielle Verlusterfahrung, die sie das ganze Leben lang begleitet. Die persönlichen Trauerwege der Eltern erfordern sensiblen Beistand von Familienmitgliedern, Freunden und Seelsorgern. Anhand der Auswertung von Interviews mit verwaisten Eltern beleuchtet dieses Buch den individuellen Umgang mit dieser Lebenskrise. Aus einer praktisch-theologischen Perspektive wird der Zusammenhang von Erinnerungen der Eltern an ihre Kinder ebenso wie die Rolle bestimmter Rituale sowie die Bedeutung des christlichen Glaubens und der Trauerseelsorge aufgezeigt.
Bd. 24, 2017, 318 S., 34,90 €, br., ISBN 978-3-643-13756-2

Ute Oskamp
Bibliotherapeutische Arbeit mit sequentiellen Bildern
Zur narrativen Funktion von Bild-Text-Gefügen im Religionsunterricht der Grundschule
Das vorliegende Buch stellt eine Vernetzung von Religionspädagogik, Bibliotherapie und Comicforschung vor und ist damit ein Novum in der Innovation des Religionsunterrichts. Es geht um die Bedeutung des Bildes für religiöse Lernprozesse, um umfassende Ausführungen zur Bibliotherapie sowie zur Religionspädagogik und Comictheorie. Drei Unterrichtseinheiten mit kinderliterarischen Comics verweisen darauf, dass mit der Verbindung von Bild und Text differenzierte Lernangebote für heterogene Lerngruppen realisiert werden können. Im Rahmen einer explorativen Studie werden ermutigende Lernprozesse belegt.
Bd. 23, 2017, 280 S., 34,90 €, br., ISBN 978-3-643-13372-4

LIT Verlag Berlin – Münster – Wien – Zürich – London
Auslieferung Deutschland / Österreich / Schweiz: siehe Impressumsseite

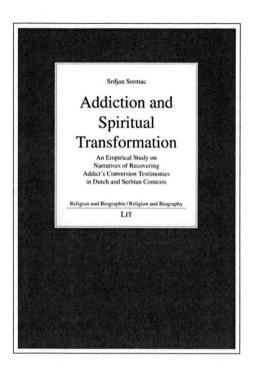

Sdrjan Sremac
Addiction and Spiritual Transformation
An Empirical Study on Narratives of Recovering Addict's Conversion Testimonies in
Dutch and Serbian Contexts
The study explores the relationship between addiction and spiritual transformation. More specifically
it examines how recovering drug addicts employ testimonies of conversion and addiction to develop
and sustain a sense of personal unity and create meaning from varied experiences in life. Drawing
on 31 original autobiographies it analyzes conversion and addiction testimonies in two European
contexts (Serbia and The Netherlands).
Bd. 22, 2014, 200 S., 34,90 €, br., ISBN 978-3-643-90451-5

Werner Eichinger (Hg.)
Endlich leben
Wozu uns Grenzen herausfordern
Das sind Erfahrungen, die wir Menschen immer wieder machen: Ein „Schicksalsschlag" setzt uns
eine Grenze; unsere Begabung, unsere Kraft, unsere Ausdauer sind beschränkter als erwartet; die
Fähigkeit zu lieben wird zu einer knappen Ressource. Da kommt etwas in unserem Leben an ein
Ende, da wird der gewohnte Lauf der Dinge abgebrochen. *Endlich* ist das Leben ja nicht nur, weil es
im Tod beendet wird, sondern weil es immer wieder Abbrüche bewältigen muss.
Das kann zu der Haltung führen, nur noch provisorisch zu leben: vielleicht betriebsam, aber nicht
intensiv. Nichts wird dann mehr wirklich ernst genommen. Eine andere Möglichkeit ist es, der Le-
benszeit gerade wegen ihrer Endlichkeit(en) Gewicht zu geben.
Dazu will dieses Buch provozieren. Es bietet dazu Einsichten aus Philosophie, Psychologie, Bibliotherapie und Theologie an und lässt Menschen zu Wort kommen, für die die Erfahrung von Grenzen
zum Impuls geworden ist, endlich zu *leben*.
Bd. 21, 2011, 128 S., 19,90 €, br., ISBN 978-3-643-11371-9

LIT Verlag Berlin – Münster – Wien – Zürich – London
Auslieferung Deutschland / Österreich / Schweiz: siehe Impressumsseite

Nordic Studies in Religion and Culture / Nordische Studien zur Religion und Kultur
edited by / hrsg. von Dr. Hans Bringeland (NLA University College, Bergen),
Prof. Dr. Ingvild S. Gilhus (University of Bergen)

Kai Merten
Färöische Religionsgeschichte
Von den Anfängen bis zur Gegenwart
Die Inselgruppe der Färöer bildet den kleinsten selbständigen Teil Skandinaviens. Dennoch weist sie eine mehr als tausendjährige Geschichte und Kultur auf, die von Anfang an ein eigenes Gepräge entwickelt hat. Besonders auffällig ist die außerordentlich starke Bindung der Menschen an die Religion. Rund 23% der Färinger besuchen jeden Sonntag einen Gottesdienst!
Das vorliegende Buch bietet deshalb einen umfassenden Überblick über die gesamte Religionsgeschichte der Färöer.
Bd. 4, 2017, 320 S., 29,90 €, br., ISBN 978-3-643-13580-3

Peter Nynäs; Ruth Illman; Tuomas Martikainen (Eds.)
On the outskirts of "the church"
Diversity, fluidities and new spaces of religion in Finland
Through exploring the diversity of contemporary religious phenomena, this volume sheds new light on religion in the twenty-first century: Is religion going through a decisive change? What are the resources that make religion so persistent and what happened to secularisation? How do the traditional religious institutions fare? How do people identify themselves with regard to religion?
Firmly rooted in analyses of the rich and fluid spiritual life on the outskirts of religious institutions – from angel healing and prayer clinics to LGBT activists and yoga entrepreneurs – this volume engages with topical discussions on religious change and post-secularity. The book suggests that there are profound changes occurring in the ways in which religion is involved in people's lives today and looks at how religious institutions have responded to these changes.
Bd. 3, 2015, 288 S., 34,90 €, br., ISBN 978-3-643-90571-0

Nils G. Holm
The Human Symbolic Construction of Reality
A Psycho-Phenomenological Study
The book sums up several years of research into religion from a perspective informed by history, phenomenology and psychology. It is typical of humans to create forms of understanding at a symbolic level of the biological and physiological reality which confronts them. This gives meaning and a coherent structure to the often chaotic nature of that reality. Religion has been a means of creating such symbolic understandings. The similarities between various religions are actually very great, although their differences tend to dominate our view of them. Everything in the world of religion can be traced back to everyday and simple circumstances which, through the construction of symbols at both the cognitive and the behavioural levels, acquire a more elevated and "sacred" character. This book provides an introduction to the key aspects of a psycho-phenomenological study of the forms of expression within religions.
Bd. 2, 2014, 152 S., 34,90 €, br., ISBN 978-3-643-90526-0

Hans Bringeland; Arve Brunvoll (Hg.)
Die Religion und das Wertefundament der Gesellschaft
Studien zum 200. Jahrestag des norwegischen Grundgesetzes 2014
Diese Aufsatzsammlung, die anlässlich des 200. Jahrestages des norwegischen Grundgesetzes entstanden ist, besteht aus Beiträgen von norwegischen Forschern in Fächern wie Theologie und Philosophie, Religionswissenschaft und Soziologie, Jura und Literaturwissenschaft. Die Aufsätze sind den Themenbereichen „Werte, Grundgesetz und Menschenrechte", „Religion und Wertefundament" und „Christliche Ideologen, Nationaltagsfeier" zugeordnet. Obwohl der Primärkontext nordisch ist, dürfte diese Anthologie auch für deutschsprachige Leser von Interesse sein.
Bd. 1, 2015, 278 S., 34,90 €, br., ISBN 978-3-643-90466-9

LIT Verlag Berlin – Münster – Wien – Zürich – London
Auslieferung Deutschland / Österreich / Schweiz: siehe Impressumsseite

Nordic Studies in Theology / Nordische Studien zur Theologie

Edited by / hrsg. von Prof. Dr. Kirsten Busch Nielsen (University of Copenhagen),
Prof. Dr. Dr. Jan-Olav Henriksen (MF Norwegian School of Theology),
Dr. Hans Bringeland (NLA University College, Bergen)

Asle Eikrem; Atle O. Søvik (Eds.)
Talking Seriously About God
Philosophy of Religion in the Dispute between Theism and Atheism
Talk about God is often the source of controversy. Theists and atheists are equally passionate when making their stand for or against belief in God.
In this book a wide range of philosophers of religion have come together to discuss how serious talk about God ought to be conducted for theists and atheists alike in what should be their common pursuit for truth. The essays both address methodological questions and provide a range of concrete samples of serious God-talk, spanning from political religion and classical proofs of God's existence to the problem of evil.
Bd. 4, 2016, 184 S., 29,90 €, br., ISBN 978-3-643-90741-7

Gunnar Innerdal
Hans Urs von Balthasar on Spirit and Truth
A Systematic Reconstruction in Connection to the Theoretical Framework of Lorenz B. Puntel
The doctrine of *the Spirit of truth* (cf. John 16:13) stands at the center of *Hans Urs von Balthasar on Spirit and Truth*. To articulate a coherent systematic theology of this aspect of pneumatology, Gunnar Innerdal analyzes Balthasar's *Theo-Logic* and related texts, followed by critical assessments in connection to the theoretical framework of Lorenz B. Puntel's structural-systematic philosophy and in dialogue with other contemporary theological proposals. In Part I philosophical questions concerning truth are discussed. Part II shows the relevance of Christology and Trinity for theological truth talk, discussing the doctrine of analogy and negative theology. Part III elaborates on the relationship of Son and Spirit, and the Spirit's work as the Spirit of truth inside and outside the Church. The Spirit, as breath of life and Spirit of Christ, has ontological and epistemological significance for all truth.
Bd. 2, 2016, 328 S., 49,90 €, br., ISBN 978-3-643-90628-1

Jonna Bornemark; Mattias Martinson; Jayne Svenungsson (Eds.)
Monument and Memory
A century after the Great War broke out, studies on politics of memory and commemoration have grown into a vast and vital academic field. This book approaches the theme "monument and memory" from architectural, literary, philosophical and theological perspectives. Drawing on diverse sources – from the Augustine to Freud, from early photographs to contemporary urban monuments – the contributing authors probe the intersections between memory and trauma, past and present, monuments and memorial practices, religious and secular, remembrance and forgetfulness.
Bd. 1, 2015, 272 S., 49,90 €, gb., ISBN 978-3-643-90467-6

LIT Verlag Berlin – Münster – Wien – Zürich – London
Auslieferung Deutschland / Österreich / Schweiz: siehe Impressumsseite